CULTURAL
THREADS

Cultural Threads
Transnational Textiles Today

Edited by Jessica Hemmings

Bloomsbury Academic
An imprint of Bloomsbury Publishing Plc

50 Bedford Square	1385 Broadway
London	New York
WC1B 3DP	NY 10018
UK	USA

www.bloomsbury.com

Bloomsbury is a registered trade mark of
Bloomsbury Publishing Plc

First published 2015

British Library Cataloguing-in-Publication Data
A catalogue record for this book is available
from the British Library.

ISBN:
HB: 978-1-4725-2499-7
PB: 978-1-4725-3093-6

Library of Congress
Cataloging-in-Publication Data

Cultural threads: transnational textiles today /
edited by Jessica Hemmings.
      pages   cm

Includes bibliographical references and index.
ISBN 978-1-4725-2499-7 (hardback) -- ISBN
978-1-4725-3093-6 (paperback) 1. Fiberwork--
Social aspects. 2. Textile crafts--Social aspects.
3. Postcolonialism and the arts. 4. Art and
globalization. I. Hemmings, Jessica, editor of
compilation.
N6494.F47C85 2014
746.09'051--dc23
2014004297

A catalog record for this book is available from
the Library of Congress.

Design by Evelin Kasikov
Typeset by Precision Graphics
Printed and bound in China

CULTURAL THREADS

TRANSNATIONAL TEXTILES TODAY

edited by
JESSICA HEMMINGS

BLOOMSBURY
LONDON · NEW DELHI · NEW YORK · SYDNEY

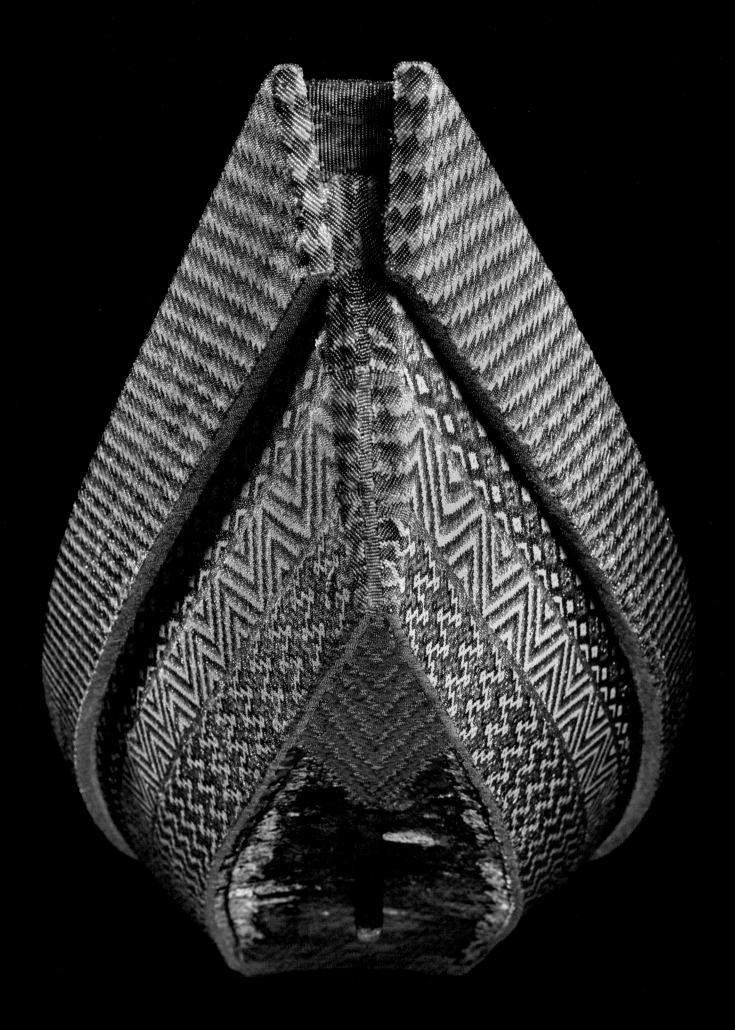

Contributors acknowledge the support
from the following organizations:

OPPOSITE   Jorge Lizarazo and
Hechizoo Studio, *Inga*, 2013.
Wood canoe, glass beads. 28 ×
50 × 401 cm (11 × 20 × 158 in.).
Courtesy of Cristina Grajales
Gallery and Andres Valbuena.

Contents

Introduction

Jessica Hemmings

Korean artist Meekyoung Shin creates objects that look like ceramics. Her versions are disarmingly precise, but soap rather than clay is her material of choice. Swapping materials allows Shin to poke fun at our ability to discern authenticity and value from the knock-off or replica. Even the crates printed with 'fragile' used as plinths for her objects tell a story of half-truths. The objects on display are indeed fragile, but in a soapy way, rather than ready to shatter. When installed outside, Shin's work literally slips away from us. Her installation in Cavendish Square, London *Written in Soap: A Plinth Project* (2012–ongoing) recreates the equestrian statue of the disgraced Duke of Cumberland whose original statue was removed in 1868, nearly 100 years after installation, when public opinion of his military career earned him the nickname 'the Butcher'. In 2013 the work travelled to exhibitions in Korea and Taiwan, further complicating history and context. Shin's statement about her exhibition of the

work at the Taipei Museum of Contemporary Art in November 2013 asks:

> As the new audience in Taiwan and beyond participate in the translation of this sculpture, we can ask: what does it mean when a statue that was originally erected to celebrate a one-time war hero over a hundred years ago as a personal tribute by an individual, brought down a century later, [is] now resurrected as a work of art by an emigrant artist in the twenty-first century in a museum dedicated to contemporary art 5,000 miles away? (Written in Soap, 2014)

Opinions change. Facts change. Popularity wanes in the face of new information. Shin's choice of material allows her to question the viability of any

OPPOSITE AND RIGHT   Meekyoung Shin, *Translation* (details), 2009. Soap, pigment, varnish. Couriers of Taste exhibition, Danson House (1 April to 31 October 2013). Photograph by Ann Purkiss. Courtesy of Bexley Heritage Trust.

FAR LEFT Meekyoung Shin, *Written in Soap: A Plinth Project* (2012– ongoing), summer 2012. Photograph by Peter Mallet.

LEFT Meekyoung Shin, *Written in Soap: A Plinth Project* (2012– ongoing), autumn 2012. Photograph by Peter Mallet.

FAR LEFT Meekyoung Shin,*Written in Soap: A Plinth Project* (2012– ongoing), spring 2013. Photograph by Peter Mallet.

LEFT Meekyoung Shin, *Written in Soap: A Plinth Project* (2012– ongoing), summer 2013. Photograph by Peter Mallet.

Meekyoung Shin,
*Written in Soap:
A Plinth Project*
(2012–ongoing),
winter 2013.
Photograph by
Peter Mallet.

sense of a singular or 'authentic' sense of history – of people, but also of objects.

The impossibility of a single historical truth is also a central theme of the work of Egyptian artist Wael Shawky, whose 2013 Serpentine Gallery exhibition in London 'explores history, culture and the effect of globalisation on contemporary societies through fact and fiction'. (Serpentine 2014) Fiction and the potential of stories to reveal alternative perspectives is another recurring theme in *Cultural Threads*. In Shawky's case 'marionettes enact key events that occurred during the Crusades', but perspective is shifted to a retelling of this history from a Middle Eastern rather than Eurocentric point of view, with characters speaking classical Arabic, 'the language spoken in news bulletins and in the Quran, to frame his narrative with a voice of authority'. (Serpentine 2014)

Shin's slippery objects and Shawky's alternative perspectives on familiar histories exemplify the types of narratives this book aims to explore. Both ask the materials of their practice to communicate cultural perspectives that are far more complex than first glance may assume. The need to reappraise the perspectives that each of us occupies in this world is a lesson visited by each of the contributors to *Cultural Threads*. Content is drawn from contemporary artists and designers who work at the intersection of multiple national or cultural influences and use textiles as their vehicle. Ideas about belonging to more than one place, which in reality results in a sense of connection to everywhere and nowhere simultaneously, are pertinent to society today more than ever. So too are the multiple, often overlooked, histories behind the objects that make up our material world. It is interesting to note that many of the contributors write from a position of personal experience, negotiating multiple cultural allegiances. In my own case, several childhood years living with my family in Yogyakarta, Indonesia, taught me at an early age that the world is far bigger than the immediate culture of my family. As an adult I returned to this experience in an effort to learn why, a process shared with many of the *Cultural Threads* contributors.

How we negotiate our understanding of complex cultural influences is central to this inquiry. So too is postcolonial thinking, in particular an attention to hybrid cultural identities and contemporary migration, and the ways in which these ideas inform textile practice. Content includes examples from regions that were once literally colonized, as well as broader notions of multiple, often contested, cultural influences not literally from former colonies. The term transnational was selected for the book's title largely because of its encompassing nature. In reality all the potential terms on offer – postcolonial, multicultural, transnational – quickly become too loaded to serve accurately or usefully as descriptors of the content included here. Postcolonial thinking is used as a starting point because of its attention to ideas of the so-called centre versus periphery, and the acknowledgement that we live in a world in which individual identities are now built from multiple points of cultural reference.

Curiously, attention to the complex narratives of multiple cultural influences told by textiles has gone somewhat unnoticed outside the field of textile scholarship. While postcolonial thinking is important to this book, the ways in which objects, rather than texts, manifest these ideas is of primary concern. In 2000, Paul Sharrad and Anne Collette wrote in their introduction to *Reinventing Textiles: Postcolonialism and Creativity*, 'the textile object and its material history of exchange adds to and critiques the sometimes overly textualised and abstracted practices of literary and cultural studies scholarship'. *Cultural Threads* intends to build on Sharrad and Collette's concern for the somewhat overtextualized and often impenetrable tone of postcolonial discourse by focusing on contemporary versions of some of the very objects that were central to the agenda of colonization. Interestingly, many of the contributors to *Cultural Threads* distance themselves from conventional academic writing, electing instead to preserve the spoken word in interview transcripts and monologues by artists, as well as 'piecing' texts in sections that punctuate points of focus. A short story is also included, 'The End of Skill' by Mamle Kabu, as a reminder of how creative as well as critical writing can contribute to our understanding of textiles today.

Wael Shawky, installation view, Serpentine Gallery, London (29 November 2013 to 9 February 2014). © 2013 Hugo Glendinning.

Christopher Frayling evokes our present reality when he observes that the future craftsperson 'will think of culture*s* rather than culture and they will come from culture*s* rather than culture', and he notes multiple national and cultural allegiances as an increasing norm. (2011: 134) It is crucial to remember that the reasons behind engagement with multiple cultures range from the luxury and privilege of international travel and education, through to the absolute need for migration on economic or political grounds. Contributors to this book consider both ends of this spectrum.

While the examples selected for this book use materials we associate with textiles, function is not always the first priority. Much like the cultural references of their makers, many contemporary textiles exist in an in-between world, not wholly embraced by the establishments of art or design, nor functional objects in the conventional sense of craft. Instead, the contributors and examples included occupy diverse positions ranging from commercial design to art made for the gallery context, as well as craft made for economic survival and craft made as an expression of creativity. These perspectives admittedly command vastly differing agendas, from the preservation of brand identity to the (relative) autonomy of academic research. In my role as editor, I have tried to resist the temptation to impose synchronization on these differing agendas, instead aspiring to respect that while differences

Wael Shawky,
installation view,
Serpentine Gallery,
London. © 2013 Hugo
Glendinning.

Elaine Reichek, installation view of *Elaine Reichek: A Précis 1972–1995*, including (from left to right): *Bikini*, 1982, knitted metallic yarn, coloured pencil on graph paper, and silver-toned gelatin silver print. Overall 104 × 213 cm (41 × 84 in.). *Blue Men*, 1986, knitted wool yarn and oil gelatin silver print. 3 parts. Overall 160 × 244 cm (63 × 96 in.). *Whitewash (Galway Cottage)*, 1992–1993, knitted wool yarn, hanger and gelatin silver print. Overall 114 × 338 × 3 cm (45 in. × 11 ft. × 1 in.). Photograph by Christopher Burke.

in priorities appear, these differences when taken as a whole provide a legitimate contribution to our understanding of contemporary textile practice.

Contemporary textile practice engages with ideas of the postcolonial more frequently than in other disciplines such as ceramics or jewellery perhaps because textiles, one of the most portable material disciplines, move with such relative ease around our world. The influence of feminist thinking on textile scholarship also offers an explanation for why postcolonial ideas, in particular the margin – the academic margins that textile scholarship inhabits, as well as the geographic margins that the colonies represented to the colonial powers – is a site of potential as well as a source of cultural damage. Elaine Reichek, speaking at the *Subversive Stitch Revisited: the Politics of Cloth* conference in London in 2013, reflected on the development of her own practice, acknowledging that the doors opened by feminist discourse were, at least in part, responsible for the prevalence of postcolonial thinking in textile practice today. In her recent exhibition *Elaine Reichek: A Précis 1972–1995* at the Zach Feurer Gallery in

New York, three early works comprised of knitted garments and photographs, *Bikini*, 1982, *Blue Men*, 1986, and *Whitewash (Galway Cottage)*, 1992–3, illustrate this progression of thinking from the politics of the female body to concerns about the 'other'. The exhibition's press release explains that by:

> deliberately misinterpreting the objects and symbols in photographs … [Reichek's] method emphasizes a colonizing culture's tendency to misinterpret and aestheticize the artefacts it comes across in its travels, and the translation from the photographed form to the knitted form replicates the way information is passed from language to language and in the process reshaped and altered, its content never quite the same. (Feuer 2014)

Ironically Reichek, in her artist's statement included in this book, also addresses part of the problem with the term postcolonial and the reason for its exclusion from the book's subtitle:

Theaster Gates, *Migration Rickshaw*
for Sleeping, Building and Playing,
2013. Wood, fabric, Huguenot
House wallpaper and wheel.
144.8 × 322.6 × 69 cm
(57 × 127 × 27 3/16 in.). ©
Theaster Gates. Photograph by
Edouard Fraipont. Courtesy of
White Cube.

the instability of meaning created by differing contemporary associations in different geographic contexts. Nonetheless, the portability of textiles – and increasingly our own lives – seems to go some way to answering why a density of interest in these ideas can be found in contemporary textile practice.

American artist and social activist Theaster Gates's exhibition *My Back, My Wheel and My Will* (2013) held simultaneously at the White Cube São Paulo and the White Cube Hong Kong makes real just how small the world has become. But in the same breath, Gates creates work that is grounded in a specific physical location: the South Side of Chicago, where many of the materials that appear in his work are harvested. Both recent exhibitions included hand-built rickshaws described as 'migration rickshaws … which function as metaphors of forced migration'. (White Cube 2013) Built from salvaged materials, the two rickshaws suggest the

modest worldly goods and tools of a life in constant motion. To add even further geographic complexity to the mix, Port au Prince, Haiti and Guadalajara, Mexico are cited as places the artist visited and found inspiration. (White Cube 2013)

In this 'small' world where travel can be accomplished with relative ease and there is conceivably a gallery-going audience taking in both São Paulo and Hong Kong in the same month, questions regarding how our material world is made and distributed must continue to be asked. The April 2013 collapse of the Rana Plaza in Bangladesh is now acknowledged as 'the deadliest disaster in garment industry history'. (*New York Times* 2014) Historically, economies of scale allowed colonial textiles produced with mechanized equipment to swamp the colonies' markets. But in amongst the real and countless stories of loss and displacement of cultural traditions, it is worth remembering that

Theaster Gates, *Rickshaw for Hardware*, 2013. Wood, metal and wheel. 57.2 × 388.6 × 66 cm (22 ½ × 153 × 26 in.). © Theaster Gates. Photograph by Vincent Tsang. Courtesy of White Cube.

not all tales of cultural exchange born during the colonial era are tales of erasure and loss. Jasleen Kaur's *Dear Lord Robert Napier* project (2010), completed while Kaur was a postgraduate student at the Royal College of Art in London is one positive example. In Kaur's words, 'the main focus in my work is design as a cultural unifier'. (Kaur 2013) For the photographic project, Kaur first wrote to the current Lord Robert Napier explaining:

> During my time here [at the RCA] I have developed a passionate interest in researching my family's stories about their journeys from India to Britain and what made them want to move here. My work is evolving as a means by which to comment upon the way in which immigrants like my great grandfather – who first moved to Britain in 1950 – adapted to his new surroundings, and how subsequent generations of 'British Asians', including myself, retain their traditional roots whilst simultaneously experiencing a constant cultural evolution …
>
> The statue of your grandfather – Sir Robert Napier – stands next to the college. He was a central figure in the story of British India and, due in part to his role in the annexation of the Punjab, someone who helped to open up the migratory relationship between India and Britain that enabled my Sikh great grandfather to come to Britain.
>
> As part of my graduation work I would like for you to allow me to tie the revered turban of the Sikhs upon your head. This act, presented as a photograph, is intended as a celebratory statement of the dialogue between two communities of different cultures, religions and languages. With this intervention I will not be claiming to make a radical new statement, but simply to draw attention to a rich historical relationship and understanding between India and Britain. (Kaur 2013)

After clarifying a humorous misunderstanding over whether the turban would be tied on the statue's head or that of the current Lord Robert

Napier, the turban, as photographed, was tied to the current Lord Robert Napier's head with the guidance of the artist's Sikh father. Kaur's gesture brings to the foreground the often unspoken assumption that the flow of cultural influence since the colonial era has been a one-sided affair.

We can also find positive examples of the emergence of new aesthetic traditions generated during colonization and inspired not by trade and exchange of the very best textiles, but ironically by the influence of flawed cloth. For example, in the southern African country of Lesotho, a gift of industrially woven blankets is thought to have been presented to the founder of the Kingdom of Lesotho, King Moshoeshoe, in the nineteenth century. The blankets contained a production flaw that created lines across the finished design, but rather than reject this cloth as inferior, the lines became part of the style of the design from the 1860s onwards when 'Sotho insisted that these "faults" should be incorporated into all future designs.' (British Museum 2013) It is interesting to note that these stripes are combined in the 'Lehlaku' (feathers) motif with a motif thought to be based on the Prince of Wales' emblem of feather, crown and ostrich feather 'said to have been adopted after Prince Edward, the then Prince of Wales, visited Lesotho on a royal visit in 1925.' (British Museum 2014)

More recently, in the interview included in this book, Vlisco's creative director Roger Gerards explains that the veining of dye on wax-resist cloth originally attributed to poor quality mechanized production, and therefore seen as a flaw in the cloth, is currently being developed and enhanced in contemporary production as protection against copies of the cloth flooding the African market from countries such as China. A production flaw, much like the lines on the Lesotho blankets, has become an aesthetic attribute. In Vlisco's case the flaw offers a way to ensure that cloth produced in the Vlisco factory in the Netherlands is unique and therefore impossible to copy with digital printing; a solution to a contemporary problem found by revisiting a production mistake of the past.

A final example of creative inspiration found in what could have been understood as a problem with production appears in the work of American

Jasleen Kaur, *Dear Lord Robert Napier*, 2010.
Lambda C Type print. 102 × 77 cm (40 × 30 in.).
Photograph by Rachel Louise Brown.

Seana Marena, circa 2012. Jacquard woven blanket in the 'poone' ('mealie'/maize) design, wool and cotton. 155 × 165 cm (61 × 65 in.). Sotho, South Africa. © The Trustees of the British Museum.

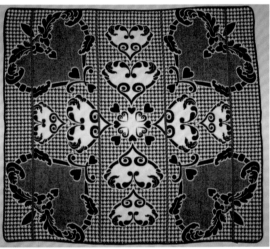

LEFT *Motlatsi*, circa 2012. Jacquard woven blanket in the 'Khosana' (chief) motif, wool and cotton (?). 154 × 169 cm (61 × 66 in.). South Africa. © The Trustees of the British Museum.

RIGHT *Victoria England*, circa 2012. Jacquard woven blanket in the 'Lehlaku' (feathers) motif, wool and cotton (?). 154 × 169 cm (61 × 66 in.). South Africa. © The Trustees of the British Museum.

Liza Lou, White Cube Hoxton Square, London (20 April to 26 May 2012). Photograph by Ben Westoby. Courtesy White Cube. © Liza Lou/White Cube.

artist Liza Lou, who from 2005 to 2012 based herself in South Africa to work with the local bead-weaving tradition. Lou's practice is based on the creation of large-scale installations that require assistants to fabricate. Her first interest in relocating to South Africa was to create a sculpture with women from the townships of KwaZulu-Natal, both to realize a sizable project and bring work to unemployed women in the region. Anitra Nettleton explains that crafts such as bead weaving and basket making were sanctioned by South Africa during apartheid because they were seen as safely inferior. 'Basket making is one of the forms of creative production, defined as "craft", which was encouraged among black South Africans under the apartheid regime,' Nettleton writes. 'It fell within the ambit of what was derogatorily labelled "Bantoekuns" (Bantu art) in Afrikaans, because it was seen as inferior to European arts and crafts.' (2010: 56)

Lou grappled with the political realities of production in South Africa as well as the material impact this context had on her work. Tellingly, the final works in her series made in South Africa allow mistakes, imperfections and dirt into the bead weavings – a belated acceptance of the complex reality of their production that brought a new aesthetic sophistication to the artist's practice. In a sobering reflection on the place of bead weaving – a pastime that could be misunderstood as frivolous – Lou writes of the project:

> Working with beads is a connection to an ancient struggle, a struggle I did not know. Since being in Africa, I have met women who can weave faster than other people can walk. Weaving is a way of getting somewhere. It puts food on the table, has agency in the marketplace. If you can weave something with beads, you've got skill. Maybe you can survive. (2012: 19)

The harsh economic realities of craft production are a further theme discussed throughout this book. For much of the world, the production of cloth and other craft activities is an economic necessity, a far cry from an elected pastime or hobby.

While textiles may not be as ephemeral as the soap sculptures of Meekyoung Shin, they do leave our material world after a relatively short lifespan. Robyn Healy suggests that this inability of textiles to adhere to the conservation standards aspired to by museums can be read as a meta-narrative. (Healy 2012)

Liza Lou, *Untitled #3,* 2011–2012.
Glass beads and cotton. 141 ×
133 cm (55 × 52 in.). Photograph
by Ben Westoby. Courtesy of White
Cube. © Liza Lou/White Cube.

Liza Lou, *Untitled #13*, 2011. Glass
beads on linen. 66 × 69 cm (26 ×
27 in.). Photograph by Ben Westoby.
Courtesy of White Cube. © Liza
Lou/White Cube.

Jorge Lizarazo, *Inga*, 2013. Wood canoe, glass beads. 28 × 76 × 401 cm (11 × 30 × 158 in.). Courtesy of Cristina Grajales Gallery and Andres Valbuena.

Just as Shin's *Written in Soap* replaces the timeless equestrian statue with a more short-lived counterpart, Healy suggests that fashion and textiles collected by museums similarly point to the impossibility of a fixed history. 'The continuing breakdown creates a disorder that cannot be contained – one that symbolically challenges the authority of the museum itself.' (2012: 91) Textiles traded with flaws that become admired, the veining of dye that now offers a solution to the problem of digital knock-offs and the aesthetic sophistication of Lou's practice that accepts the realities of a production context beyond her control all offer versions of Healy's uncontained disorder – discrete material moments that refuse conformity.

The image chosen for the cover of this book is a final example of an object with multiple narratives to tell, an object playing between the worlds of fiction and fact. The exhibition *Hechizoo: Voyages/*

Explorations at the Cristina Grajales Gallery in New York City in 2013 presented *Inga* as the centrepiece of an installation that sought to 'transform the gallery space into the Amazon, bringing its flora and fauna indoors through the use of handmade textiles ... invit[ing] the viewer to move through this magical environment much like a nineteenth century botanical expedition'. (Grajales 2013) The exhibition is the work of weaving atelier Hechizoo, founded in 2000 by Jorge Lizarazo and based in Bogotá, Colombia. The canoe 'alludes to the coca gathering river forays of the Inga people caught up in Colombia's narcotics trade'. Lizarazo explains, 'Since the history of conquest by the Spanish, it is always the same, indigenous culture is treated as the weakest part of the [cultural] chain.' (2013)

Colombia has rich sources of minerals, petroleum and wood, but its equally rich culture, Lizarazo laments, suffers because it is not immediately important for the economy. While the boat once stood as an 'element very important to life and culture; fishing, transport, connecting parts of the jungle' it has now come to symbolize the prominent role Colombia plays in the global narcotics trade. *Hechizoo: Voyages/Explorations* seeks to 'give dignity back to this object', to 'dress the canoe'. (Lizarazo 2013)

While the object looks in photographs to be a canoe of cloth, it is in fact an original wood canoe from the Putumayo region of Colombia covered in a geometric pattern of imported glass beads that represent the water, sky, land and jungle. (Lizarazo 2013) Lizarazo purchased the canoe, which

> had been used to transport coca leaves on the Putumayo river. The Indians and *campesinos* who plant coca (the sole crop that gets a decent price in those remote and isolated areas) are the weakest link in the drugs trade, a booming industry fuelled by consumption in First World countries, which has had devastating effects in terms of deforestation of the jungle, violence and the breaking up of whole communities'. (Roca 2013: 13)

Lizarazo purchased the canoe from an Inga family. Eight members of the family then worked for nearly six months at the Hechizoo studio to cover the canoe in glass beads, 'expanding on their traditional patterns as they worked on a familiar but completely unexpected surface'. (Roca 2013: 13)

Literal function is no longer the role of this impossible object: a boat that has adopted a new poetic identity in an attempt to move beyond the troubles of its cultural and national location. Beauty present in the face of such grave cultural loss is another recurring theme that appears throughout *Cultural Threads*. As *Inga* exemplifies, textiles like to travel. But the patterns, materials and meanings they carry are often not what first glance would confirm. As the population of the world becomes increasingly itinerant – driven by political or economic necessity at one extreme and cultural thirst at the other – the ease of the textile to travel with us means that textiles continue to absorb and record our peripatetic lives.

BIBLIOGRAPHY

British Museum (2014), <http://www.britishmuseum.org/research/collection_online/collection_object_details.aspx?objectId=3460612&partId=1&people=186385&peoA=186385-3-7&page=1> [Accessed 20 June 2014].

British Museum (2013), exhibition wall text from 'Social Fabric: Africa Textiles Today', British Museum, London, 4 February to 21 April 2013, curated by Chris Spring.

Feuer (2014), <http://www.zachfeuer.com/wp-content/files_mf/er_pressrelease13.pdf> [Accessed 9 January 2014].

Frayling, C. (2011), *On Craftsmanship: Towards a New Bauhaus*, London: Oberon Books.

Grajales (2013), <http://www.cristinagrajalesinc.com/exhibitions/hechizoo-voyages-explorations> [Accessed 8 January 2014].

Healy, R. (2012), 'The Parody of the Motley Cadaver: Displaying the Funeral of Fashion', in J. Hemmings (ed.), *Textile Reader*, London: Bloomsbury, 89–98.

Kaur, J. (2013), email correspondence with the author, 12 July 2013.

Lizarazo, J. (2013), interview with the author, 22 December 2013.

Lou, L. (2012), *Durban Diaries*, London: White Cube.

Nettleton, A. (2010), 'Life in a Zulu Village: Craft and the Art of Modernity in South Africa', *The Journal of Modern Craft*, vol. 3, no. 1, 55–78.

New York Times (2014), <www.nytimes.com/2013/12/24/business/international/40-million-in-aid-set-for-bangladesh-garment-workers.html?pagewanted=1&_r=0> [Accessed 4 January 2014].

Roca, J. (2013), 'Jorge Lizarazo: Weaving Through the Putumayo River', *Hechizoo: Voyages/Explorations* catalogue, New York: Cristina Grajales Gallery, 8–13.

Serpentine (2014), <http://www.serpentinegalleries.org/exhibitions-events/wael-shawky> [Accessed 8 January 2014].

Sharrad, P. and Collette, A. (2000), *Reinventing Textiles, Volume 3: Postcolonialism and Creativity*, Bristol: Telos.

White Cube (2013), <http://whitecube.com/exhibitions/theaster_gates_my_back_my_wheel_and_my_will_sao_paulo_2013/> [Accessed 8 January 2014].

Written in Soap (2014), <http://www.writteninsoap.com/about.html> [Accessed 8 January 2014].

1

Chapter one

Artist statements

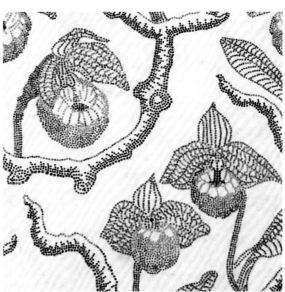

Julie Ryder, *Generate: Charles* (detail), 2008. Hand-cut leaves, tapa cloth, archival glue. Photograph by Barry Brown. © DACS 2013.

Julie Ryder, *Generate: Charles*, 2008. Hand-cut leaves, tapa cloth, archival glue. 50 × 80 cm (20 × 32 in.). Photograph by Barry Brown. © DACS 2013.

Five statements from artists and designers with connections to Australia, Colombia, Peru, South Africa and the United States comprise the opening chapter of *Cultural Threads*. Their voices are foregrounded at the outset to ensure that the intentions, explanations and the questions raised by artists, designers and makers remain central to our reading and seeing of the practices included in this book.

Australian Julie Ryder opens the chapter with her discussion of *Generate*, a series of works inspired by Charles Darwin's journey across the South Pacific to Australia. Working with the format of the portrait, Ryder translates the uncomfortably close genealogy of Darwin's own family tree in meticulously collected and cut discs of plant materials both introduced and native to Australia. Ryder explains that her series of textiles addresses 'eighteenth- and nineteenth-century fascination with scientific exploration, botanical and zoological specimen collection and the appropriation of the "exotic other"'.

Much like Ryder's interest in early botanical expeditions, Jorge Lizarazo builds a poetic interpretation of the Colombian rainforest, which the Cristina Grajales Gallery refers to as a 'magical environment much like a nineteenth-century botanical expedition'. As its centrepiece is a bead-covered canoe. Before colonization of the region, the canoe acted as a primary form of transport and exchange of indigenous culture. Today it is tarnished by associations with the country's coca production and rampant drug trade. Lizarazo refers to a desire to dress up the original canoe for the occasion of his New York City exhibition and supported the family who owned the canoe to embellish the surface with coloured glass beads based on traditional patterns that would have originally been carved in wood or decorated with seeds. Installed alongside the vessel are tree-like sculptures of industrial rubber and copper; below the floor is covered with a woven carpet of silver thread suggestive of waterways and *cumare*, a fibre found in the Andes.

From Colombia we travel with Chilean artist Cecilia Vicuña to her installation *Quipo Austral* at the 18th Sydney Biennial. Vicuña references the ancient Andean communication system of *quipos*, which were forced out of use during the Spanish conquest of the region in the sixteenth century. Vicuña's installation of unspun wool 'connects two ancient traditions of the southern hemisphere: Quipo and Songlines' – both systems of understanding the land that exist beyond the printed word.

From South America, via Australia, we then visit the United States where American artist Elaine Reichek reflects on the reinstallation of *Postcolonial Kinderhood*, a recreation of her childhood bedroom first exhibited nearly twenty years ago. In this context the colonial – in contemporary parlance – is noted as a style of interior decorating. Reflecting on her childhood, Reichek explains that the colonial style of the home was an identity conspicuously foregrounded while her family's Jewish identity was not. As the work included throughout this book begins to show, in the twenty years separating the conception of Reichek's show and the reinstallation, the textile's engagement – via feminism – with postcolonial thinking has grown significantly.

Finally, we visit South Africa where designers Sharon Lombard and Heidi Chisholm, also known as Mr Somebody and Mr Nobody, discuss the complexity of white South African identity today. Mr Somebody and Mr Nobody, both expatriates now living in the United States, describe themselves as 'immigrant artists, finding ourselves "neither here nor there", grappling with personal identity construction, puzzling over genealogical fuzziness, navigating political shifts and revising culture/cultural production'.

Jessica Hemmings

OPPOSITE Julie Ryder, *Generate: Emma*, 2008. Hand-cut leaves, tapa cloth, archival glue. 50 × 80 cm (20 × 32 in.). Photograph by Derek Ross. © DACS 2013.

ABOVE Julie Ryder, *Generate: Emma* (detail), 2008. Hand-cut leaves, tapa cloth, archival glue. Photograph by Derek Ross. © DACS 2013.

Artist Statement

Reflections on Charles Darwin's South Pacific

Julie Ryder

In 2008 I developed a solo exhibition, *Generate*, for the Australian National Botanic Gardens to coincide with the bicentenary celebrations of the nineteenth-century naturalist Charles Darwin.[1] My inspiration was drawn from Darwin's five-year voyage in the *HMS Beagle*, the impact this exotic journey had on his ideas of social and natural history, and the controversy surrounding his publication *On the Origin of Species* (1859). In response I created a collection of decorative works that reference the eighteenth- and nineteenth-century fascination with scientific exploration, botanical and zoological specimen collection and the appropriation of the 'exotic other'.

Julie Ryder, *Regenerate: 1808* (detail),
2008. Silk, reactive dyes, direct digital
print. 120 × 300 cm (47 × 118 in.).
Photograph by Margot Seares.
© DACS 2013.

Julie Ryder, *Regenerate: 1835* (detail),
2008. Silk, reactive dyes, direct digital
print. 120 × 300 cm (47 × 118 in.).
Photograph by Margot Seares.
© DACS 2013.

Julie Ryder, *Regenerate: 1859* (detail),
2008. Silk, reactive dyes, direct digital
print. 120 × 300 cm (47 × 118 in.).
Photograph by Margot Seares.
© DACS 2013.

After reading Darwin's diary from the
HMS Beagle journey, I became interested in his
observations about the indigenous inhabitants
of the lands he visited. Of particular interest was
his journey from Tierra del Fuego through the
Galápagos Islands and across the South Pacific to
Australia, which he eventually reached in 1836. In
Darwin's opinion the people of Tierra del Fuego
were 'savages' because they were dirty, did not wear
clothing or live in houses replete with the furnishings
of civilized Victorian society. But contrary to the
racist polygenist theories of the time, Darwin
firmly believed that human beings were all of the
same species. His encounters with these 'savages'
eventually lead to his publication *The Descent of
Man and Selection in Relation to Sex,* a book that
sets out his concepts of human evolution and sexual
selection, including the differences between human
races and sexes, and the relevance of evolutionary
theory to society.

These facts led me to explore a fascinating
aspect of Darwin's own life: his genealogy and the
intermarriages between the Darwin and Wedgwood
families. Both Charles and his sister Caroline
married their first cousins (Emma and Josiah III),
thus sharing a mutual grandfather, Josiah Wedgwood
I, founder of the Wedgwood pottery company. To
illustrate these concepts I created two sets of triptych
'portraits' exploring Darwin's family and the many
indigenous peoples he encountered on his voyage
with the *HMS Beagle.*

The first triptych, *Generate: Emma, Charles
and Josiah,* is constructed from thousands of
hand-punched leaves, both native to Australia and
introduced. I meticulously rearranged the leaf
pieces onto tapa cloth to form abstract 'portraits'
of Charles, his wife Emma and their mutual
grandfather, Josiah Wedgwood I. Tapa cloth was
deliberately chosen as the base for the collages
because of its use as wearable or ceremonial cloths
by peoples from South America right through the
Pacific Islands that Darwin encountered. Leaves
became perfect metaphors for the way Darwin, and
other explorers of his time, amassed botanical and
zoological collections from around the world.

To create the works the leaves – free, abundant and easy to collect and hole-punch – were sorted by size, shape and colour. The circular pieces were then stored in petri dishes and later reassembled with archival glue on the tapa cloth.

Redesigned historical textiles provided the starting point for each 'portrait'. The intricate leaf collages are bordered on the top and bottom by piercings into the tapa cloth that reference the tattoos and body decorations of the Mocoví, Tahitian and Marquesa Islands peoples that Darwin recorded on his journey. This reference to influences that are skin deep, or that lie just beneath the surface, is apparent in the meeting of two cultures, whether consciously acknowledged or not.

The other triptych 'portraits' are not of individual people, but are symbolic of the indigenous societies that Darwin came into contact with. *Pollinate: Originate*, *Infiltrate* and *Eliminate* represent the effect of colonization on another culture: the eradication of traditional values and beliefs, languages, customs as well as sacred and symbolic objects and imagery. The three works carry a tapa cloth design from Samoa that is slowly being supplanted by an English damask design rendered with actual grains of pollen, adhered to the tapa cloth with archival glue.

My use of pollen as a medium references the theory of pangenesis (the process of hereditary transmission) that was advanced by Darwin in his book *Variation of Plants and Animals under Domestication* (1868). The pollen used in *Originate* is from *Acacia pycnantha*; in *Infiltrate* it is a blend of *Acacia pycnantha* and *Acacia genistifolia*, and in *Eliminate* I have used pollen from an introduced plant, the Oriental lily, to reference the introduced culture overtaking the indigenous one. The pin-pricked borders of these works reflect the Victorian textile designs from the *Generate* triptych.

In the series of digitally printed textiles *Regenerate: 1808, 1835* and *1859*, I explore the avenues open to textile designers to produce or 'generate' patterns and designs. The dates in each title refer to specific events: the year of Emma's birth; the year Darwin arrived in the Galápagos Islands; and the year that *Origin of Species* was published. Images and motifs are re-worked to form new meanings, each one being generated from the cloth before it. As with our understanding of life, it is a mixture of the past, the present and the future. The blue colourings of the three textiles reference the tones found in the famous Wedgwood jasperware pottery, founded by Emma and Charles's mutual grandfather Josiah Wedgwood I.

Generate reflects my ongoing fascination with nature as a way of understanding our inner and outer worlds, challenging perceptions of chaos and control, perfection and imperfection, and questioning concepts of beauty and veracity.

OPPOSITE   Julie Ryder, *Pollinate: Originate*, 2008. Pollen, tapa cloth, archival glue. 50 × 80 cm (20 × 32 in.). Photograph by Derek Ross. © DACS 2013.

NOTE

1.   This project was funded by artsACT.

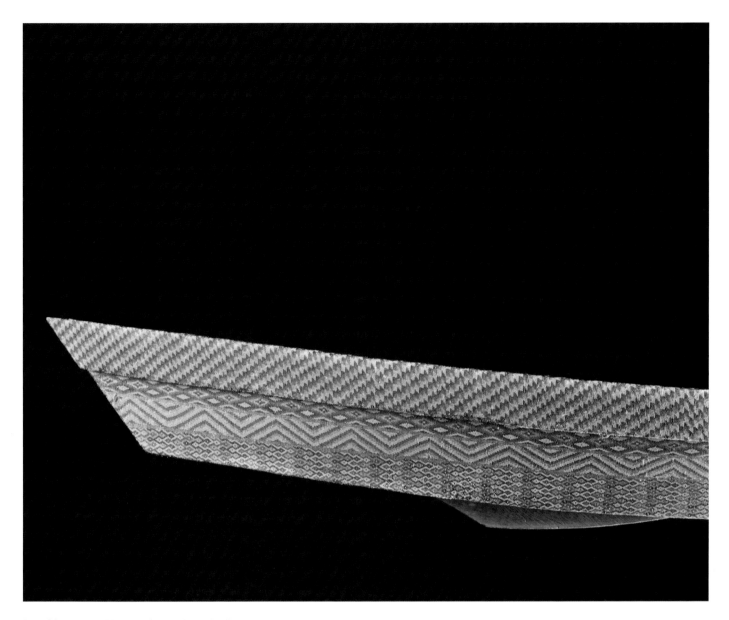

Jorge Lizarazo and Hechizoo Studio, *Inga* (detail),
2013. Wood canoe, glass beads. Courtesy of
Cristina Grajales Gallery and Andres Valbuena.

RIGHT Jorge Lizarazo and Hechizoo Studio, installation, Cristina Grajales Gallery, New York, (7 November 2013 to 14 March 2014). Courtesy of Cristina Grajales Gallery and Andres Valbuena.

Artist Statement

Colombian voyages and explorations

Jorge Lizarazo and Hechizoo

Observing ... this is my main working tool.

Hechizoo intends to understand and get to know its own history through the hands of its craftsmen. In a world of unique and particular stories of pain and uprooting, our craftsmen become narrators of their own history. With this narrative we seek to heal through craft and we help to tell horror stories in a sensitive and aesthetic way. We want to show that behind these stories there is an aesthetic that has always been present, the aesthetic of towns that do not connect with the media because the media is not interested in them. We become the instrument by which the world gains interest in those who have no voice. Along with our craft, which is our only tool in common, we begin a journey through the painful world of displacement, drugs and oblivion.

We ride on a beautiful canoe, dressed in an elegant gown for the occasion, to an expedition that will travel through two forgotten and devastated regions of my country, Putumayo, an Amazon region, and lower San Juan, on the Pacific coast. Each of the objects collected in this journey expresses their story through our most precious legend of El Dorado. Each object shines. Some have crystals, others are metal. They shine from the jungle where they were fabricated to narrate their stories, and paradoxically they are harmless.

LEFT Jorge Lizarazo and Hechizoo Studio, *Cacho*, 2013. Horn. 366 × 183 cm (144 × 72 in.) Courtesy of Cristina Grajales Gallery and Andres Valbuena.

OPPOSITE Jorge Lizarazo and Hechizoo Studio, *Single Sailor*, 2013. Candleholder in copper, bronze, crystal. 279 × 25 cm (110 × 10 in.) Courtesy of Cristina Grajales Gallery and Andres Valbuena.

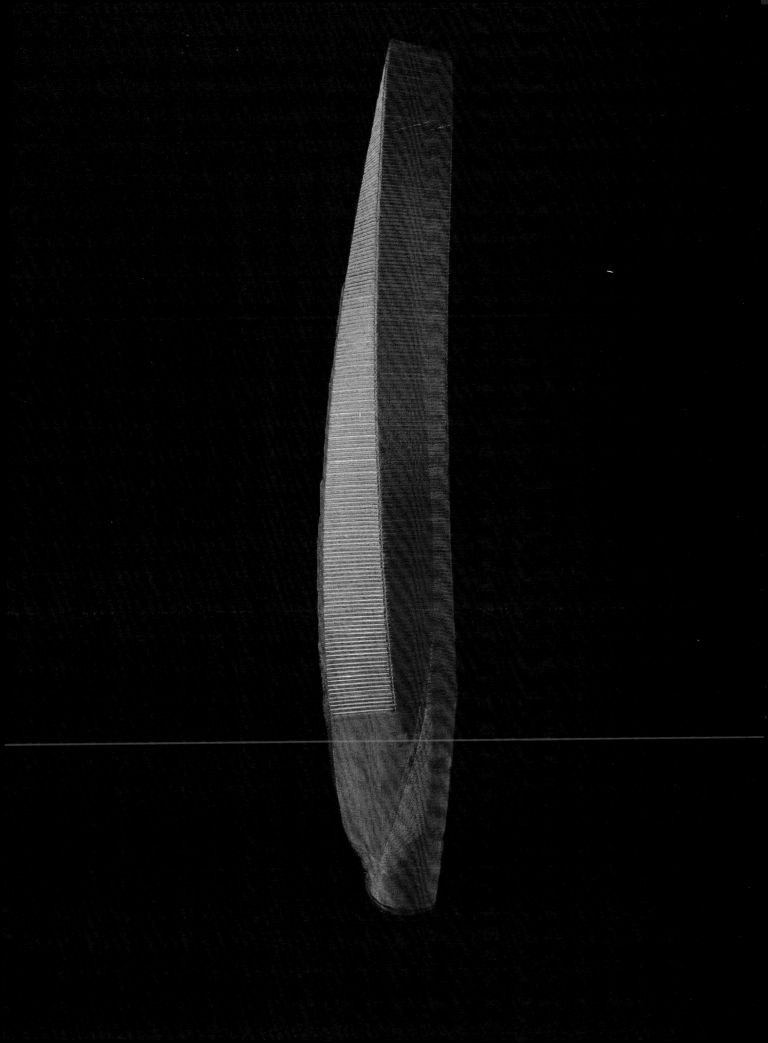

ABOVE Jorge Lizarazo and Hechizoo Studio, *Werregues: Woun, Wouna and Chanco*, 2013. Aluminium and copper. 23 × 68.5 cm (9 × 27 in.). Courtesy of Cristina Grajales Gallery and Andres Valbuena.

OPPOSITE Jorge Lizarazo and Hechizoo Studio, *Barcas del Putumayo* fabric (detail), 2013. Woven ribbon. Courtesy of Cristina Grajales Gallery and Andres Valbuena.

Jorge Lizarazo and Hechizoo Studio, *Neymar Area Rug* (detail), 2013. Woven fique. Courtesy of Cristina Grajales Gallery and Andres Valbuena.

Jorge Lizarazo and Hechizoo Studio, *Jade* fabric (detail), 2013. Woven ribbon. Courtesy of Cristina Grajales Gallery and Andres Valbuena.

Jorge Lizarazo and Hechizoo
Studio, *El Dorado's Autumn* (detail),
2013. Copper, gold-plated and
silver-plated leaves. Courtesy of
Cristina Grajales Gallery and
Andres Valbuena.

Jorge Lizarazo and Hechizoo
Studio, *Moreira Rug*, 2013.
Fique, cumare, aluminium,
silver-plated leaves. Courtesy of
Cristina Grajales Gallery and
Andres Valbuena.

OPPOSITE AND ABOVE Cecilia Vicuña, *Quipu Austral*, 2012. Tasmanian wool fleece, installation, 18th Sydney Biennale, Australia (27 June to 16 September 2012). Photograph by the artist.

Artist Statement

QUIPUing from Santiago, Chile to Sydney, Australia

Cecilia Vicuña

Quipu: knot (Quechua)

In the ancient Andes people did not write; they wove meaning into textiles and knotted cords. Five thousand years ago they created the *quipu* (knot), a poem in space, a tactile, spatial metaphor for the union and interdependence of all. The *quipu*, and its virtual counterpart, the *ceque* (a system of sightlines connecting all communities and sacred sites in the Andes) were banished after the Spanish conquest of the Americas. *Quipus* were burnt and they ceased to be used, but the vision of interconnectivity they represent endures underground.

Cecilia Vicuña, *Quipu Austral*, 2012. Tasmanian wool fleece, installation, 18th Sydney Biennale, Australia. Photograph by the artist.

I first encountered *quipus* as a teenager, and something in me knew they belonged – like poetry – outside time and space, despite being in time and space. This non-local quality of the *quipu* acts as a connector between dimensions. Touching the threads or thinking about them I re-enter a different scale of the imagination. The *quipu* knots me into new ways of being and seeing.

I began making *quipus* in the mid 1960s as an act of poetic resistance. *El quipu que no recuerda nada* (the *quipu* that remembers nothing), an imaginary cord laid out in my bedroom in Santiago, was my first *quipu* work. I wrote: 'an empty cord is the core, the heart of memory, the earth listening to us'.

A decade later, in exile in London, while enduring the pain of loss from the military coup in Chile, I created a large *quipu* above my bed and I slept under it for the memory of the pain not to leave my body.

Years later, walking along Lake Titicaca in Bolivia I observed that alpaca herders tied unspun wool dyed in rainbows to the ears of their alpacas. The fibres hung and danced in the wind as prayer flags do in Tibet. In the Andean worldview ritual tying increases the fertility of the herd.

Unspun wool is all potential, nothing holds it together, except the desire of togetherness in each hair. Unspun wool stands for the cosmic gas from

Cecilia Vicuña, *Quipu Austral*, 2012. Tasmanian wool fleece, installation, 18th Sydney Biennale, Australia. Photograph by the artist.

which stars and galaxies are born. The gluon the Large Hadron Collider can't find.

Emptiness is connection.

I began making monumental *quipus* and precarious weavings of unspun wool in the early 1990s. *Cloud-Net* (1999) was dedicated to global warming, and *Canoes of Light* (2000), to the indigenous view of the life force.

In my book *Chanccani Quipu* (2012) I metaphorically wrote with breath on the unspun wool by printing words on the outer hairs of fleece. The Quechua word *quipucamayoc*, or *quipu* maker, means 'the one who animates and gives life to the knot'. A *quipu* depends on the interaction of breath and thread, hand and voice. To write with breath is to see the body and the cosmos in a continuous reciprocal exchange.

Chanccani Quipu condenses the clash and collaboration between two cultures and worldviews: the Andean oral universe of threads and the Western world of print.

In *Quipu Austral*, created for the 18th Sydney Biennale, I connected two ancient traditions of the southern hemisphere: the Andean *quipu* and the aboriginal Australian songline. *Quipus* and songlines participate in the web of life by creating complex interactions between land, memory and sound enacted through song and speech.

OPPOSITE AND ABOVE Cecilia Vicuña, *Quipu Austral*, 2012. Tasmanian wool fleece, installation, 18th Sydney Biennale, Australia. Photograph by Farhan Mahmud.

Quipu Austral was installed in a building without walls on Cockatoo Island in Sydney's Harbour. It interacted with the wind and the sun, the smells and sounds of the place. Long streams of unspun wool hung from the tall beams. They were dyed in the earthen colours of aboriginal rock paintings and Andean weavings. The combined palette of the two traditions merged with the southern light, radiating intensely at sunrise and sunset. As people entered the *quipu*, they became the living knots walking about the threads.

My work responds to an awareness of place, a sensory memory of the land. To respond is to offer again. Desire is the offering – the body is only a metaphor. Precarious means prayer, uncertain, exposed to hazards, insecure. Prayer is change, the dangerous instant of transmutation. An object is not an object. It is the witness to a relationship. In complementary union, two opposites collide to create new forms. Seeing and naming the beauty of the exchange creates the space for it to unfold. Weaving is awareness of the exchange.

Quipu Austral was dedicated to the union of all.

Elaine Reichek, *A Postcolonial Kinderhood*, 1994. Installation view, The Jewish Museum, New York (6 February to 31 March 1994). Collection of The Jewish Museum, New York. Photograph by John Parnell.

Artist Statement

Revisiting
A Postcolonial Kinderhood
in America

Elaine Reichek

Given the inquiry into issues around history, identity and representation in my work of the 1980s and 1990s, it was not illogical that curator Susan Goodman of The Jewish Museum, New York, should visit my studio in 1992 and ask, 'Done anything Jewish?' And yet I was startled, perhaps less by the question itself than by its making me realize that I had never even considered the idea of working with issues of Jewish identity. When Susan left I filed 'Jewish' in the catacombs of my psyche and went on reading about Native Americans, Fuegians and Ireland's Easter Rebellion of 1916, the subjects I was exploring in my work at the time. But of course the idea could not stay entombed, and the result was *A Postcolonial Kinderhood*, an installation at The Jewish Museum recreating my childhood bedroom.

I was brought up in Brooklyn in a large Dutch Colonial house full of reproductions of

Elaine Reichek, *A Postcolonial Kinderhood Revisited*, 2013. Installation view, The Jewish Museum, New York (23 August to 20 October 2013). Collection of The Jewish Museum, New York. Photograph by Paul Kennedy.

early American furniture. In the United States, the term 'colonial' as often as not refers to a style of architecture and interior design. The celebrations surrounding the country's first centennial, in 1876, set off the first of many subsequent waves of colonial revivals, all reflecting the national wish to define what was really 'American' (important in a nation of immigrants) and to invoke the period before the revolution when we in the colonies declared and fought for our independence. My house was built in 1903, during a wave of colonial nostalgia. When I was growing up there in the 1950s, there were many family conversations about good taste and bad taste, particularly in furniture – my father was in the furniture business – and by contrast a great deal of silence surrounding our Jewishness.

In my recreation of my bedroom, I explored decor as a means of assimilating and Americanizing the family. For us it was a way of 'passing' and of connecting to a desirable past. The installation was dimly lit, and the furniture – all store bought from the '1776' collection of Ethan Allen, to this day a popular manufacturer of old-fashioned home decor – had been slightly reduced in size by subtle carpentry, creating an environment that I hoped felt melancholy, unsettled and off-kilter.

In addition to the furnishings, the olive-grey walls were lined with embroideries I'd made based on American samplers. But instead of the usual Christian homilies or historical quotes that I'd replaced those homilies with in earlier works of this kind, I sewed these samplers with quotations from my relatives and friends, mostly gathered from conversations during family get-togethers. In my family the occasions for these meetings were less Passover or Chanukah, more Thanksgiving,

Elaine Reichek, *A Postcolonial Kinderhood,* 1994. Installation view detail of towel rack and washstand, The Jewish Museum, New York. Collection of The Jewish Museum, New York. Photograph by John Parnell.

Christmas and the Fourth of July. Becoming an anthropologist of my own culture, I discovered the same kind of shifting border territory that I had been exploring from a safe distance in my studies of the nineteenth-century politics of colonialism.

Last spring, to celebrate its twentieth anniversary, The Jewish Museum decided to reprise the exhibition. In the text accompanying *A Postcolonial Kinderhood Revisited*, Norman Kleeblatt, chief curator at the Museum, described the 1994 installation as having 'probed the fears and embarrassments – real or imagined – that still prevailed among many American Jews'. The reinstallation allowed me to revisit the material, and in thinking about the response to the first show I configured two separate bulletin boards: the first

displayed documentation of the original installation, and the second included information about making the exhibition, along with family pictures and other personal memorabilia. I also included a video, *Bon Voyage*, made from a 1934 home movie of my in-laws' honeymoon, and I borrowed an earlier sampler, *Self-Portrait (E. R.)*, from the Pennsylvania Academy of Fine Arts in Philadelphia. This sampler seemed an apt postscript to the installation, as it includes my personal, professional and married names, and my initials embroidered in a variety of monogram styles. In restaging an exhibition made at the apex of American multiculturalism and identity politics, I was hoping to clarify my feeling that issues of identity, immigration and assimilation still resonate in this age of globalism.

Elaine Reichek, *A Postcolonial Kinderhood,* 1994. Installation view of samplers, photograph and table with family photographs, The Jewish Museum, New York. Collection of The Jewish Museum, New York. Photograph by John Parnell.

ABOVE Elaine Reichek, *A Postcolonial Kinderhood Revisited,* 2013. Installation view with Bulletin Board #2, 2013, and samplers, photograph and table with family photographs, The Jewish Museum, New York. Collection of The Jewish Museum, New York. Photograph by Paul Kennedy.

LEFT Elaine Reichek, *Untitled (John P. Engel),* 1993. Hand embroidery on linen, 53 × 31 cm (21 × 15 in.). Collection of The Jewish Museum, New York. Photograph by Paul Kennedy.

RIGHT Elaine Reichek, *Untitled (Susan Engel Golden),* 1993. Hand embroidery on linen, 41 × 37 cm (16 × 14 ½ in.). Collection of The Jewish Museum, New York. Photograph by Paul Kennedy.

LEFT Elaine Reichek, *Untitled (Jesse Reichek),* 1993. Hand embroidery on linen, 30 × 32 cm (11 × 13 in.). Collection of The Jewish Museum, New York. Photograph by Paul Kennedy.

Elaine Reichek, *Untitled (H.R.)*, 1993. Hand embroidery on linen.
38 × 23 cm (15 × 9 in.). Collection of The Jewish Museum, New York.
Photograph by Paul Kennedy.

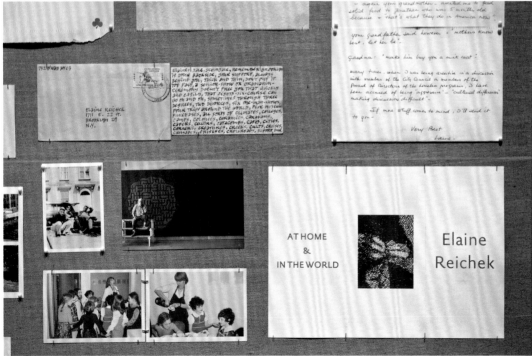

ABOVE Elaine Reichek, *Bulletin Board #2*, 2013. Printed matter, family photographs, letters and ephemera pinned to linen stretched over board. 112 × 163 cm (44 × 64 in.). Collection of the artist. Photograph by Paul Kennedy.

LEFT Elaine Reichek, *Bulletin Board #2* (detail), 2013. Collection of the artist. Photograph by Paul Kennedy.

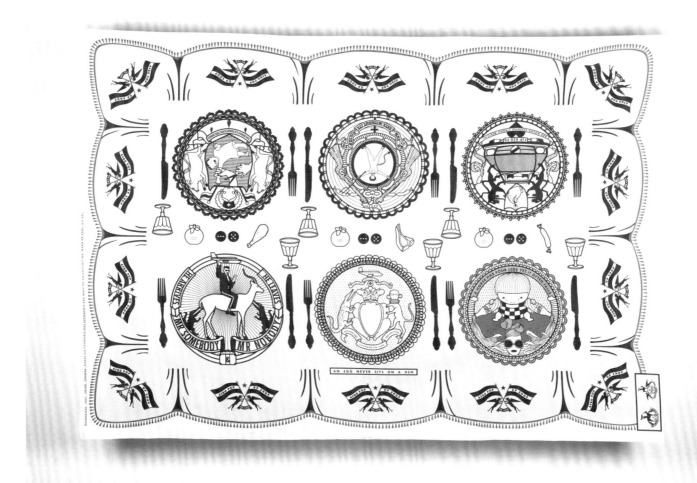

ABOVE Heidi Chisholm & Sharon Lombard for Mr Somebody & Mr Nobody, *An Egg Never Sits on a Hen*, Baby Blue Khanga, 2013. Digital print on cotton. 107 × 163 cm (42 × 64 in.). Photograph by Richard Bock.

Artist Statement

African design exported

Mr Somebody & Mr Nobody

Mr Somebody & Mr Nobody is a collaborative practice between South African born Heidi Chisholm and Sharon Lombard who now reside in the United States. We are immigrant artists, finding ourselves 'neither here nor there', grappling with personal identity construction, puzzling over genealogical fuzziness, navigating political shifts and revising culture and cultural production. As South Africans we were socialized to believe that we were inherently Europeans, momentarily trapped in a 'foreign' land. Our current realities challenge this assumption. Culture is not a hermetically sealed and symbiotic exchange between indigenous Africans and 'us', it is a dynamic force.

Like pre-colonial African traders we peddle our wares. In the place of old trade routes, we exchange objects and ideas over the internet and in 'souvenir stands' or design installations that become pop-up market stall realities, where goods are viewed and sold. The online flash sales site Fab Europe aptly describes us: 'Mr Somebody & Mr Nobody are two stand-up (female) gents. Their collection of … African-flavoured domestic curiosities runs a spectrum of quirky cool, from radio cushions and golden chickens to multipurpose khangas that you, your bed or your dining room table can wear.' Khangas are our special interest.[1]

Historically, buckskin khangas (karosses) were used by San women as carrying cloths, garments and blankets. 'In !kung thought, the kaross is so characteristic of women and their work that the term knot (!kebi)[2] that ties the kaross at a woman's waist is also an affectionate colloquial term for "women" (!kebisi). (Lee 1984: 37) In the nineteenth century, cotton was picked by African slaves in the USA, shipped to England, then exported to East Africa by slavers in the form of white cloth. This trade met the demand to 'adequately' clothe female slaves captured in East Africa. (Awaaz Magazine 2013)

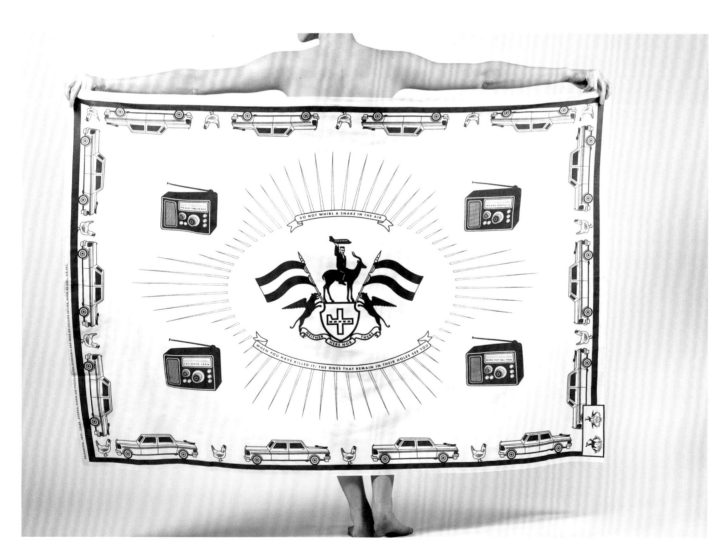

Heidi Chisholm & Sharon Lombard for Mr Somebody & Mr Nobody, *Whirl a Snake*, White Khanga, 2013. Digital print on cotton. 107 × 163 cm (42 × 64 in.). Photograph by Richard Bock.

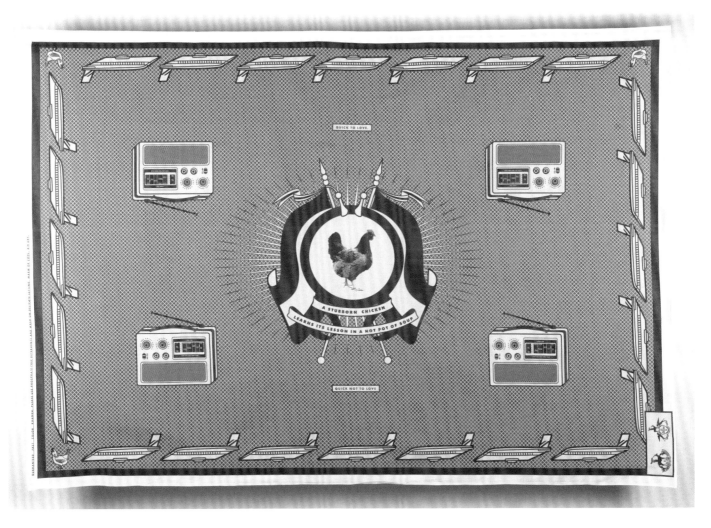

ABOVE AND LEFT Heidi Chisholm & Sharon Lombard for Mr Somebody & Mr Nobody, *Stubborn Chicken*, Rusty Red Khanga and Baby Blue Khanga (detail), 2013. Digital print on cotton. Photographs by Richard Bock (above) and Daniel Portnoy (left).

BELOW Heidi Chisholm & Sharon Lombard for Mr Somebody & Mr Nobody, *Stubborn Chicken*, Rusty Red Khanga in package, 2013. Digital print on cotton. Photograph by Sharon Lombard.

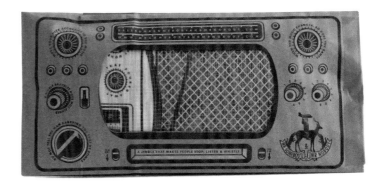

Artist statements

Heidi Chisholm & Sharon Lombard for Mr
Somebody & Mr Nobody, *He Arrives Mr
Somebody & He Leaves Mr Nobody*, installation,
Fountain Art Fair Miami, 2012. Photograph by
Sharon Lombard.

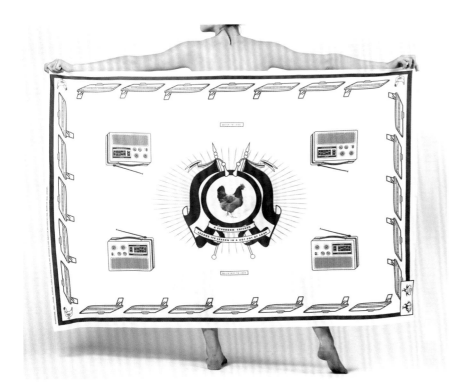

LEFT Heidi Chisholm & Sharon Lombard for Mr Somebody & Mr Nobody, *Stubborn Chicken*, White Khanga, 2013. Digital print on cotton. 107 × 163 cm (42 × 64 in.). Photograph by Richard Bock.

ABOVE Heidi Chisholm & Sharon Lombard for Mr Somebody & Mr Nobody, 2013. Photograph by Sharon Lombard.

RIGHT Heidi Chisholm & Sharon Lombard for Mr Somebody & Mr Nobody, 2014. Illustration by Heidi Chisholm.

ABOVE   Heidi Chisholm & Sharon
Lombard for Mr Somebody & Mr
Nobody, *Piggybacking Goat*, Blue Criss
Cross Khanga, 2013. Digital print on
cotton. 107 × 163 cm (42 × 64 in.).
Photograph by Daniel Portnoy.

RIGHT & FAR RIGHT   Heidi Chisholm
& Sharon Lombard for Mr Somebody &
Mr Nobody, *Piggybacking Goat* (details),
Afro Pop Dots Khanga and Red Flags
Khanga, 2013. Digital print on cotton.
Photographs by Daniel Portnoy.

After abolition, this practical cloth was reclaimed by Africans and revamped with surface decoration. Around 1910, text appeared on khangas and words became crucial to their selling potential. These cloths began to express suppressed women's voices.

Khangas evolved as important vehicles for communication and are frequently used to create awareness or mobilize people and issues. (Swahili Proverbs 2013) This communication aspect really interests us. Like giant posters (though much more useful!), our portable cloths broadcast humorous African proverbs inspired by the Africa we love. For decades hand-stamped khangas were produced in East Africa, and up until the 1960s, most machine-printed versions came from Europe, then later India, China and Japan. Now khangas are principally produced in Tanzania, Kenya and India, for the African market. Some of our khangas are digitally printed in North Carolina (enabling small multi-coloured runs) and sewn in Miami. Presently the *Stubborn Chicken* khanga, marked 'made in South Africa', is silkscreened in Cape Town on Indian cotton, finished by a women's cooperative there, then exported back to Miami for distribution.

Khangas 'are an ongoing part of the great trading network which has thrived for at least two thousand years between the many peoples of the Indian Ocean littoral'. (British Museum 2013) Khangas reflect and document the times. The design collaboration of Mr Somebody & Mr Nobody is a page in this human story. We view the process and results as 'ours', recognizing that larger cultures and cultural productions are shared human experiences.

NOTES

1. Two spellings of the term are found in common usage: khanga and kanga. The meaning is the same.
2. The !Kung language is spoken in parts of Namibia, Botswana and Angola.

BIBLIOGRAPHY

Awaaz Magazine (2013), <http://www.awaazmagazine.com/index.php/component/k2/item/258-language-of-the-kanga> [Accessed 1 March 2013].
British Museum (2013), <http://www.britishmuseum.org/research/projects/kanga_and_printed_textiles.aspx> [Accessed 1 March 2103].
Lee, R.B. (1984), *The Dobe !Kung: Case Studies in Cultural Anthropology*, New York: Holt, Rinehart and Winston, CBS College Publishing: 37.
Swahili Proverbs (2013), <http://swahiliproverbs.afrst.illinois.edu/kangas.htm> [Accessed 1 March 2013].

Chapter two

Dutch wax-resist textiles: Roger Gerards, creative director of Vlisco, in conversation with Jessica Hemmings

The transnational identity of wax-resist textiles emerges from the numerous cultures that have in the past, and continue today, to identify with wax-resist cloth. Present-day Indonesia has a history of refined wax-resist cloth production known as batik. During Dutch colonization of the region, batik production was taken up in the Netherlands, as well as other textile manufacturing centres such as Manchester, England, intended for trade with the islands. (Kent 2008: 12) But the market proved unsuccessful. Aesthetic concerns are often cited as the reason for this failure, with the presence of 'veins' of dye on the cloth occurring during mechanical production deemed inferior by a market familiar with the subtleties of hand production. (Picton 2001) But taxation imposed, ironically, by the Dutch government, to protect the value of cloth produced in the islands is also cited as a reason why importing cloth to the region was a marketing failure. (Hobbs 2008 and Vergès 2014) Instead, the textiles found a welcome reception in West Africa, becoming symbols of national pride associated with independence gained by a number of nations in the late 1950s and 1960s.

The Dutch company Vlisco has been designing and manufacturing wax-resist cloth since the late nineteenth century for the African market. (Arts 2012) Based in Helmond near Eindhoven, Vlisco today produces wax-resist textiles that are sold globally. In this chapter Roger Gerards, creative director of Vlisco, discusses the company's brand identity, speculates on the reasons for Vlisco's longevity and proposes that fashion, by default, always seeks out the unfamiliar.

Jessica Hemmings

OPPOSITE Vlisco, Theo Maas, fan design, 1985. Wax-resist on cotton. © Vlisco Netherlands B.V.

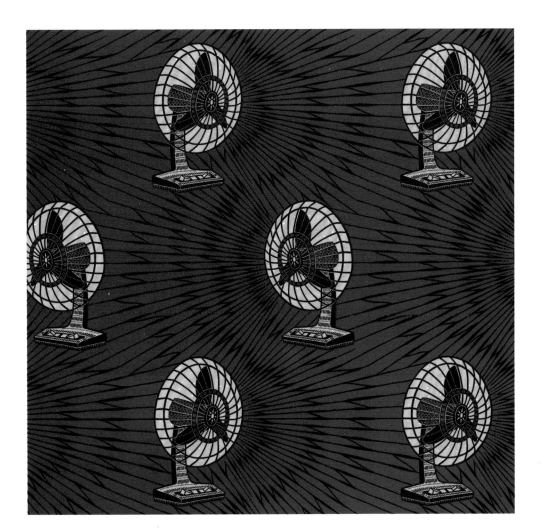

LEFT Vlisco, Theo
Maas, fan design, 1985.
Wax-resist on cotton.
© Vlisco Netherlands B.V.

OPPOSITE Vlisco campaign
Funky Grooves, 2012.
Wax-resist on cotton.
Photograph by Wendelien
Daan. © Vlisco Netherlands
B.V.

**JESSICA HEMMINGS: There are many
explanations put forward to explain why Dutch –
and English – wax-resist cloth produced for what
is present-day Indonesia was not a successful
business during Dutch colonization of the
islands. What is Vlisco's understanding of this
'failed' trade route?**

ROGER GERARDS   The story I know is that there
was a law in Indonesia that it was forbidden to import
batik from outside. The import rates on imitation batik
were so high – imposed by the Dutch government –
that it was no longer profitable for the Dutch and the
English to export to Indonesia. There was also a kind
of print technique of batik that we [the Dutch] were
not allowed to do. The original batik is not printed
by wood but with handmade copper plates. We were
not allowed to do that anymore. So there were a lot
of complications in making the batik product for
Indonesia. In Indonesia they also discovered a new
stamping technique (*Tjap*) for certain simple designs
to replace the hand-drawn technique (*Tjanting*), so
they could produce their own product easier, cheaper.
But the most important thing, which made it difficult,
was that we were not allowed to export to Indonesia.

**JH   Mechanized production of batik can
introduce 'veining' where small cracks in the wax
allow dye to seep onto the cloth. I understand
that Vlisco is now developing production
techniques to enhance this veining because
it allows each cloth to be unique and affords
protection against digitally printed copies. I had
originally understood that the veining was a
problem for some markets and another reason
why imported cloth was unpopular in what is
now Indonesia?**

RG Yes. In the design image the vein is caused by an uncontrolled break in the wax [that] became part of the image. This is a very specific, unique aspect of the product. Besides the drawing meant and designed by the designer, we allow the manufacturing technique to 'draw' as well: there are design-related image effects in the bubbling, and also in the veining aspect of the image. So when you look to the old cloths made by the wax technique, the vein (which is in the image by accident) became a stylized ornament to refer to the wax process and it happened a lot. Since 2000 we have a lot of copies on the market made by rotation printing. They don't have the natural uncontrolled vein and other effects anymore in the image and consumers like that better than the original wax.

JH So the design development is also a market response?

RG Yes. On the other hand, we also have products which use work that is called 'spec' to refer to 'special breaking' in which you have very long veins through the whole image that ignore the planned design. We have wax 'spec' products now, which I am going to use in every season to show the technique. But the arts and crafts technique in the image has become less important for our key consumers now. On the other hand, outside our key markets the arts and crafts – the vein – becomes much more important because people love the speciality of the technique.

JH Is there an aesthetic split among Vlisco consumers that is driven by differing cultural tastes?

RG Yes, and from a design aspect. I discovered in West Africa a blue t-shirt with a white vein printed on it as an African image. It was originally a mistake, which had been stylized, then became a design ornament, and now stands for Africa. So you have these layers of ornament, some derived from uncontrollable techniques.

JH In your West and Central African markets where Vlisco is so popular at the moment, do you think your customer has an interest in the complex history of the product?

RG [Vlisco's history] has meaning when you talk to consumers, but also professionally. The mothers and grandmothers are around the table immediately and the [company's] history is apparent through the generations.

JH When did Vlisco's market in Africa begin?

RG It started in the 1920s, but it really became big in the 1960s and 1970s. Almost fifty years ago. But I have seen dresses [made with Vlisco fabric] from 1900 and 1910. The first shipment we have documented is dated 1876. That is the real first order for Vlisco. Before that time there had been trade with the Ashanti in Ghana, where imitation batik was traded for water and supplies when the boats stopped halfway before they completed their journey to Indonesia. Before 1876 and the opening of the Suez canal they had to sail around Africa to get to Indonesia. In the nineties (last century – so that is not that long ago) the Nana Benz in Togo played an important role in the market growth. By then the trade became important in Togo, Benin and Nigeria. And Nigeria is huge.

JH How important to Vlisco is it be thought of as 'authentic'? Admittedly, our material world is hardly ever authentic if we define authenticity as a single history or source of reference.

RG The printed [Vlisco] selvedge is not that old. It is not from the beginning [of the company], that is the first thing. The selvedge also has a legal reason. In a lot of countries you were obliged to show that you were 'made in Holland'; it has to do with import duties. But talking of authenticity in general, I always challenge that: give me one authentic company. What you see in the history of Vlisco, and not only Vlisco but also other brands that worked with wax [resist textiles] for West Africa, is a follow-up of reasoning and circumstances and facts which made the product as it is. And the image of the product now is totally different than the image of the product in the beginning, because then it was a copy of the Indonesian product for West Africa. But by making the batik technique industrial you get a kind of roughness in the technique, which made the ornament more rough and bigger, which was appreciated for storytelling or other aspects.

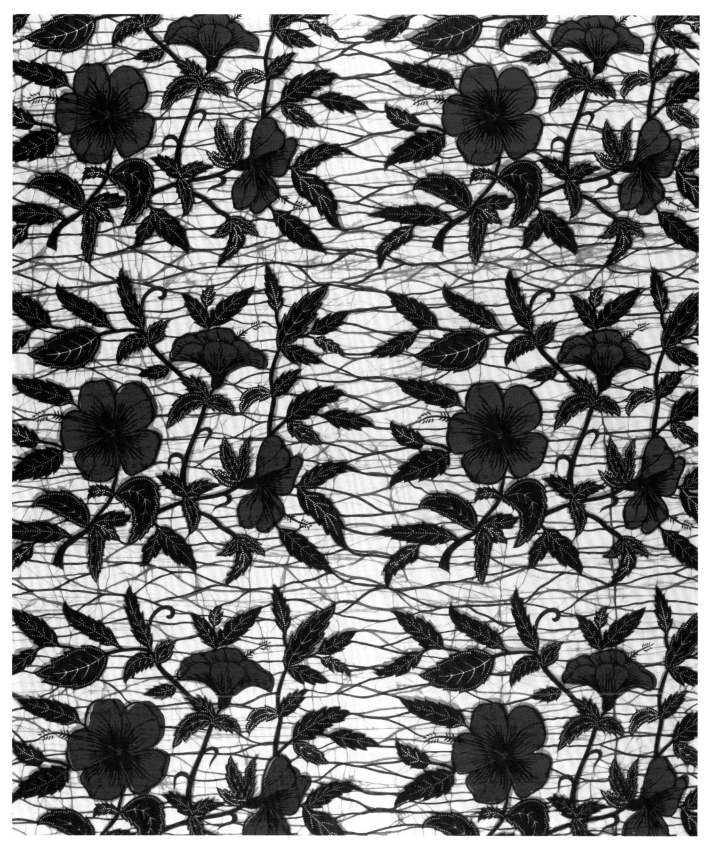

Vlisco, Dries van de Ven, *Hibiscus – Hiisque – Fiorba,* 1952. Wax-resist on cotton. © Vlisco Netherlands B.V. In the background the stylized breaking of the wax – the vein – is visible and part of the design.

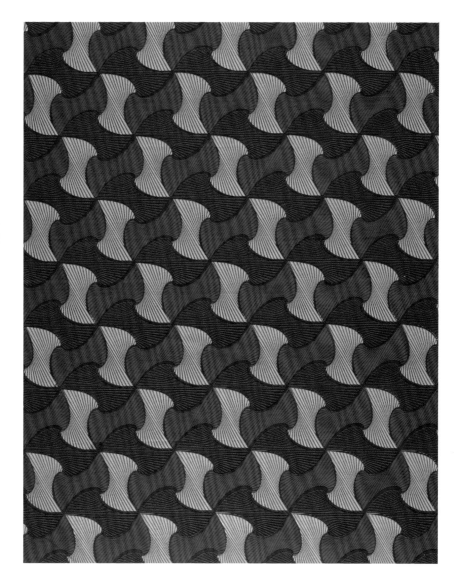

THIS PAGE Vlisco, Johan Sleegers, *Santana – Cherie, ne me tourne pas le dos,* 1984. Wax-resist on cotton. © Vlisco Netherlands B.V.

OPPOSITE Vlisco, Ankersmit design, *Big Step – Staircase – Death Men's Ladder,* 1927. Wax-resist on cotton. © Vlisco Netherlands B.V.

However, the style changes were appreciated. So it is the dialogue which made the image as it is now. Then I don't know anymore if you can say it is authentic.

We keep it authentic because we have our own designers working on it, and we have our own technique that nobody else has. So we have aspects of authenticity, because the designs we bring now are from the brains and craft of the designers, and made in an industrial technique, which is also authentic as such. But at the very end, I often hear, 'but you copied Indonesian batiks'. Yes, it is true. But the image now is different than the Indonesian batik. There are new authenticities. That is also what I like. The batik has had time to react to environmental aspects, to legal aspects, to appreciation aspects, to consumer and trader aspects, which all give influence to how the product is now. And in all the interpretations, or reactions, or dialogue the brand also took some authenticity to answer it. We are the ones who are copied now, with the same products but made using different techniques.

There are other brands that are also Vlisco group owned: Uniwax and GTP. So we have a factory in Côte d'Ivoire making Uniwax and we have a factory in Ghana making GTP.

JH   This is where some of the production equipment from Helmond [the Netherlands] moved?

Vlisco, Willie Kartner, *Small Star – Petits Etoiles – Kilikilistar – Stars,* 1952. Wax-resist on cotton. © Vlisco Netherlands B.V.

CHAPTER TWO

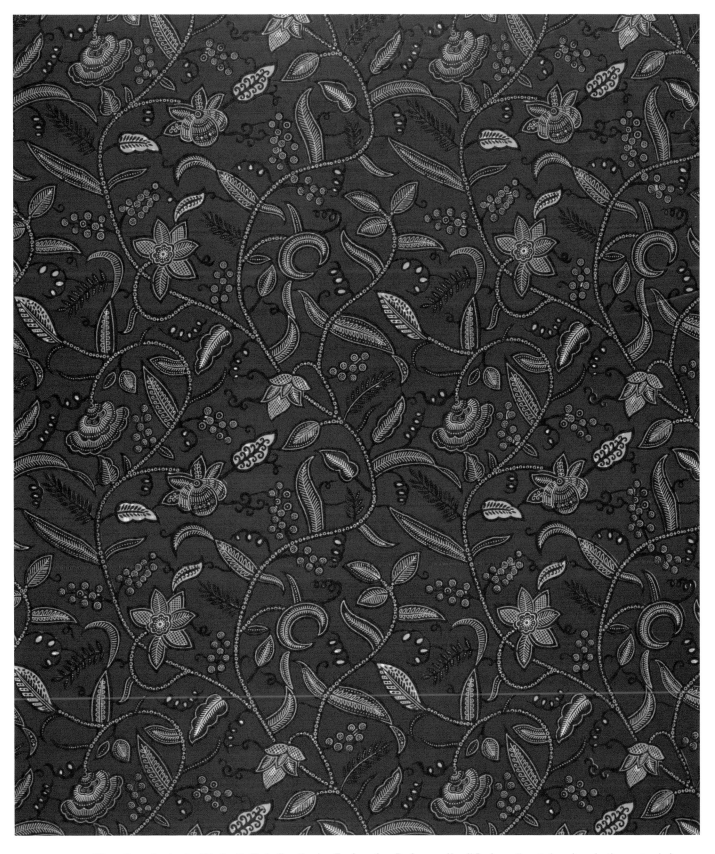

Vlisco, Frans Jacobs, *Leaf Trail – Feuille-feuille – Zamba- Zamba – Agre Pankassa – Ahoudi Pankassa* ('empty barrels make the most noise', Ghana) – *Makaiva*, 1933. Wax-resist on cotton. © Vlisco Netherlands B.V.

RG   Yes, in the early 1970s there were opportunities to start manufacturing in West Africa, and in the beginning the existing designs of Vlisco were reproduced under other names. Uniwax was produced in Abidjan, Côte d'Ivoire and GTP – Ghana Textiles Printing – in Accra, Ghana. But that did not work, so now there are also design departments in Abidjan and Accra who design for the Uniwax and GTP brands. I work closely with the [entire] Vlisco group[1] as the creative director. But the Vlisco products made in Helmond have the best quality and the best quality perception with the consumer still. One aspect is because it is not made in West Africa. In Africa there is a perception that it is better if made 'abroad' than there. The aspect of exoticism is always important in fashion and design – it is the same as when we perceive products from other cultures as more inspiring.

JH   And are the various West and Central African markets particular – quite different – for Vlisco?

RG   Yes every country, or market, or tribe or cultural group.

JH   So talking about a country is not a very useful way to talk about organizing design, production, marketing … ?

RG   No. We offer new designs, but also existing designs every year. We order more existing designs than we take on new designs. And the order on existing designs really relates to the symbolism some designs have in specific areas. It can be different areas within one country. The most famous is the Igbo wax product, which only has a palette of five colours and is always ordered because of the design. There is a red, a green, a blue and a yellow on indigo. They are ordered for the Igbo market in Nigeria. And that is only one part of Nigeria.

JH   And these orders are stable? Is this because the cloth has ceremonial use that generates a steady demand?

RG   Yes, it is very traditional and it is very static. On the other side, we are a fashion brand in the sense that people are longing to see what we are doing the next season. So we have that aspect, but also what we do is release some classic designs and the new seasonal concepts. So we link the new with the history and the heritage: past, present and future as a concept.

JH   You have one of the most productive relationships with a company archive that I have seen, helped by your designers' studios being located on site next to production and next to the company archive.

RG   Yes, now I will take this more to the foreground. It has always been that designers use the archive to get inspiration, or designers look to old designs for reinterpretation, that happens also. So we have some designs that we can follow through, that are reinterpreted. I discovered in our archive a period in which our known old designs are used on a smaller scale. The ornaments have shrunk in size so that there is more density of ornaments in the repeated design. Then I heard from colleagues in West Africa that there was a trend that all the designs should be smaller to allow for other use in fashion. So we have all these interpretations. But now more and more we work in concepts, which started six years ago. I went to [trade fairs such as] Première Vision, but I stopped that because now we just look to ourselves and make our own concepts. And of course on colourways and on ways of communicating we catch up on things that are going on because we are in the middle of the world. But for the designers' inspiration I am making the heritage and the archive much more important.

OPPOSITE   Vlisco, Marjo Penninx, 2008. Wax-resist on cotton. *Touch of Sculpture* collection, August 2009. © Vlisco Netherlands B.V.

JH The current colourways are suited for bright sunlight and dark skin. I can't get out of my head the image of your designers' studio and the grey winter sky of the Netherlands. Production and the archive are on your doorstep, but your market – the sounds, the smells, the heat – how do you make sure that the design team comprehend that?

RG Vlisco designers go once every year or two to the market and when they have been they are flabbergasted for half a year or a year. You really feel the strong bond with the users. You see, you feel. I have seven new designers. The design department is nearly fifty people now, but there are seventeen designers. We have design support, technical people for translating designs for the factory. I try to answer this question for the new designers who have not been to the market yet. It takes you a year to learn to develop just technically. We only have two hundred colours to add to the indigo so that already also gives a lot of influence to the design image. Even when you don't know Africa, if you want to make dark colourways, it is still bright because we have a bright, fully saturated palette. There are a lot of technical restrictions. On the other hand, I have designers that love to design ornament. They are more and more difficult to find.

JH Textile design education isn't preparing the type of designer Vlisco needs?

RG I think it is a significant difference between England and Holland, but in Holland everything is conceptual. When people like to design illustration or ornament they do it with Photoshop and not by hand. I see a lot of work where I see more the Photoshop function than the handwriting of the designer. These designers that we choose are almost already Vlisco designers who discover Vlisco. They already have this urge to design strong ornaments, detailed and illustrative. So it is also choosing the good designers – in fact I discover that they are Vlisco already.

JH Is it a benefit to train in another discipline outside textile design? Is there a concentration of designers of different nationalities working with Vlisco?

RG Now more and more we become known since we have a brand strategy. So now we have designers from Mexico, England, everywhere. I just had a request for a designer from Peru to do a work placement. And applications from Nigeria, Denmark and Poland. So it becomes international. What also happened is that a graphic designer who had his own career discovered that he has a lot of affinity with our way of working, our techniques and designs, and wants to work with us. And he does now. More and more we find the people that fit Vlisco and in that way we guide our DNA. I also have my own theory that fashion (in the perspective of a consumer) is when you see something that is different from what you know. My theory is that when designers have a totally different environment of reference compared to the environment of the consumer, that fact in itself is already a strong fashion condition. Because when designers have a different cultural heritage from the users, then there is already a fact of inspiration by definition. There is already one very important restriction on newness that you always feel new because you are different. So the fact that you are Dutch, with a European culture, making a product for a West African or African culture makes it aspirational in the design image. Similarly, it works the other way. And this immediately touches our unique story: our image is perceived everywhere as African, and by that inspires non-Africans as well.

JH Do you think – ironically – it works better if the designers don't know the market?

RG In some perspectives (brand and design positioning) it is better. The point is when you make it for yourself it is not fashion in a sense. And then the concept becomes important because you need to have a difference in the product. We have a kind of circumstantial law that it already is fashion. That is why even big fashion houses take other times or other cultures as inspiration for concepts. When I first started at Vlisco I was also wondering, how can it work? But it does work. One of these circumstances is some guarantee that there is some fashion in what you do. Mixed with exceptional technique, mixed with heritage, mixed with exceptional inspiration. You have a lot of laws that keep the brand the brand.

Vlisco, Marjan de Groot, 2010. Wax-resist on cotton. *Dazzling Graphics* collection, May 2011. © Vlisco Netherlands B.V.

JH   Is the new work that is now developing with the woven fabrics (rather than prints) for a global market? Is it located in the way that the print heritage is located, or is this a crossover moment?

RG   It is a crossover moment. Before I worked for Vlisco, I thought Vlisco was as exceptional as Liberty is, or a [William] Morris design. It is so typical in its image. I found it strange that it was only for Africa; I never understood [this]. I can understand from the colours and the size, but it is a taste product and you can like it or not. There are a lot of non-Africans who like it as well. That is now what we are creating. We want to be relevant for everyone and the only critical factor for that is looking to your design DNA to communicate. But it is a crossover for all consumers of our products. A big change that is typical of Africa now is that we are not only making the pagne[2], I call it pagne because pagne means that there are thousands of tailors, a lot of designers that make fashion for you. We [also] need to make finished products for consumers who are used to buying finished products, who never make a dress for themselves – with or without the help of a designer or tailor – from bought fabric.

JH   But the two types of production run in parallel? The two cultures of dressing [ready-made and cloth bought for bespoke tailoring] are so different. Does the Central and West African textile market have no hunger for the ready-made garment?

RG   Yes. When you look to Ghanaian or West African music clips on YouTube, all the music bands wear five, six types of clothing: casual, pagne, African artisanal, chic, ready-to-wear, ceremonial, cocktail dress, fashion. Only in West Africa can I see consumers' huge range of different clothing styles or types. As a man I can wear a suit with an artisanal hat, I can wear smoking [a tuxedo suit], a booboo made of wax [resist cloth] or lace. I can wear jeans with a polo – you can do that.

You can mix all these different types of clothing as one person. In Europe we don't have that.

JH   Our clothing traditions are much more rigid?

RG   Yes. We don't have an artisanal, or cultural or African clothing set within our wardrobe that we can use. In West Africa everyone has. I see the people in our company working in offices in West Africa in all types of clothing. It can be very African to very Western. The range is massive. The exclusivity of the pagne dress made for you as a woman is also exceptional because you make dresses for every new moment you want to dress up. When you can afford it, you want to wear it once. People [have] a haute couture habit of making a dress for a moment, which is something special that we don't have any more. In fact, the best use of fashion as a language exists in West Africa. We could learn from that.

JH   Does a Vlisco dress then become a family heirloom?

RG   Of course you have rich people who can buy many and will do it this way. But I also talked with tailors in Lagos who explained you don't need to finish the dress that well because it is only for one day: the image of the moment. I love it, it is really styling because then it can collapse! But you also have dresses where the seams are not cut so that as you grow…

JH   More like a sarong or whole-cloth garments?

RG   In the past I have heard – nothing is statistically proven – but I have heard that the problem with Vlisco is that you don't cut into it because it is too expensive. So there were a lot of other folding techniques to use it. The young women I speak to don't wear pagne, but they say that 'my mother wore it' and they [the garments] are all kept. That is my next task, to get all the dresses.

OPPOSITE   Vlisco, Marjo Penninx, 2010.
Wax-resist on cotton. *Dazzling Graphics*
collection, May 2011. © Vlisco Netherlands B.V.

JH   Vlisco has a good archive, with the exception of the damage caused by fire in 1883. But it sounds as though your customer base also has a rich archive.

RG   And traders also – in that sense it is very complicated. Even today, we still have some textile designs that are only going by one channel to West Africa. So the trader has his own exclusive products; all trade will go via him to maximize profit. That was the system for everything in the past. In the beginning nobody from here [Helmond] went to Africa. Traders from Paris or other countries came to Helmond and said I want to have one pagne for Africa and then they gave it to other ones and other ones and other ones and that is how it came to West Africa. In this relationship, these designs became really attached to certain people who knew this is my exclusive design. So in Togo you had traders in the market who had all pagnes, which were only traded via them. More and more we allow them to come to us to show this old design and we re-engrave [the printing plates] and make it again. There is a very emotional relationship – also a business relationship – with the traders. Some [textile design] names are named after traders. People knew, even if you lived in Togo, this [design] is traded in Lagos. On everything there is emotion attached to it.

JH   And the trade monopoly would stay in a family?

RG   Yes, in Togo this is the case. I know a lot of mother-daughter relationships. The 'Nana Benz'[3] originally started in Togo in Lomé (the capital city) and there it was said that only a few families were able to trade in the pagne. So it was only women who were allowed to trade in textiles. I am sure there were also certain products that only women were allowed to trade. I think it was around fifty families. Madam Krepe made a union of female traders in the 1990s and the trade is going from the mother to the daughters. The Krepe family still have a shop, Manatex. There is an older woman working there and I discovered that she had four sons and she had to wait for a granddaughter to pass on the trade. In the markets in Lomé I often meet young women who studied abroad, in London or Paris, and come back to take over the trade of their mothers. In this African environment, women educated in London, Canada, Paris, are coming back to do the trading because it is really big business and very relevant. The 'Nana Benz' is named after the first lady of the Krepu family because she bought the first car; the first car in Lomé was a Mercedes Benz, and Nana means 'woman'. That is why all these women in Lomé are called 'Nana Benz'. The young daughters in business are called Nannettes nowadays. And Lomé is only one part of the big market we have. People think that 'Nana Benz' is everywhere, but it is originally Togo.

JH   Why did Vlisco survive? There were so many other Dutch textile companies producing wax-resist cloth.

RG   I don't know, but I think it could be the culture of the company. I think other companies took more risks than Vlisco. Besides Vlisco there were companies in Haarlem (HKM), in Leiden (LKM), in Rotterdam (KKM) and Deventer (Ankersmit).

I know that Vlisco was not the first to improve on colours; I know that Vlisco was not the first to improve on how to print the wax. Some of our very old designs are not Vlisco-owned but from other archives: the Ankersmit Company, which was based in Deventer, and the HKM in Haarlem. They really discovered the new techniques. But it is very important to mention that Vlisco only became a focused West African textile business in the 80s of the last century. Until the 1880s, Vlisco also made fabrics for Europe, and from the beginning of the 1950s the African textiles became more important than the Euro textiles. In the 1980s Vlisco stopped producing for European markets.

JH   With entirely different production techniques?

RG   Yes – rotation printing. And there were different names to the company.

JH   So Vlisco is one strand of the company that has survived.

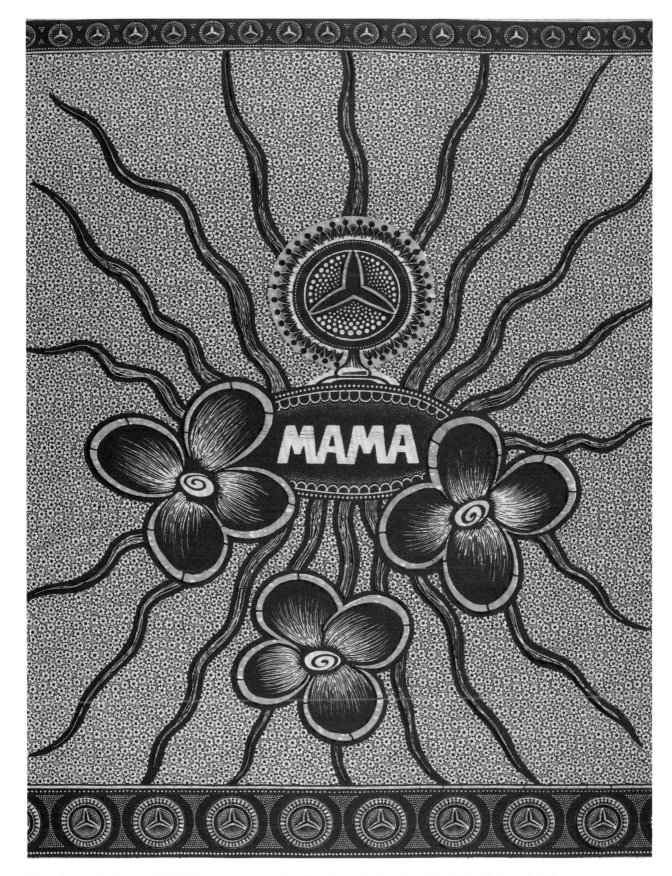

Vlisco, Cor van den Boogaard, 2009. Wax-resist on cotton. *Sparkling Grace* collection, May 2010. © Vlisco Netherlands B.V.

REPUBLIC OF REPUBLIC OF
NIGERIA NIGERIA

1946
1956
1960
1963

1963

1963

REPUBLIC OF REPUBLIC OF
NIGERIA NIGERIA

RG   Yes, and the other strands were very important to survival. I have never thought about this before, but maybe the other companies [that did not survive] only had one strand and that was, at the time, much more difficult. In the 1960s and 1970s a lot of West African countries became independent. We have textiles in which the independencies are celebrated. And I know from Congo, by law, or by government, the president has said to the people that they have to wear wax [resist textiles] to express their African identity, to tell this story to the Belgians [the colonizers]. By government you needed to wear wax and suddenly the wax of Vlisco became very important. So this circumstance gave a big boost to the volume of Vlisco.

JH   Which is interesting today because the Indonesian government dress uses batik, so their version of the batik tradition is also alive as well.

RG   I really want to see the [Indonesian] batiks more because I saw a collection some time ago. A lot of small drawings we are still using but I want to make that Indonesian connection again. I see a lot of old wax – I call them the Indonesian wax – with a lot of Indonesian ornament in it. When I started [working at Vlisco] some years ago, the [company] image then was the image made by the last twenty years; and people always think when they see us that we made this product in the 1960s. I am now changing the design more and more because it changes every year. Our story is so layered and surprising for people that when they meet it they think this was it for 160 years. And that is a big mistake. But that is always in fashion and textiles: what you see today is a result of the past and the start of new design tomorrow.

JH   Can your newest developments in woven jacquard fabrics inspired by the wax-resist printing process be understood as yet another type of adaptation?

RG   This is a big step. When you see the other products, made by rotation printing until the 1980s,

you can't say it is Vlisco. It is a totally different image than the wax image. I even met an interior designer some months ago who worked for Vlisco in the [19]80s, but she worked for the Euro fabric style at the opposite [side] of the street and she was never involved in the wax design. I heard from her that there was really a split between the designers working for the European markets and the wax prints. What is happening now is that we are making new textiles. Now maybe I make it a kind of static design DNA and translate it to new textile qualities or arts and crafts techniques in which we ask questions, also inspired by our own wax technique. Because we print on both sides of the fabric, our product has two good sides – which is exceptional for printed fabrics.

We ask our printed and leather and even logo designers, 'what is the other side'? We ask different questions because of our own technique. And that reflection on what you are as a designer is something of the recent years because we made a DNA book and we made DNA laws. More and more people are working for us and we need to have laws otherwise it goes in all directions. That was not necessary in the past.

JH   Because the production and the design teams were much smaller previously?

RG   [Vlisco] designers in the past were not called designers, but called 'drawers'. And they had no design department. They were working in the drawing room in the factory and after they drew, it went to the walls department and they engraved it by hand on the walls. And then the colour was added on a commercial level because the traders were allowed to say what colours would you like to have. Everything was focussed on production and trade. And since the 1970s/1980s when the wax became more important in West Africa the drawers – and we still have designers who have now worked here for forty-one, forty-two years – they became more stubborn and said we are designers and we do our own funny things.

OPPOSITE   Vlisco, Dries van den Ven, untitled (Republic of Nigeria), 1962. Wax-resist on cotton. © Vlisco Netherlands B.V.

Vlisco, Marjon de Groot, 2011. Wax-resist on cotton (front). *Delicate Shades* collection, November 2011. © Vlisco Netherlands B.V.

Vlisco, Marjon de Groot, 2011. Wax-resist on cotton (back). *Delicate Shades* collection, November 2011. © Vlisco Netherlands B.V.

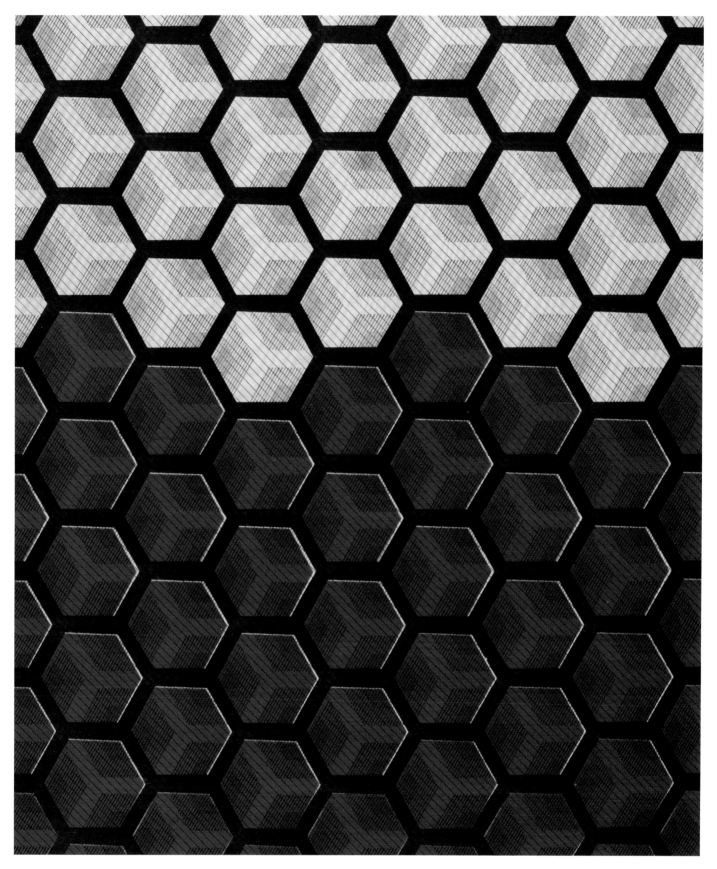

Vlisco, Marjon de Groot, 2011. Wax-resist on cotton (front). *Delicate Shades* collection, November 2011. © Vlisco Netherlands B.V.

Vlisco, Marjon de Groot, 2011. Wax-resist on cotton (back). *Delicate Shades* collection, November 2011. © Vlisco Netherlands B.V.

For instance in 1998 Vlisco started to work digitally also. In 1998 you see a lot of digital designs with wax effects. So the drawers became much more autonomous designers, and the [new] requests from the markets [traders] slowed down. Vlisco said 'we are going to draw this' because in the past it was much more on request, and then it became design driven. In that sense we honour all designers, because they really made it a design house.

JH   To have such a core design team is unusual. Many design houses would bring in freelancers.

RG   To be honest, we have some freelancers in other departments. But if you do not understand the key to Vlisco this is a big risk. My philosophy is that we never work on wax design with freelancers because you can't. You need to know the technique. For other products we do use freelancers but still the laws and the questions we ask and the design image and the colour we use and the perfect imperfections of image in it – in your veins you need to understand it. I want to work more with students again because it is always good to challenge yourself with new insights. But people who have a degree or experience in other fields of textile design find Vlisco quite difficult. The other thing and this is what I said earlier is sometimes I discover people who are Vlisco designers but they don't know yet. But they have something: largeness or strangeness or humour or surrealism in them and I discover they are Vlisco even when they don't know themselves. And that is what is happening more and more. In some ways for a long, long time the company has always been a factory making products and traders asking for something. There was almost no sales or marketing. For the last six years I see we are telling stories but you need to be clear who you are. We could copy all the designs to other qualities but in two years it would be over.

JH   Cannibalized?

RG   Yes, so I am making the translation much more clever. That is design. There are a lot of open questions still. People buy textiles and beautiful design products because you love it. And even when

you think it is an important brand, when you hate the Louis Vuitton bag on a taste level, you don't buy it. Your taste level could be organized because your friends have it, or the brand has changed, but still when you don't like the product you never buy it. I am now developing design that is so beautiful and individually made that when you love it you want to buy it and then you discover the whole world of Vlisco behind it, because we will tell our story in books and on the website and that is what I want.

JH   Do you think your clients in West and Central Africa have a better appreciation of the textile? I shouldn't speak for the Dutch, but a lot of English people walking down the street don't know or care that what they bought is going to fall apart tomorrow. They have not even noticed that the seam is not straight. They are really not that bothered. Is there a different value system in West Africa about the material world?

RG   In the past, textiles were sixty per cent of your individual expression because you don't have a swimming pool, you don't have a home interior. It is stupid to say, but because you don't have an interior, the textile is very important for your personal expression. I think it is still an important part of the culture in West Africa – showing off. That is one thing. The other thing is that when you don't have a lot of money and you pay a lot of money, you want quality. The quality awareness is quite huge. This said, the fact that we can buy updated fashion design very cheap at several popular retail chains has destroyed quality perception. But be aware, this again can be the start to [how we] differentiate on quality – it makes you exceptional.

I think Africa is much more international than the rest of the world. Proactive and not proactive; not proactive because families have been torn apart because they had to flee to other countries and continents. Proactive because of money and studying. But there is a huge international audience, much more than we have in Europe. Africa is changing and its global awareness is huge.

NOTES

1. In addition to the two wax-resist related brands Uniwax and GTP, the Vlisco Group also has an Accra-based brand Woodin, which makes rotation printed fabrics and fashion. Gerards describes the brand as 'totally African in perspective, designed and made in Africa'. In contrast with the wax-resist textiles that are the focus of the interview conversation, Woodin designers draw inspiration from and market the fabric at international textile trade fairs such as Première Vision and Indigo. Gerards explains, 'The product is perceived as "African" as well, but the design process is global, using universal laws of designing and producing. The product of Woodin is a so-called "fancy" product. In the textile world of West Africa, "fancy" stands for all products that are not artisanal and/or wax, but made by screen rotation printing.'

2. *Pagne* refers to the tradition of buying cloth that is then made into a garment, rather than buying a ready-made garment.

3. Roger Gerards explains, 'About the M and the N; the official Togolese name is Nana Benz. Nana is how mothers are referred to in French (the official language in Togo). Benz of course refers to the Mercedes Benz. Also, the daughters of the Nana Benz nowadays are called the Nannettes. The Mama is the designer, Cor van den Boogaard's, freedom [poetic license] of the Nana word. In Dutch (here the Vlisco triangle is coming in) mama means mother.' (Gerards 2014)

BIBLIOGRAPHY

Arts, J. (2012), *Vlisco*, Zwolle: WBOOKS and ArtEZ Press.
Gerards, R. (2014), email correspondence with the author, 13 January 2014.
Hobbs, R. (2008), 'Yinka Shonibare MBE: The Politics of Representation', in R. Kent, R. Hobbs and A. Downey (eds), *Yinka Shonibare MBE*, London: Prestel, 24–37.
Kent, R. (2008), 'Time and Transformation in the Art of Yinka Shonibare MBE', *Yinka Shonibare MBE*, London: Prestel, 12–23.
Picton, J. (2001), 'Undressing Ethnicity', *African Arts*, vol. 34 no. 4: 66–73.
Vergès, F. (2014), 'The Invention of an African Fabric', SMBA Newsletter N° 124, n. pag. <http://www.smba.nl/en/newsletters/n-124-a-sign-of-autumn/> [Accessed 9 January 2014].

Chapter three

An imagined Africa: stories told by contemporary textiles

Jessica Hemmings

Places evoke images that can be real, or entirely imagined. Africa may be one of the most extreme examples of this. Our imagined image of Africa has created an entire continent that never really existed, and does not exist today, in the manner constructed by those beyond its borders. But rather than think of fiction as the opposite of truth, stories can expose thinking that is entrenched and unexamined, as well as presenting us with new alternatives. The artists and designers discussed in this chapter, Yinka Shonibare, Susan Stockwell, Dan Halter, Walter Oltmann, Vincent Vulsma, Studio Formafantasma and Victoria Bell, confront in various ways ideas of an imagined Africa. Shonibare, one of the most well-cited examples of an artist who uses cloth to speak

of cultural influences and question the possibility of authenticity, chooses to work with wax-resist cloth, the same type of textile discussed in the previous chapter's interview with Vlisco's creative director Roger Gerards.

This chapter considers a number of recent exhibitions that use textiles to confront the fabricated, fictional image of Africa that so many of us carry in our mind's eye. The works discussed here convey the complexity of cultural influences that textiles carry, and question concepts held dear to the creative arts: authenticity and originality.

Jessica Hemmings

Yinka Shonibare MBE, *Scramble for Africa*, 2003. 14 life-size fiberglass mannequins, 14 chairs, table, Dutch wax printed cotton. The Pinnell Collection, Dallas. © Yinka Shonibare MBE. All Rights Reserved, DACS 2014.

Susan Stockwell, *Pattern of the World*, 2000. Tea stains on dress making patterns with dress making pins. 180 × 120 × 2 cm (70 × 47 × 1 in.) © Victoria and Albert Museum, London.

The oft-cited example of an artist who plays with notions of appropriation and authenticity is the British born, Nigerian artist Yinka Shonibare MBE.[1] Shonibare is best known for a practice that actively engages with the complex journeys of material trade and production communicated by the one constant in his art: wax-resist textiles. As Françoise Vergès observes, 'African wax belongs to the history of cultural appropriation, of the unexpected and unforeseen that is inseparable from the history of imperialism and postcolonialism.' (2014) Shonibare knowingly refers to this complex heritage when he uses the cloth in his sculptures. The artist's interest in cultural authenticity began when he was questioned as a student about the assumed connection between his personal identity and the art that he should aspire to produce. He explains:

> The fabrics are signifiers, if you like, of 'Africaness' insofar as when people first view the fabric they think Africa. When I was at college in London my work was very political. I was making

work about the emergence of *perestroika* [restructuring] in the then Soviet Union and I was also quite intrigued by the idea of the Cold War coming to an end. However my tutor, upon seeing this work, said to me: 'You are African aren't you; why don't you make authentic African art?' I was quite taken aback by this but it was through the process of thinking about authenticity that I started to wonder about what the signifiers of such an 'authentic' Africaness would look like. (2008: 39)

As noted in the introduction to the preceding chapter about Vlisco's Dutch wax-resist textiles, the hallmark of Shonibare's practice – wax-resist cloth – points to a complex set of cultural references. By repeatedly dressing his figures in wax-resist cloth Shonibare suggests that identity is fraught with layers of complexity.[2]

Shonibare draws on this complex history of the 'inauthentic' precisely to question the notion of any culture resulting from a single set of references or influences. This commentary is epitomized in

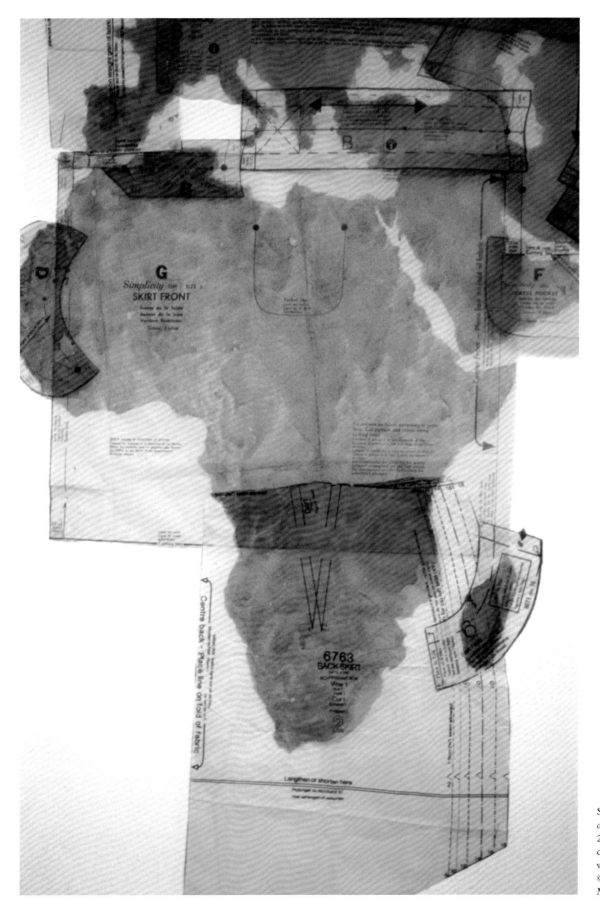

Susan Stockwell, *Pattern of the World* (detail), 2000. Tea stains on dress making patterns with dress making pins. © Victoria and Albert Museum, London.

Scramble for Africa (2003), a sculpture depicting European colonial powers at the Berlin Conference of 1884 where agreements to colonize, annex and occupy much of the continent were negotiated. As the author and playwright Wole Soyinka explains:

> One hundred years ago, at the Berlin Conference, the colonial powers met to divvy up their interests into states, lumping various tribes together in some places, or slicing them apart in others like some demented tailor who paid no attention to the fabric, colour or pattern of the quilt he was patching together. (1994: 20)

In *Scramble for Africa* fourteen headless colonial authorities sit around a table, a map of Africa spread before them. Heedless of the havoc they will wreak on the African continent, the committee creates an essentially arbitrary map apportioning the continent among them.

British artist Susan Stockwell speaks to a similar concern for the arbitrary nature of Africa's colonial mapping in *Pattern of the World* (2000), a Mercator projection made of tea stains on paper dressmaking patterns.[3] Mercator projections were first introduced in 1569 by the Flemish geographer and cartographer Gerardus Mercator, and are drawn so that straight lines meet at right angles on the meridian points. But in order to achieve this, the projection must become increasingly distorted as it moves away from the equator and towards the North and South Poles. Despite the fact that the Mercator projection distorts our impression of the world, it is often this image of the world map that is held in our mind's eye – a fiction compared to the reality on the ground, or sea.

Stockwell's knowing placement of the instructions to 'lengthen or shorten here' meant for the hemline of a skirt pattern find new meaning when placed at the tip of Africa. As the artist explains, 'darts and pleats resemble the shipping lanes [used] in ship maps' to trade produce, including the materials used to create the map, and people around the world. (2013) 'Lengthen or shorten here', a throwaway comment that in reality

determined national boundaries, could have easily been overheard spoken by Shonibare's headless men. Both Shonibare's *Scramble for Africa* and Stockwell's *Pattern of the World* critique a vision of Africa constructed by colonial powers from afar.

But Shonibare is far from being the only artist to reference the complex network of postcolonial signifiers that cloth can provide. Zimbabwean artist Dan Halter's *Space Invader* (2008) project of sculptures, video and photographs was staged at the Refugee Centre, Customs House in Cape Town, South Africa, where refugees seeking asylum queue to renew documentation of their legal status in South Africa (IOL News 2014), as well as at taxi ranks in Harare, Zimbabwe and Johannesburg, South Africa – respective points of entry and departure. In each location Halter has installed and recorded large woven synthetic carrier bags similar to those often owned by migrants to transport their material possessions. Halter explains that the large woven plastic bags, referred to as 'Ghana-must-go-bags', appeared in Marc Jacobs's 2007 collection for Louis Vuitton, a luxury brand celebrated for their iconic logo-patterned luggage. Françoise Dupré uses these very same bags (discussed in chapter seven 'From Brixton to Mostar') as the common material of her own collaborative-participatory art practice, which involves co-production with local community groups.

Nii Thompson acknowledges that the original plaid pattern of the bags may have originated in China by the third century, but is a history also claimed by Scottish Falkirk tartan dating to 1707. Much like the complex history of multiple national and cultural references found in wax-resist cloth, plaid cloth, as Thompson explains, has an equally transnational history:

> Our plaid bags are the physical proof of the way in which the boundaries that meant nothing in our pre-colonial past now loom large in Africa. Indeed their name stems from the 1983 Expulsion Order giving illegal immigrants 14 days to leave Nigeria. But more broadly the bags refer to repeated upheavals in our lands and sub-Saharan Africa knows upheaval all too well. (2012)

ABOVE Dan Halter, *Space Invader*, 2008. Lambda print mounted on aluminium of woven plastic bags at the Refugee Centre, Customs House, Cape Town, South Africa. 25.5 × 37.5 cm (10 × 14 in.). Photograph by Matthew Partridge.

ABOVE Dan Halter, *Space Invader (Johannesburg taxi rank)*, 2009. Lambda print mounted on aluminium of woven plastic bags at the Wanderers taxi rank, Johannesburg, South Africa. 83 × 125 cm (32 × 49 in.). Image made in conjunction with a video showing Space Invader character making its way into the city. Photograph by Dan Halter.

OPPOSITE Walter Oltmann, *Caterpillar Suit I*, 2007. Anodized aluminium and brass wire, woven. 118 × 59 × 42 cm (46 × 23 × 16 in.). Collection of the Seattle Art Museum, USA. Photograph by John Hodgkiss. Image courtesy of the Goodman Gallery and the artist.

Photographed from above, the bags suggest icons from a video game. Halter's chosen title adopts a veneer of science fiction or gaming culture in work that has a far harder narrative of displacement and economic inequality to tell:

> Although particularly focused on Zimbabwe, his work draws attention to a broader discourse around the postcolonial African state … specifically … a spate of xenophobic attacks directed at Zimbabwean refugees living in South Africa. Through looking at the plight of refugees his work deals with issues of forced migration and the root causes and results of mass movement on the continent. (Volta 2014)

In the global world we inhabit today, transnational identities are both sought and forced, a reality difficult to reconcile with the decorative gesture of the exotic used by the luxury brand Louis Vuitton. Notions of the exotic often fuel misrepresentations of the African continent. Some, like the Louis Vuitton collection, are recent, but many are informed by images collected during early colonial encounters. South African artist Walter Oltmann weaves with wire to create suits based on early colonial drawings of the region. Oltmann explains that his woven hybrids are based on an interest in:

> imagery associated with the first contacts between Africa and Europe, for example visual records by European explorers arriving on African shores, and also representations of such explorers by African carvers. Scrutiny and the detail of documentation of the foreign and exotic in such depictions was something that I felt would align well with my particular techniques of weaving (at times the weaving would take on features similar to line drawings, engravings and carvings). (2012)

Oltmann's *Caterpillar Suit I* (2007) references the conquistador-like dress of early European colonizers shrunk and mutated into an insect. While the original images highlighted a sense of male power and authority, Oltmann undermines this original intention by reworking the imagery to suggest an insect rather than human costume. 'My works engage with themes of the re-examination of the "other"', he explains, resulting in 'the inversion of power and the slow metamorphosis into a new hybrid identity'. (Oltmann 2012) *Caterpillar Suit I* makes strange the scientific and supposedly rational documentation of a region new to its colonizers.

The carvings and images Oltmann cites as references for his contemporary work have fuelled artists' and designers' impressions of Africa for centuries. In 1935 the Museum of Modern Art in New York City held the exhibition *African Negro Art*, now considered one of the first 'institutional attempts to apply a modernist reading to the so-called primitive objects'. (Vulsma 2013) At the time, work made by African artists, if exhibited at all, tended to be categorized as ethnographic objects. (Winking 2014) In fact, the separation of art and ethnographic objects can, as Kerstin Winking observes, also be categorized as 'the cultural production of the colonizers and the people of the colonized territories' with the former categorized as art and the latter ethnographic objects. (2014)

Our knowledge of the textiles included in the 1935 exhibition is today gleaned through the photographs that American Walker Evans took of the exhibition now in the Photographic Corpus of African Negro Art by Walker Evans held at the Metropolitan Museum of Art in New York City. Of particular interest were a number of Kuba textiles made from raffia with distinctive geometric patterns.

WE 455 (I-XIII) (2011) is Dutch artist Vincent Vulsma's response to this moment in curatorial history, his attempt to find 'ways to accumulate multiple layers of historical information into one piece' and speak to the legacies of appropriation that surround African art. (2013)

Vincent Vulsma, *WE 455*, 2011.
Installation view, Galerie Cinzia
Friedlaender, Berlin (2 December
2011 to 28 January 2012).
Photograph by Nick Ash.

Vincent Vulsma, *WE 455 (IX)*, 2011. Jacquard
woven fabric, rayon raffia and cotton. 170 ×
170 cm (67 × 67 in.). Photograph by Nick Ash.

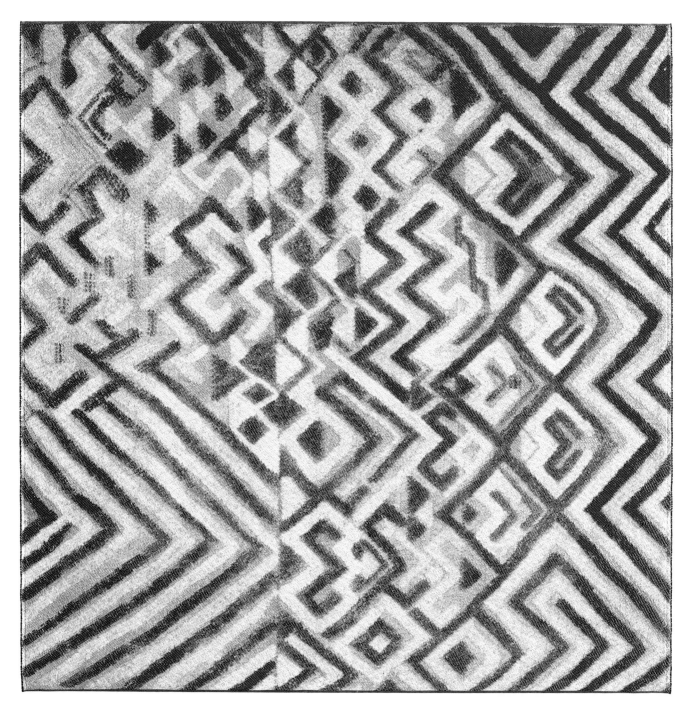

Vincent Vulsma, *WE 455 (X)*, 2011. Jacquard woven fabric, rayon raffia and cotton. 170 × 170 cm (67 × 67 in.). Photograph by Nick Ash.

The title of the work is drawn from the catalogue number of one image in Evans's photographic archive, which became the basis of a series of thirteen Jacquard weavings. In one version, Vulsma's exhibition has also included a Baulé mask from the Ivory Coast/Guinea region, brought to Europe by German ethnographer Hans Himmelheber circa 1933, and included in the 1935 exhibition, nineteenth-century Mangbetu stools and examples of Ray Eames's walnut stools in an 'African style'. Together the objects old and new tell of a legacy of curiosity and appropriation.

As Kerstin Winking, co-initiator of Stedelijk Museum Bureau Amsterdam's Project '1975' and organizer of Vulsma's exhibition *A Sign of Autumn*,[4] which included the textiles, mask and stools explains:

> One of the many questions triggered by Vulsma's installation at Stedelijk Museum Bureau Amsterdam is whether the re-positing [and repositioning] of African art objects (which were presumably produced in the early twentieth century) from the colonial museum into the contemporary art institution is a way of finally breaking with colonial methods of classification. At the same time, the installation considers whether the repositioning of these objects might accentuate artists' and the art institutions' involvement in contemporary forms of colonization. (2014)

Vulsma studied Evans's original photographic prints, but the digital files he was able to work from in his studio were low-resolution versions of the originals. The visible pixelation in these reproductions led Vulsma to computerized Jacquard weaving, a system of weaving first operated by punch cards when invented by Joseph Jacquard in 1801, and considered to be the forerunner of modern computing.[5]

He explains that the creation of contemporary weavings suited his concept to 'materialise research' in direct response to the photographs of the Kuba textiles. Using a 'low tech but systematic' working process he cropped, rotated and enlarged sections of a single digitized image. (Vulsma 2013) Each section was rotated because, as Vulsma explains of

his source image, 'Kuba panels are already arbitrary to put on the wall. They don't have a specific orientation'. (2013)

Vulsma's 'abstraction of the original' uses the distinctive geometry of the Kuba textiles, woven this time on a white cotton warp with a black weft of artificial raffia made of viscose rayon. (2013) The more pixelated the portion of the image he referenced, the coarser the weave used in the contemporary version. The colour palette of black and white refers back to Evans's black and white photography of the 1935 exhibition and results in a textile from a digital image of a photograph of a textile. Wary of misunderstandings and the accusation of stylistic appropriation, Vulsma explains that his process uses 'appropriation only in so far as they [Kuba textiles] have a history of appropriation in the context of Modernist art'. (2013) Much like Shonibare, Vulsma exposes the impossibility of a single 'original' source. As Joshua Simon observes, 'he displaces these objects from where they were displaced to'. (2014)

WE 455 (I-XIII) brings into focus the role museums and exhibitions have played in constructing Africa's identity from afar. Weltkulturen Museum director Clémentine Deliss writes of the challenge now facing a post-ethnographic museum, heir to a collection of objects often acquired and catalogued in ways we would wish to revise:

> To remediate implies to remedy something, for example, the ambivalent resonance of the colonial past. To satisfy this end, something like a post-ethnographic museum needs to be developed, for we can no longer be content to instrumentalise earlier examples of material culture for the purpose of depicting the ethnos, tribe, or an existing range of grand anthropological themes. Our earlier assumed epistemological authority does not extend comfortably to the postcolonial situation. We can respect and critically integrate earlier narratives and hypotheses written by anthropologists and experts from the field, just as we need to take on

Trading Style, 2012. Exhibition view
of global style collage, Welkulturen
Museum, Frankfurt, Germany
(8 November 2012 to 31 August
2013). Exhibition design Mathis
Esterhazy, Bausprache, Vienna.
Photograph by Wolfgang Günzel.

Trading Style, PERKS AND MINI: Tempo Top, Goude Trouser, Deep Echo Long Sleeve Top, Vibrations Leggings, Rousseau Sandals. Cotton jersey, linen, lycra jersey, leather, wood, plastic. Deep Forrest Remix A/W 2012. Photograph by Max Doyle.

Trading Style, Buki Akib. Kuti Trouser. FELA A/W 2011. Photograph by Milly Kellner.

the existing testimonials that originate from the producers and users of these artefacts. But we also need to expand the context of this knowledge by once again taking these extraordinary objects as the starting point and stimulus for contemporary innovation, aesthetic practice, linguistic translation, and even future product design. (2011)

In the 2012–2013 exhibition *Trading Style*,[6] Deliss tests her curatorial strategy for this legacy – mixing old and new, jumbling geographies, chronology, materials and customs. Contemporary fashion, she explains in the context of the *Trading Style* exhibition, is 'smuggled into the sequence, breaking down the hierarchy that may seem to exist between cultures, periods and fashions'. (2013: 11)

The exhibition included a wall of twinned photographs of fashion old and new showing similarities in adornment and dress that reach across time and culture. Contemporary designers were also invited to work and live with the museum's archive, generating contemporary responses to archival materials they selected.

Rather than revealing difference, *Trading Style* exposes the desire for adornment that humans have long held dear. The cover image of the exhibition catalogue says more than thousands of words of 'theory' could capture: somewhere in Uganda, a topless white woman stands beside a dressed black man. For once it is white skin that is treated as object and curiosity, while the black male gaze knowingly confronts the camera lens: a reversal of colonial expectations of race and gender.

Cover image of *Trading Style* catalogue, Weltkulturen Museum, Frankfurt. Original photograph by Gert Chesi, 1967.

Studio Formafantasma,
Colony, 2011. Exhibition
view of *Studio
Formafantasma: The
Stranger Within* at the
MAK Geymullerschlossel,
Vienna, Austria (14 August
to 1 December 2013).
Colony blanket series on
loan from Gallery Libby
Sellers, London and the
TextielMuseum, Tilburg.
Photo © MAK Austrian
Museum for Applied Arts/
Contemporary Arts and
Katrin Wißkircken.

108

Studio Formafantasma, *Moulding Tradition*, 2009. Exhibition view of *Studio Formafantasma: The Stranger Within* at the MAK Geymullerschlossel, Vienna, Austria. *Moulding Tradition* object series on loan from Gallery Libby Sellers, London and Studioformafantasma. Photo © MAK Austrian Museum for Applied Arts/Contemporary Arts and Katrin Wißkircken.

Another recent exhibition, this time by the young Italian design duo Simone Farresin and Andrea Trimarchi, who work as Studio Formafantasma, also rearrange the hierarchies of place and material. *The Stranger Within* (2013) confronts what is today so often considered to be politically incorrect: an interest in the exotic. Here Studio Formafantasma installed seven interventions in the MAK museum's Geymüllerschlössel branch, a building on the outskirts of Vienna, Austria that began life as Viennese merchant and banker Johann Jakob Geymüller's summer home for entertaining. Amongst furniture circa the home's beginnings which are thought to date to 1808, Studio Formafantasma inserted *The Stranger Within*, explaining, 'Society's ambivalent stances toward the "foreign" or "strange" fuel the exhibition's paradoxical theme of yearning for distant places and Biedermeier-era coziness or homeliness that one can experience at the Geymüllerschlössel.' (Formafantasma 2013a) Acknowledgement that the exotic continues to fascinate us is something not many are comfortable admitting. More usually we see the exotic banished out of concern for racist undertones or the objectification of women. Here the curiosity of the past is confronted.

Included in the exhibition is Formafantasma's *Colony* (2011) series, bed blankets woven (like Vulsma's *WE 455*) at the Textiel Museum in Tilburg and displayed here on a single bed in the master bedroom. Each blanket in the series contains urban and architectural plans from an African city – Tripoli, Asmara, Addis Ababa – that experienced a version of Italian colonization. (Ethiopia, admittedly, was never officially colonized by anyone.) Studio Formfantasma explain of the imagery woven into the bed blankets:

> [*Colony*] represents three different versions of the colonial encounter. Addis Ababa never really became a colony. Tripoli is an example of an ongoing relationship between Libya and Italy, now and when Gaddafi was there. And Asmara is the most curious of the cases … It is absolutely Italian. There are lots

of fantastic buildings; the greatest example of futurist architecture is there. (2013b)

In the MAK, the blankets are twinned with an existing image of a turbaned woman and, nearby, a contemporary photograph taken in southern Italy of a refugee, presumably from Africa. The mohair blankets refer to the beds on which they belong, sites of intimacy, refuge and rest, but details in the designs take these references a step further. 'We started to use the language of the blanket and textile for our purpose so there are labels on the blankets. The labels refer not to the objects' materiality, but to the key references we used.' (2013b) Instead of washing instructions the blanket labels offer instructions for interpretation such as key dates and the currency used.

All three mohair blankets follow the same system of composition: the Italian city plan, plans for a key building such as a town hall and, in the final layer, references to the complex contemporary relationship between Europe and North Africa. The blanket dedicated to Eritrea includes blueprints of the futurist building Fiat Tagliero built in 1938 in Asmara. The Libyan blanket references a poster from the fifth triennial in Milan that includes text on how to build colonial architecture. As Studio Formafantasma explain, 'Le Corbusier was participating in this. We find it fascinating that with the growth of the International Style, instead their response was local.' (2013b)

The last layer of the African map carries contemporary content, such as 'the recent concordat between Italy and Libya to stop illegal immigration from Africa to Europe.' (Formafantasma 2014) One exception is the blanket dedicated to Addis Ababa that includes text describing the city written by a journalist visiting at the beginning of nineteenth century. Describing the blankets as 'three gigantic postcards' suggests that the care labels can also be read as stamps. (2013b) As missives from an imagined colonial project, each blanket refers to an Italian image of Africa that did not come to pass.

The centrepiece of the exhibition is *The Stranger Within, Nodus Rug* (2013).

THIS PAGE AND OPPOSITE Studio Formafantasma, *Colony* (details), 2011. Mohair wool, cotton, ceramic tiles. Blanket's full size 220 × 110 cm (86 × 43 in.). Photograph by Studio Formafantasma. Courtesy of Gallery Libby Sellers.

OPPOSITE Studio Formafantasma, *Colony: Asmara*, 2011. Mohair wool, cotton, ceramic tiles. 220 × 110 cm (86 × 43 in.). Photograph by Luisa Zanzani. Courtesy Gallery Libby Sellers.

ABOVE Studio Formafantasma, *Nodus Rug*, 2013. Wool, hand-knotted. Exhibition view of *Studio Formafantasma: The Stranger Within* at the MAK Geymullerschlossel, Vienna, Austria. Rug loan from Nodus Milan Rug. Photo © MAK Austrian Museum for Applied Arts/ Contemporary Arts and Katrin Wißkircken.

The rug's imagery is a totem-like mask (painters of the past and their sojourns to tropical idylls spring to mind) matching the palette of the landscape painted on the room's walls and reflecting the window design found throughout the house. The rug is unnervingly anachronistic as an object of contemporary design, but perhaps it is not anachronistic in its immediate setting. In contrast to the other interventions included in the exhibition that suggest more functional roles, *Nodus Rug* hangs suspended, 'placed before the fictitious, Oriental landscape … of the kind that was fashionable when this villa was put up, reminiscent of an oversized mask – a mythical metaphor of the "foreign" derived from the texture and coloration of the surrounding rooms'. (Formafantasma 2013a)

Vincent Vulsma and Studio Formafantasma's contemporary creation of what Vulsma has referred to as the 'materialisation of research' draw into question imagined versions of Africa from the past. In contrast, New Zealand-based artist Victoria Bell's *Resisting Africa* (2011) mocks clichés of what the artist admits she had been brought up to expect of Africa from more recent popular European and North American cinema and literature. Taking issue with the image of Africa inherited from films such as *The Sheltering Sky* (Bernardo Bertolucci, 1990) and *Out of Africa* (Sydney Pollack, 1985), Bell creates a world where, in her words, 'the drawing room and safari collide'. (2012: 5)

Bell brings ironic stereotypes of the African safari indoors: flamingo chandeliers, baboon-bottom

Victoria Bell, *Resisting Africa*, 2011. Exhibition view Temple Gallery, Dunedin, New Zealand (12 August to 2 September 2011). Mixed media. Photograph by Craig Mcnab. Courtesy of the artist.

dining room chairs, a printed animal skin carpet, and a chaise longue impossible to occupy because of the presence of a languishing mythical black velvet lioness. The artist explains that her 'collection of animal/furniture sculptures ... refers especially to the deployment of British campaign furniture, which can be seen as symbolic of Western culture, to the site of Africa and the consequential redeployment of animal "trophies" to the drawing rooms of Britain'. (2012: 5) The temporary comforts of military tent furnishings – quite literally a colonial home away from home – are contrasted with the desire to decorate the fixed 'real' home with hunting trophies of the exotic. Bell explains:

> One of my intentions for the work was to explore a re-ordering of power hierarchies, and I've been interested in feminist

perspectives on how I might achieve that. One of the things that postcolonialism provides, I think, is a reflection on our colonial activity – and desire is an important aspect of that. Desire to posses, to take. The thing about considering desire is that one must also think about pleasure. (2012: 23)

Bell's use of the textile and its connection to our sense of touch establishes a tension in her work. While her choice of materials invites the viewer to enjoy the surfaces optically and tactilely, the content they allude to – hunted wild animals – reminds us that a high price is paid for our desire of the exotic.

Imagining Africa has distorted our understanding of the complex and diverse cultures that populate the vast continent. On the one hand, images of famine and war are reported by the

Victoria Bell, *Heart of Darkness*, 2011. Exhibition view Temple Gallery, Dunedin, New Zealand. Mixed media. 20 × 140 × 180 cm (8 × 55 × 71 in.). Photograph by Craig Mcnab. Courtesy of the artist.

international news; on the other exotic landscapes and cultures tinged with a frisson of danger and the strange. As Bell reflects of her own experience:

I have and have not been to Africa.

Africa: not a single imagined country but many nations. As a tourist I have been to places in Africa, within a bubble of my own, unrecognized fantasies and cultural constructions. I have travelled through landscapes, savannahs, across lakes, rivers and the Indian ocean, entered cities, temples, markets and slums … always contained within a vehicle, a vessel, a room, a space, by my guide, by my language, by my skin … kept in close proximity to 'Africa' but always at a distance.

I have not been to Africa. (2012: 12–13)

Each of the artists discussed in this chapter approaches the notion of an imagined Africa differently – from Dan Halter's allusion to gaming that confronts immediate and ongoing immigration concerns to Vincent Vulsma's reflection on an exhibition archive from eighty years ago. In many cases, scrutiny of fact reveals it to be based on fiction. But rather than reject fiction, the artists in this chapter confront the fictions of the past by telling new stories, creating new fictions that teach us to question and challenge the established narratives of our material world.

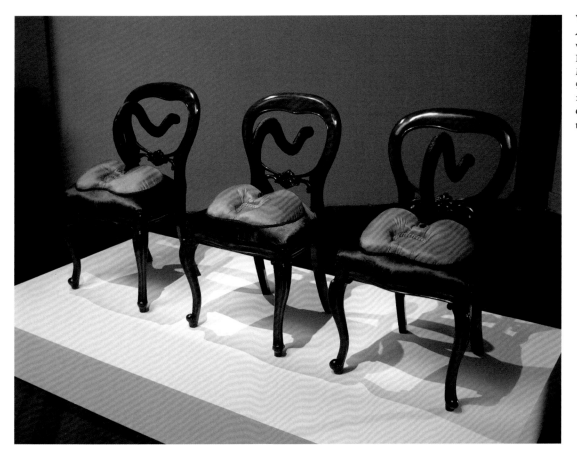

Victoria Bell, *I Dreamed of Africa*, 2011. Exhibition view Temple Gallery, Dunedin, New Zealand. Mixed media. Each chair 90 × 52 × 66 cm (35 × 20 × 26 in.). Photograph by Gary Blackman. Courtesy of the artist.

Victoria Bell, *Out of Africa*, 2011. Exhibition view Temple Gallery, Dunedin, New Zealand. Mixed media. 105 × 180 × 110 cm (41 × 71 × 43 in.). Photograph by Gary Blackman. Courtesy of the artist.

NOTES

1. Yinka Shonibare was awarded the decoration of Member of the 'Most Excellent Order of the British Empire' or MBE in 2004 by the Queen of England. The honour now accompanies his professional name. The irony here for an artist whose career is built on postcolonial critique to adopt the nomenclature of Britain's colonial past is of course palpable.

2. See Hemmings, J. (2013), 'Postcolonial Textiles: Negotiating Dialogue', in J. Gohrisch and E. Grünkemeier (eds), *Cross/Cultures: Postcolonial Studies Across the Disciplines*, Rodopi: Amsterdam, New York, 23–50; and Hemmings, J. (2010), 'Material Meaning', *Wasafiri* 25. 3 September 2010: 38–46.

3. See Hemmings, J. (2005), 'Susan Stockwell: Revisiting the Colonial', *Surface Design Journal*, Spring: 42–43; and Hemmings, J. (2004), 'Postcolonial Discourse in Garment Form', *FiberArts* Magazine, March/April: 39–42.

4. Vulsma explains, 'The exhibition title *A Sign of Autumn* refers to the writings of French historian Fernand Braudel. As political economist Giovanni Arrighi explains, Braudel used the phrase "a sign of autumn" to describe "the time when the leader of the preceding expansion of world trade reaps the fruits of its leadership by virtue of its commanding position over world-scale processes of capital accumulation. But it is also the time when that commanding position is irremediably undermined"' (Arrighi, G. (1999), 'The Global Market', *Journal of World-Systems Research*, vol. 2, Summer: 225) (Vulsma 2014).

5. See Plant, S. (1997), *Zeroes and Ones: Digital Women and the New Technoculture*, London: Doubleday.

6. See Hemmings, J. 'Trading Style: Weltmodeim Dialog at the Weltkulturen Museum, Frankfurt (8 November 2012 to 31 August 2013)', reviewed in *Selvedge* Magazine May/June 2013: 86.

BIBLIOGRAPHY

Bell, V. (2012), *Resisting Africa* catalogue.

Deliss, C. and Shahverd, T. (2013), *Trading Style*, Berlin: Keber Verlag.

Formafantasma (2013a), *MAK Design Salon 02 Studio Formafantasma: The Stranger Within* exhibition pamphlet, n. pag.

Formafantasma (2013b), interview with Simone Farressin and Andrea Trimarchi with the author, 30 October 2013.

Formafantasma (2014), <http://www .formafantasma.com/home_the_stranger_ within.html> [Accessed 9 January 2014].

IOL News (2014), <http://www.iol.co.za/news/ south-africa/western-cape/guards-turn- hose-on-desperate-refugees-1.1522852#. UsukfmRdVbx> [Accessed 7 January 7 2014].

Oltmann, W. (2012), email interview with artist, 30 July 2012.

Shonibare, Y. (2008), 'Setting the Stage: Yinka Shonibare in Conversation with Anthony Downey', in R. Kent, R. Hobbs and A. Downey (eds), *Yinka Shonibare MBE*, Munich, London, New York: Prestel, 39.

Simon, J. (2014), 'Privatisation as the Highest Stage of Colonisation: Contemporary Processes of Primitive Accumulation and Exhibition Display', SMBA Newsletter N° 124, n. pag. <http://www.smba.nl/en/newsletters/n-124-a- sign-of-autumn/> [Accessed 9 January 2014].

Stockwell, S. (2013), email correspondence with author, 25 November 2013.

Soyinka, W. (1994), 'The Bloodsoaked Quilt of Africa', *Guardian Newspaper*, May 17: 20.

Thompson, N. (2012), 'To Those Who Mock "Ghana Must Go"', <http://www.ghanaweb .com/GhanaHomePage/NewsArchive/artikel .php?ID=177138> [Accessed 22 August 2012].

Vergès, F. (2014), 'The Invention of an African Fabric', SMBA Newsletter N° 124, n. pag. <http://www.smba.nl/en/newsletters/n-124-a- sign-of-autumn/> [Accessed 9 January 2014].

Volta (2014), <www.voltashow.com/Dan-Halter .6285.0.html> [Accessed 2 January 2014].

Vulsma, V. (2013), interview with the artist, 6 December 2013.

Vulsma, V. (2014), email correspondence with the artist, 14 January 2014.

Winking, K. (2014) 'Vincent Vulsma – A Sign of Autumn', SMBA Newsletter N° 124, n. pag. <http://www.smba.nl/en/newsletters/n-124-a- sign-of-autumn/> [Accessed 9 January 2014].

Chapter four

Weaving, tradition and tourism in Ghana: 'The End of Skill'

Mamle Kabu

Mamle Kabu's short story 'The End of Skill' tackles the complex question of how traditional crafts can incorporate change, the quandary that is tourist art and the immersive state of mind that can be found in the rhythms of hand weaving. Set in Ghana, Kabu writes a story of rural flight to an urban centre that ironically brings the narrator Jimmy back to his family's traditional craft, because he discovers how lucrative it can be when repackaged for the urban market. However, his knowledge of the traditional use of kente cloth taught by his father comes into stark conflict with the commercial opportunities of the urban setting. When a wealthy client uses the cloth in an inappropriate way, Jimmy is torn between the sense of sacrilege – from a traditional perspective – and the profit gained from the sale. The short story raises the question of how traditional crafts can negotiate the difficult territory of change: on the one hand is the desire to preserve their quality and historical integrity, and on the other, the harshness of economic realities and the need to adapt in order to remain relevant and commercially viable. Through the medium of fiction, and told from the perspective of the weaver, 'The End of Skill' tackles questions about the future of traditional forms of weaving that are also raised in Damian Skinner's interview with Margaret White in chapter five.

Jessica Hemmings

The second time Jimmy had a soul exchange with his father was the day they talked about the fate of the *Adweneasa* cloth. It was exactly what Jimmy had hoped to avoid for he knew that if it happened, his father would speak to that part of him over which he had no control. When their eyes locked in that inexpressible way, he heard the word come out of his lips. The one he had promised himself he would not say. His father's reaction shattered his daze.

'He did what?'

There was a painful silence.

'Speak up boy, and let me open my ears well this time because I didn't hear you right.'

Jimmy looked into his father's face again and knew he had heard him very well. He could not stand the burning gaze, full of pain and angry questions. He dropped his eyes.

'I said he put it on the ...'

'Silence!'

Obediently, he swallowed the last word. He dared not protest against being ordered to speak and to shut up at the same time. He might be a grown

OPPOSITE Drawing of kente cloth by Anthea Walsh, 2014.

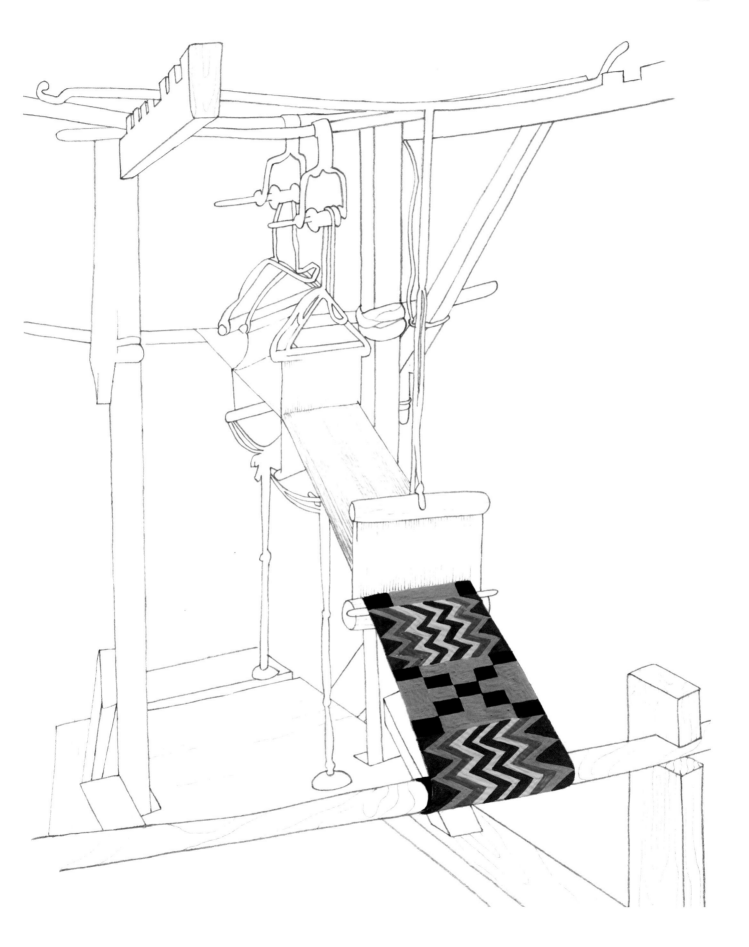

Weaving, tradition and tourism in Ghana: 'The End of Skill'

man now – a 'guy' in town, a hero to his younger brothers, a success story – but when his father spoke to him like this, he might as well be five years old again. He kept his eyes on the floor and his hands behind his back.

'Let us not offend the ancestors with this talk.'

His father put down the shuttle he had been gripping tightly throughout their conversation and climbed out of the loom. For an angry man, his movements were gentle, contained, and even graceful.

They walked out into the compound. After the inner sanctuary of the old man's weaving room, the heat and glare of the dry-season March day were like a blow to the senses. They walked past the fragrant cooking fire and the main weaving shed where twelve boys and young men were engrossed in their work, pretending not to notice the troubled pair pass by. As he skirted the line of warp threads stretched out before the looms, Jimmy caught the eye of his younger brother. Kwabena kept his fingers moving so that their father would not catch the look that passed between them. 'You fool,' it said. 'You went and told him, didn't you?'

The sound of clicking shuttles receded as they stepped over the little gutter that circled the compound, stopping finally at a disused weaving shed. Jimmy quickly pulled out the weaver's stool, dusted it off with his hands and set it down for his father. He shooed away a hen and her chicks and perched on a rusty tin trunk.

'Kweku.'

'Yes, Da.'

His father never called him Jimmy. That was the name he had given himself after he had left home. But it had taken over so much now that he only remembered 'Kweku' on his trips back home. His father had never given any indication that he was aware Kweku had any other name.

'What did the white man do with our *Adweneasa* cloth?'

'Father, he treasures the cloth so much. If only you could understand.'

On their short walk between his father's weaving room and the old shed, Jimmy had racked his brains for a way to convey to his father that foreigners simply had different ways of expressing

their admiration. Jimmy had never doubted the ambassador's profound appreciation of the cloth. 'Ah, what a masterpiece,' he had said the day Jimmy brought it to him. As he unfolded the great cloth, Jimmy saw the same awe in his eyes that lit them up every time he brought him a piece. 'Ken-tay is so beautiful,' he said, shaking his head with the mystery of it as he stroked the perfect web and traced the colourful geometry with his fingers. 'You really are a master.'

Jimmy did not bother to explain that he had not woven any of it. It made no difference anyway, because he could have done so. But why waste time explaining that it would take one man four months to weave such a cloth on his own, and that all his father's apprentices had worked on it. What mattered to the ambassador was that he had his cloth and it was beautiful. What mattered to Jimmy was that he would be paid. But the ambassador was not ready. He wanted to know more about the cloth. Its name, the meanings of its motifs. Jimmy was impatient for his money but he was no fool. He would not be standing in a cool, plush ambassador's residence in Accra, about to receive several crisp bills of a coveted foreign currency if he had not learned that there was more to a good sale than the exchange of goods and money. That was what set him apart from other young kente weavers. They slaved away in villages under their masters, in crowded city craft markets and in the dusty din of urban roadsides, making a pittance. Jimmy had carved a niche for himself. He had 'made connections' and was now the envy of them all.

It all started when he met Cassie at the Golden Sands Hotel. That was three months after he had arrived in Accra to seek his fortune. Jimmy had big dreams and he was smart. He had kept quiet as his father poured libation to invoke the blessings of the weaving forefathers on the loom he would carry to Accra. He had friends who had gone to Accra and found work as waiters, gardeners, and security men. Some of them worked for white people and earned far more than a village weaver could dream about. His friend Boateng had grown dreadlocks and found a white girl at the beach who had taken him to America. Jimmy had heard that he had become a taxi driver there and earned more than a bank manager back home. Someone who could barely speak English when he left Adanwomase! Jimmy knew he could make it too. After all, he had a primary school education, which was more than many of the others had. With his quick brain and flair for languages, he often gave the impression of being more educated than he was. He was also blessed with good looks and natural charisma. He was what people called 'a free man' – good natured, ready to see the humour in everything. This combination of attributes made him popular with people in general, and women in particular.

At first, he had squeezed into the stuffy chamber-and-hall in a suburb of Accra, which was shared by his friend Jonas, his brother and another friend. Jonas worked as a waiter in a fast-food restaurant and he tried, unsuccessfully, to help Jimmy get a job there. Jimmy would walk around town, asking in shops and restaurants and even at some private houses, but everyone seemed to be suspicious of a footloose new arrival. What he needed was a 'connection', but how to get it was a problem. He also started weaving. He had brought his loom to Accra mainly so that he did not have to explain to his father that he had no intention of weaving. However, he soon realised that kente cloth had taken on a new life in the big city. The roadside weavers were not wrestling with the problem of trying to sell twelve-yard pieces of cloth for chiefs and rich men to wear to festivals. They were selling single 'letterstrips' with messages like 'I Miss You' woven into them, which were snapped up by tourists and passers-by.

He went to the central craft market in Accra and saw an astonishing variety of modern fashion items made or trimmed with kente cloth. He bumped into Nana, one of his father's former apprentices. He was making things that Jimmy had never seen, like sets of table place-mats composed of a few strips sewn together and cut into pieces.

'You can sell a set of six like these to a rich tourist for the price of a full cloth back in Adanwomase,' Nana told him. 'And you don't even have to be as careful with the quality as when you are with your master back home.'

Jimmy did not need any further encouragement. He was in debt now and hardly eating properly anymore. He was also excited by the challenge of making something so different. He set up his loom under a tree in the crowded compound. Nana had agreed to sell something for him if he could take a share of the sale. Jimmy's father had given him some yarns to take to Accra, which he had secretly planned to sell. Now he brought them out and began weaving a strip, which he planned to turn into a set of place-mats.

It was good to be weaving again. He had always loved it and had clearly been a born master, evident from the time that his father began to teach him at the age of seven. He started creating new patterns as soon as he had mastered the old ones. By the time he was fourteen, his father would boast, 'As for Kweku, my first born, I can sell his work to a chief and tell him I wove it myself. And all he will say is "Egya Kwame Mensah, you've done it again."'

In his loom, Jimmy found an inner peace, which he never found anywhere else. It was another world in which he and his art became one and did not need anyone or anything else. The design flowed out of him and into the cloth. He worked for hours, feeling neither hunger nor thirst. The disappointment of not finding a job and the tension over his uncertain future were lulled to sleep by the rhythm of the loom as the heddles parted the warp threads and the shuttles flew through, trailing their colours behind them.

He had often secretly watched his father at work. Even before he ever wove himself, he knew that otherworldly look on his father's face and understood that stopping work and climbing out of the loom was a transition from one world to another. The closest comparison he could think of was waking from sleep. He knew that not all weavers felt this way. Back home in Adanwomase, weaving was an occupation which all young boys were expected to follow, and many did so simply because it was the family tradition. They learned the technique and produced acceptable pieces of cloth, but they never became masters. True kente masterpieces were made by weavers who entered another world when they climbed into their looms.

It was not a topic one ever heard discussed. He always knew which of his father's apprentices were destined to become masters simply by watching their faces as they wove. He knew his father had seen it in him too, but they never talked about it until the day of his thanksgiving ceremony. It was a great day when Egya Kwame Mensah, bursting with pride, officially declared his first son a competent weaver. After Kweku had presented the customary drinks and a fat white ram to his father, and the requisite libation had been poured for a prosperous weaving career, they sat down to discuss his future. That was when the old man first realised that his son did not want to be a weaver. He could not take it seriously.

'Kweku, I have always been so proud of you. You are my first-born and the best weaver in the family. Yes, one day you will be even better than me. I know it already and I thank God for it. What more could a father ask?'

Kweku was ready. He had rehearsed this scene in his head dozens of times, made a mental catalogue of all his father's possible protestations and prepared answers for each one of them. He was deeply sorry to spoil his father's joy on such a day, but he knew this discussion could not be postponed any further. He was certain it would not end acrimoniously, for the two of them had an understanding beyond the usual filial relationship, which hinged mainly on respect from the son. Although he was not altogether conscious of it, this special understanding was not unrelated to their mutual belonging to that other realm, which they entered through the loom.

It was also due to this special understanding that Kweku knew he could no longer keep up the pretence of wanting to be a weaver. If he was dishonest about it on such a momentous day, it would be even more difficult for his father to forgive him later on. He had never actually misled the old man on this point. However, the assumption that he would become a weaver was so strong that nothing short of a direct refutation would shake it. Kweku's silence on the issue had never been interpreted in any way as ominous. Now, finally, it was time to speak.

'Father, I know that in the olden days weavers rubbed shoulders with royalty, and that our great grandfather wove for the King himself, but how many weavers today can make a living only from weaving?'

If it would not have been disrespectful to his father, Kweku would simply have come out and said that he did not want to be like most weavers today – a poor man. That he did not just want to be a respected village master-weaver. He wanted to live in the city, own a car and a beautiful house, travel abroad ... He wanted a completely different life from his father. He was talented and driven and it showed in his weaving, but he knew he could apply that talent to other things and be successful. He could never realise his dreams through weaving, much as he loved it. However, it was precisely this love that complicated things. Even as he argued, as respectfully as he could, against his father's objections, Kweku felt guilty in doing so. He did not intend to admit it, but he fully sympathised with the old man's failure to comprehend that he should want to give up something he clearly loved so much. Still, he was not prepared for what his father said next. What he had prepared for was something like: 'But Kweku, you enjoy weaving so much, how can you talk about giving it up?'

And his response would have been: 'Yes Father; I do enjoy it, but times are just too hard now. If I get a good job and make money, it will benefit all of us.'

Instead, his father said something so simply and quietly that Kweku would not have been sure he had heard him correctly if his meaning had not been unmistakable:

'My son, I have seen the look in your eyes when you weave.'

Kweku looked up to meet his father's direct gaze. They had never exchanged a look like that before. In the interminable few seconds that it lasted, it completed the conversation. For the first time in his life, Kweku realised that he had participated in an exchange between souls that was far more eloquent than the language of spoken words. And he knew that he could discard the rest of his set responses. His eyes had given his father the answer he wanted, and it came directly from his soul. But they had given it involuntarily, startling him in the process. He was uncomfortable with what had happened. It was as if his father had spoken to a part of him that he did not fully know himself and that had betrayed the Kweku with whom he was more familiar. The one whose dreams he was determined to pursue.

Now he tried to rally that person and focus on his ambition. One day, when he was rich and could buy the whole family everything they had ever longed for, cushioning his father in health and wealth for the rest of his life, the old man would forgive him for leaving their secret world. In the meantime, there would be no need for him to know that Kweku was not weaving. After all, he could not check up on him in Accra. It was pointless to cause any further pain now. Kweku wanted to end the conversation but he could not find the words to respond to the look that had just passed between them. As if in recognition of this, his father picked up the spoken part of the conversation.

'Kweku, the way you feel when you weave, it is not just an accident. Not all weavers feel that way. Do you know where that feeling comes from?'

Kweku felt his scalp tingle. His father's hushed tones and direct gaze did not frighten him, but they conveyed a sense of something beyond the ordinary, which he had sensed but never consciously investigated.

'Your gift for weaving is God-given and is guided by the ancestral spirits. When you settle in the loom, they invite you into their world, in which you find the peace, inspiration and perfection that make you a great weaver. These things do not belong to the ordinary world. You may not have realised it, but I am telling you now that the spirits of our great weaving ancestors are with you when you work. When you enter the loom and lose yourself in the web, you cross over to their world. It is not all weavers who can go there. Only those with a special gift, like you and I.'

These words echoed in Jimmy's head now as he wove under the tree in the squalid little compound. He had thought about them a great deal since that day. They had made certain things clearer to him. Once when he was a child, his father had caught him 'practising' on the loom in his weaving room. In his confusion at being caught and his haste to vacate his father's seat, he had tripped and fallen. He knew he was in trouble, but had not been prepared for his father's degree of horror and agitation, for which he naturally blamed himself. It was only much later that he learned it was a taboo to fall in a loom and that special rites and sacrifices had to be performed to save the person who had fallen from the curse of the offended spirits. Jimmy also knew that the fixed loom in his father's weaving room was special. Although his father often wove on the mobile looms outside, it was only on the indoor one that he created new designs. Jimmy had watched him pour libation and sacrifice fowls there before. With advancing maturity, he also came to understand that it was their menstrual periods that barred his mother and sisters from that room at certain times, and even barred them from speaking to his father while he sat there. Jimmy knew that not all weavers of his father's generation were so traditional. It was their proud history as descendants of royal weavers that made the old traditions so important to his father.

The day Jimmy met Cassie, his fortunes changed forever. He and Nana were selling their place-mats and table-runners at a craft bazaar at the Golden Sands Hotel. He had brought along his loom. He knew the hotel staff and the other vendors would find it odd, but he had thought about it and decided that it would probably attract people to their stall. He was right.

'Oh look, a kente weaver', people exclaimed excitedly, hurrying over to watch him at work.

Their goods sold out long before they had anticipated, and they even had difficulty holding back a few to serve as samples. Jimmy continued to weave while Nana took orders. Nana had to admit that it had been a good idea to bring the loom, although he would never have tried such a thing himself. That was the difference between Jimmy and other people. He always thought of that little extra that made the difference between mediocrity and excellence. What really set him apart, though, was that he had the courage to match the boldness of his ideas and translate them into action.

Cassie was the first person who asked if she could have a go on the loom. Nana smiled and was about to explain that it was too complicated for a beginner and that even weavers did not start learning on proper looms. But Jimmy stopped him with a look, that said, 'Of course' and stepped out of the loom and beckoned her into it with an engaging smile. Nana knew that Jimmy's father would never have allowed a woman to sit at a loom or to touch a weaving instrument, but he was beginning to realise that Jimmy, the obedient son and apple of his father's eye, had his own set of rules. Jimmy guided the heddle toeholds between Cassie's toes, placed a shuttle in her hand and showed her what to do. She was extremely eager but, predictably, was confounded by the complexity of it. He placed his hands over hers and guided them as well as he could from behind. It was an agreeable sensation, enveloping her small, beautifully manicured white hands in his. He sensed immediately that he was not alone in enjoying the feeling. Perhaps that was why she was having trouble co-ordinating her hands and feet.

On an impulse, he suggested that she sit on his lap, so that he could help her with the footwork. He knew it was an audacious proposition and did not bother to apprise himself of Nana's reaction. Following bold impulses could be dangerous, but he often felt that it was the only way to pull oneself out of a rut and force new opportunities to open up. The look Cassie gave him affirmed that audacity was not alien to her nature either. They felt this common trait pull them towards each other across the many gulfs of difference that lay between them. It was a tight fit in the loom but Jimmy would not have suggested it if Cassie had not been a slim, small woman. He acted as a full-body puppet-master, not pulling strings, but matching his body to hers and guiding her with his movements. He folded his arms around hers and moved his legs underneath her as a prompt. After a few bumpy beginnings, they found perfect rhythm. She clasped the heddle toeholds tightly between her bare toes and pumped them up and down in tandem with Jimmy, parting the warp threads to create a space for the shuttle, which he guided into place with his fingers – manipulating hers.

They became lovers the next day. Cassie was spending her summer vacation with a friend, Margaret, whose husband worked for a multinational company in Ghana. Margaret was well connected in the Accra expatriate social scene and soon became Jimmy's most important client and promoter. She had money to spend, time on her hands, and friends

with whom to share her new discoveries. Within weeks, Jimmy was receiving a flurry of orders, being invited to coffee mornings where he could display, sell and take new orders; he was frequently receiving foreign currency as payment. He gained a foothold as an exciting young local artisan in many expatriate households and his 'free' character made him so popular that he even started receiving party invitations. By the time Cassie left, he was quite the flavour of the month, and was well on his way to his new, exclusive niche at the top of the kente-trading ladder. Margaret and her friends would ask, 'Oh, is that a "Jimmy"?' every time they saw a beautiful piece of kente, so that his name became synonymous with the textile within the narrow but powerful confines of the expatriate community.

Of course, charisma alone was not enough to sustain this kind of success. Underpinning Jimmy's comet-like rise to artisanal fame and glory, was the outstanding quality of his work. However, it did not take long for the volume of his orders to exceed his capacity. The time had come to enlist help from home. Jimmy made his first trip home nine months after he had left, taking along money, gifts and a stack of weaving orders. It was a sweet return, for he had fulfilled his father's dreams in spite of himself. He rejoiced quietly in the knowledge that his father would never have to find out that he had attempted to be anything but a weaver since he left home. The old man was quite beside himself with joy to see his beloved Kweku again. Although he had expected his son to be successful in the city, he was amazed by the number of orders he brought back home and was speechless when Jimmy showed him the first dollar and euro bills he had ever seen.

For Jimmy's brothers and the other apprentices, his fashionable clothes, new slang expressions and sharp 'American Gigolo' haircut were the clearest signs of success. It had the desired effect when Jimmy asked them to weave letterstrips for him with the messages 'My Sweet Tanja' and 'Vanessa my African Queen'. He told them offhandedly that he did not have the time to do them himself as he had to focus on the main orders, but the truth was that he knew the foreign names and sugary messages would convey the requisite information about his new lifestyle to the boys at home without him having to brag about it. He was right, because when he approached the busy line of looms the following morning, a football match-like chant of 'Ji-mmy! Ji-mmy!' went up. He grinned conspiratorially and told them to shut up.

The message for Vanessa showed his growing awareness of the issue of African-American heritage and its value on the kente market. Vanessa had been his greatest education on this topic so far. Thrilled to meet a kente weaver, she was effusive about what kente meant to her and the sisters and brothers back home. She already owned several kente-patterned items, which she had bought in America, including a backpack, a head tie and a dressing-gown. On the day she took him to the beach and stripped off to reveal a kente-patterned thong bikini, however, the expression, 'Now I have seen everything' came to his mind. Even as he enjoyed the rear view of the tiny kente triangle pointing like an arrow to the shapely cheeks of Vanessa's bottom, he could not shake a niggling feeling of discomfiture.

'How d'you like my kin-tay bikini Jimmy?' she asked.

'It's very sexy,' he said evasively and then added in what he hoped was a casual tone, 'So you like wearing kente like this?'

'Are you kidding me? Man, you know what it means to us. I feel so African when I wear it. I love it, can't you see that? I want it around me all the time. You know Jimmy, I could wear it all day long – day and night.'

Jimmy had perfected the art of keeping his father out of his mind on such occasions, but this time the spectre of the old man rose unbidden before he could stop it. If he could see and hear Vanessa now ... what would he say to the idea of a kente thong bikini making someone feel 'African'? The cloth of kings worn day and night, a kente arrow pointing to the cheeks of a woman's bottom ... Jimmy shuddered. How could love and esteem be expressed in such different ways? He knew his father would never understand that a person who used kente in such ways could genuinely love and esteem the cloth. Vanessa, on the other hand, would never be able to understand that surrounding herself with something and making it a part of her everyday life could show anything but love. She had big plans

to help Jimmy break into the American market, and had promised to explore export opportunities for him when she returned home. She assured him that there were many African-American companies that would snap up his cloth for graduation gowns, designer clothes and all sorts of 'heritage' goods. Jimmy showered her with kente gifts. This fulfilled the multiple role of expressing affection, promoting his weaving for future marketing opportunities and compensating for his periodic blunders with regard to her racial sensitivities.

It took an exquisite stole, originally ordered by an ambassador's wife, to appease her the day his friend Nana called her white. Vanessa was one of those African-Americans who had more white blood than black. In Ghana, far darker people were called 'white'. Even Ghanaians of mixed parentage were often called white. Jimmy had actually laughed aloud the first time he had heard her call herself a black woman. He was astonished by the degree of anger and pain this caused her, and was cowed by her scathing attack on him for his failure to recognise his own brothers and sisters from the diaspora. Jimmy quickly realised that not taking her seriously on this topic would be the quickest way to end their friendship. Although he could not fully comprehend her point of view, he resolved not to make any other careless slips about her colour. He also came to realise that racial sensitivity and an awareness of the issue of heritage gained him incalculable goodwill with his African-American clients, which naturally translated into excellent profits.

However, keeping up his guard with Vanessa was harder than he had imagined, especially as it also meant worrying about his friends' blunders. The day he introduced her to Nana at the craft centre he was nervous. He had warned Nana in advance but was still fearful because he could see that Nana could not take it seriously. Nana gave Vanessa an effusive welcome, which delighted her, and when he teased Jimmy in Twi, 'So this is your black woman' and laughed heartily, Vanessa assumed that they were simply exchanging some guy gossip. Jimmy laughed too but warned him again not to slip up. Nana assured him that there was no need to worry. Everything went extremely well at first, and Vanessa took a liking to the talkative Nana. She admired his kente goods and asked about some of the patterns. Jimmy knew that Nana would be surprised by her knowledge of kente designs. She had read a book about kente and, through her persistent questions and discussions, had even taught Jimmy some new things about the cloth.

'Oh, that's "Fathia is right for Nkrumah"', she exclaimed, pointing at the cloth named for the Egyptian wife of Ghana's first president. 'And this must be "Family is strength"' Nana nodded in open-mouthed admiration and asked if she also knew the names of the newer designs. She had no idea but was eager to learn. He picked out the ones he thought she would find most interesting. 'This one, for your former president – is named "Clinton".'

She was duly intrigued. Jimmy explained to her that it was of the same pattern as the one that had been presented to President Clinton on his visit to Ghana.

'And this one call "Hippic"', continued Nana, thoroughly enjoying himself, 'for people who can't afford'.

Vanessa looked puzzled. Jimmy did not actually know the full term 'Highly Indebted Poor Countries', but he explained as best he could that the cloth had been jokingly named to mark 'Ghana going HIPC'. To their joint relief, Vanessa understood and found it extremely witty. While Nana cast about for another interesting cloth, she glimpsed a heavy rayon piece with a dazzling variety of patterns.

'Is this the Adwi … Adwen … I mean, the one that means "the end of designs" or something like that?'

'*Adweneasa* – My skill is exhausted,' supplied Nana in garbled English, impressed again.

'Oh, is that how you translate it?' Vanessa looked confused. 'So what does it mean, literally?'

Jimmy sighed. Naming kente cloths was a complicated business. His father was one of the few people he knew who could name most cloths with confidence. Young city-based weavers often referred to a popular chart of kente names and meanings when questioned by their clients. That was where Nana's version of *Adweneasa* had come from. It was a particularly challenging example with a variety of different interpretations.

'*Adwen* …' he mused. 'Nana, how do you explain *Adwen*' he asked in Twi. They discussed it for a few seconds and Jimmy said:

'Something like "ideas" or "intelligence".'

'Wisdom', chimed in Nana.

'Art … creativity, skill', mused Jimmy.

'I thought it meant "designs" or "motifs",' said Vanessa.

'Yes, it does', said Jimmy, and Nana nodded emphatically.

Jimmy tried to explain that the motifs woven into the cloth represented the inspiration and skill of the weaver, hence the use of the same word for them. 'And "*asa*" means "finished"', he concluded. 'They say that the Asante King for whom this design was first woven admired it so much that he said … er, how can I put it?'

'That the limits of weaving skill had been reached', provided Vanessa, who had read about it.

'Yes', said Jimmy, relieved for this succinct explanation. 'So it means, "the end of skill".'

'But there's another version', said Vanessa, 'that the weaver who created it used all the designs known at the time in one cloth, so it means "all designs have been used up".'

Although Nana was not able to follow Vanessa's American English with any degree of accuracy, the fact that she was displaying an impressive knowledge of kente nomenclature did not escape him. He could not contain his admiration.

'Ei sister, you have tried! You know kente proper!'

Vanessa was delighted. She liked being called 'sister' and had enough experience with Ghanaian English to know that 'you have tried' actually meant, 'you have excelled'. She thanked him for the compliment.

Shaking his head in wonder, Nana gushed, 'In fact, this is my first time to see a white who knows kente more than me.'

Vanessa's face froze. Jimmy's froze a split second later. It took Nana a few seconds to realise what he had done. With great alarm, he apologised to Jimmy first, making it obvious to Vanessa that they had discussed her sensitivities before. This did not improve things.

She said stiffly, 'I'm not white, OK, I'm black! Just because I come from America doesn't make me white. Man, don't you guys understand anything about our history? How can you say that shit when you're our brothers? I'm an African, like you!'

She stopped there because Nana was losing the battle against laughter. Jimmy was horrified. He knew exactly how Nana felt and fully understood that he had no intention of causing offence. Jimmy was slowly coming to understand that this now familiar scenario was simply a glimpse of the sea of cultural divergence, historical erosion and plain misunderstanding that churned between home Africans and their diaspora kin. To compound his horror, he was irresistibly infected by Nana's helpless mirth. His face betrayed his own struggle between Vanessa's anguish and Nana's artless incredulity. Vanessa was beside herself. She rounded on him, but before she could formulate any coherent words, her face crumpled and she dissolved into tears. She ran out, hailed a taxi and was gone before Jimmy could catch up with her.

Although he was able to make amends to some extent with the beautiful 'Gold Dust' stole, things were never quite the same between them again. Their relationship eventually petered out, taking along with it Jimmy's dreams of a lucrative export business and his secret hope of being taken to America one day by Vanessa. Although he was not short of other girls to take her place and gradually to reconstruct his ambitions, he did miss her. The lessons she had taught him about African-American heritage, her struggles with her racial identity and her amazing way of loving kente had somehow touched him, and they earned her more space in his heart and memory than any woman had ever claimed.

The day he saw the *Adweneasa* cloth on the floor of the ambassador's living room, he heard the echo of Vanessa's voice. 'I love it, can't you see that?'

It had been spread out carefully, lovingly, displaying every inch of its twelve-yard length. Few applications could have shown it off so effectively. Exhibited thus in its entirety, it proclaimed the toil, skill and creative ecstasy that had worked miles of plain thread into a spectacular web of colour and art. Its predominant tones of maroon, green and yellow denoted the royal *Oyokoman* warp pattern and its

myriad of tiny motifs symbolised a wealth of cultural and historical meaning. In the centre of the cloth stood an exquisitely carved Asante stool upon which had been placed a collection of antique brass-cast gold weights.

'Do you like my arrangement?' asked the ambassador proudly.

Jimmy stammered out a polite response, keeping his back to the ambassador. He could indeed appreciate the beauty of the artistic arrangement, but it took a while to recover from the shock of seeing the magnificent textile, of which his father had been so proud, used in such a manner. The room was so large that the space allocated to the cloth did not impede free movement and Jimmy hoped this meant it would not be trodden upon.

He had become used to seeing kente cloth used in all manner of new ways and had learned to harden himself to it because of the profits involved.

As Nana said, 'Once they have paid, you can't tell them what to do with it. Just take your money and shut up.'

But this time, Jimmy felt a strange, indefinable pain. It was one thing to see a made-in-America nylon triangle, machine stamped with the approximation of a kente pattern, sandwiched between the cheeks of a woman's bottom. It was another thing to see a full piece of *Oyokoman Adweneasa* kente cloth, hand woven in his father's workshop, on the floor. The ambassador wanted to order an identical piece as a wall hanging to complete his 'Asante kingdom' display. The thought of another generous payment helped Jimmy recover from his shock. However, he knew his father would be curious about an identical order of such magnitude so soon after the first. He knew the old man was already uneasy about the ways in which the foreigners who were buying it were using their kente. He had asked questions before, but after his reaction to the tablecloth and bedspread orders, Jimmy had passed most subsequent orders off as wall-hangings or bodily attire.

As long as the cloth was assigned a decorative rather than utilitarian function, his father could accept it. However, the idea of kente cloth having things placed on top of it was definitely unacceptable. Jimmy did not allow the cutting of strips into small items like place-mats in his father's workshop. That could be done in Accra to save awkward questions. Naturally, the old man suspected that Jimmy was not always telling the whole truth. However, he realised, in the cold light of economic reality, that there was not necessarily much to be gained by questioning his son too closely. That year, Jimmy had paid for him to have a critical operation and for the expensive medication he had been taking ever since. Jimmy knew that his father could turn a blind eye to some things but would never forgive the use of his kente as a floor-rug. He decided that it was not necessary for him to know this particular detail. He would think of a way to handle his questions. Before his trip home, Jimmy mentally prepared himself for their conversation, building up a stock of responses for the various different turns it might take.

The silence in the old shed lasted so long that the hen and her chicks wandered back to see if their rusty tin home had been vacated at last.

'Kweku', the old man said finally. 'I have only ever heard of one other instance of kente being put on the ground. Do you know when that was?'

Jimmy shook his head.

'In 1931, when our king returned from his long exile in the Seychelles, where he had been sent by the colonial British government, he came here to Adanwomase to see his chief weaver, your great grandfather. They wove three special cloths in preparation for his visit, and when he arrived, they spread them on the ground like a red carpet for him to walk upon. The people wept for joy. It was a wonderful tribute. You see, only a mighty king could tread upon the king of textiles.'

Jimmy understood what his father was saying, but he felt torn. Conflicting thoughts buzzed around his head. Several samples from his repertoire of responses should have been of help to him now but they suddenly all seemed inappropriate. His father saw the struggle on his face and said gently, 'I know, my son, we have made a lot of money but we have also paid a price.'

With that, Egua Kwame Mensah rose and walked silently back to his weaving loom. Jimmy followed at a respectful distance. His father sat back in his loom. He pulled down a short strip of *Oyokoman Adweneasa* cloth draped on the loom frame. It was a leftover piece from the long strip he himself had woven for that magnificent cloth. He looked at it for a long moment. '*Adweneasa'*, he murmured softly to no one in particular, shaking his head sadly.

Jimmy closed the door and walked away. He had never seen his father cry, and he suspected the old man would rather keep it that way.

Chapter five

Can Pākehā make customary Māori art?
A conversation in New Zealand with weaver
Margaret White and Damian Skinner

5

Damian Skinner is curator of applied art and design at the Auckland Museum in New Zealand. Here he speaks with Margaret White about the complexities of a Pākehā, or New Zealander of European descent, practicing traditional Māori craft. White is clear to differentiate her position, explaining 'A Pākehā can never be a Māori weaver, but a Pākehā can accomplish Māori weaving techniques.' White's life story is a difficult experience to hear, a biography of obstacles and rejection from the Māori and Pākehā communities alike, triggered first by her marriage to a Māori man and then her desire to engage with a culture she was not born into, but rather born near. The thorny question of how traditional crafts evolve and adapt, and for what audience, is also addressed in chapter four, the short story 'The End of Skill' written by Mamle Kabu located on the other side of the globe from New Zealand in Ghana. While Kabu addresses the dilemma of adapting kente cloth for sale to the expatriate and tourist market, White speaks about learning and later teaching traditional weaving to create objects that are given as gifts, but never sold. She speaks of the patience and respect – to the weaver's materials and to your own body – as well as the practice necessary to weave well concluding, 'traditional weaving is hard. One learns patience and can become skilful because of that.'

Jessica Hemmings

DAMIAN SKINNER: Tell me about yourself.

MARGARET WHITE: Kō Ingarangi katoa ōku tīpuna, he Pākehā ahau. All my ancestors are from England, therefore I am a Pākehā.[1] I was born in Hāwera, Taranaki, in 1938. I had two sisters and two brothers and I was the eldest. My parents Perce Duckett and Myrtle Duckett (née Coxhead) were involved in farming at Ōkaiawa at the time. All my grandparents were pioneer farmers on the same Ōpunake-Stratford road, but some distance apart. During the Second World War we shifted to Ōpunake while my father was in military camp and I started school there. Next door was a Māori family and there began my fascination for all things Māori.[2] I ate raw pāua and crayfish, but most of all I was fascinated with the language.[3] If I was forbidden to go over there, I would sit under the hedge and listen. Then the war was over and we shifted to the other side of Taranaki. When my grandfather retired we went back to the farm and later, when my father's health deteriorated, we shifted to Lepperton and then to Waitara where there is a large Māori community. Once again I became interested in Māori – the neighbours over the road, women sitting on the pavement outside the pub with their feet in the running water, strange noises from the marae next to the high school.[4] We played tennis at Manukorihi Pā,[5] now called Ōwae Marae, and had to go past a little whare in the toetoe bushes where a woman would be sitting breastfeeding her baby.[6] We would hurry past looking straight ahead.

I really wanted to go to teacher training college with my friends but I was a year too young and was made to leave school and work in my parents' florist shop. I met my husband, Moki Te Whiowhio Retimana Te Ue White, at badminton practice and once a week we went dancing. He was twenty years older than me, nearly as old as my parents, and my mother in particular did not like this. She was very scathing. Three years later I married him and went to live next to Manukorihi Pā with his family. What a shock was in store for me! I'm sure I wasn't the only one who thought Māori were the same as Pākehā, only a different colour. My husband's father said we should have our own house further away, but from the front gate we could see the Pā. While my children were small I learnt to cook Māori food and took a correspondence course in Te Reo Māori.[7] When the children were older I started to take them to the marae and we went most weekends.

DS   Why were you forbidden to go to the Māori family next door, and why would you hurry past the whare where the Māori woman was breastfeeding?

MW   I don't know why I was forbidden to go to the Māori family next door. Maybe because there were two younger siblings than me in the family and my mother needed to know where I was. I don't remember her visiting over there, but perhaps she did. Although I was sixteen when I saw the woman breastfeeding, I had never experienced that before. Māori women sat outside the hotel downtown and did that, but I would be on the school bus, not up close. Although I had a young sister when I was twelve and a brother when I was sixteen, my mother breastfed them out of sight in the bedroom. When I had my first baby she forbade me to feed it in front of the others, and it caused a stir when I packed up and went back home to my own place. Interestingly, the woman I saw feeding her baby at the Pā became a weaving student of mine later on. When I took my husband home to meet my parents,

my father was accepting but not my mother. When I had three babies I took them to see my paternal grandmother. She said she couldn't see them because they were so dark! I remember that she had told me not to have anything to do with Māori when we shifted to Waitara. I believe some Pākehā are still very ignorant in this area because they are reluctant to associate with Māori. My father was well liked by Māori when he worked in the Farmers Co-op horticulture department.

DS   How did you become a weaver?

MW   My mother-in-law, Ira Retimana, had been a weaver, but was crippled with arthritis. She was thrilled when she saw that I wanted to learn to weave. Her fingers were very bent and crippled but she could instruct me as best she could, and she could still be helpful in guiding me to make a kete.[8] She didn't live to see how proficient I became.

The kuia at Manukorihi Pā were not so kind.[9] They would say, 'You made a mistake, you fix it.' I shed many tears over that but determined to be better than any of them. I would show them! Years later I realized that maybe they didn't know themselves how to fix someone else's work. What I did learn from them was that I was not to sell my work. I became proficient at working in the Pā kitchen and at weaving. Then my son turned five and I went back to work. I still went to the Pā, but there was no time for weaving. When I sold my wool and babywear shop I wanted to learn to spin. I did that and started weaving again, firstly by myself and then in one group or another. These groups were always starting somewhere, then there would be a bit of raruraru over something and that would be it until the next one.[10]

DS   When you say the kuia at the Pā would tell you to fix your own mistakes, what kind of mistakes are you talking about?

MW   The main problem is and always will be to get the row to meet after you have made the corners. There is maths involved, and after many years of giving a sigh of relief when it worked out, I have solved that problem and now teach others how to do that. The kuia would not show me how to cast off at the top either.

Margaret White, *Feather Kete*, 2004. Muka and
pheasant feathers with cotton taniko border.
20 × 24 × 5 cm; 12.5 cm long handles (8 × 9 × 2 in.;
5 in. long handles). Courtesy of the collection of
Anna-Marie White, Nelson, New Zealand.
Photograph by Craig Potton, 2013.

DS   What did people say to you when your work was good?

MW   When my work was good sometimes I would get a pat on the back. Sometimes people would say, 'Very nice darling, but it looks like a Pākehā made it.' Most people didn't say anything but showed their respect for me in other ways by telling others I knew what I was doing. Some would ask me to help them. My husband always used one of my kete to go to the tide for mussels and pāua or to take his gear to the Pā, or to do the shopping. He never commented on what I did but because he used them, I knew he approved. The days of using kete, kono, whitebait nets and so on in customary fashion are almost gone.[11] Making a hundred or more kono for a hangi to sell at the gala days, or using a kete for shopping or going to the tide to gather shellfish is unusual now, too.[12]

DS   What models of weaving did you have?

MW   People made useful kete and floor mats when I first started. A few used black and purple dyes but did simple patterns, not kete whakairo.[13] Everything was useful. No one I knew did kete whakairo and I could never find a tutor. I never went to the museum or saw old examples until I started teaching weaving to women of my own age, who were accepting of me in most aspects of how I lived as well as the weaving. I could hold my own amongst them at the marae, and although they didn't really like that, they put up with me and my ways.

Because no one would fix my mistakes I became self-taught. Books on weaving were few and far between. After a while it became easy to examine a kete and work out the pattern. I acquired the knowledge I have now mostly from practice, and am happy to pass it on. Digeress Te Kanawa's book *Weaving a Kakahu* was extremely helpful to me.[14] *Taniko Weaving* by Sydney Moko Mead[15] and *Te Aho Tapu* by Mick Pendergrast[16] were also helpful for patterns and measurements in particular. Initially my mother-in-law helped as best she could, and I joined groups but had no luck there.

DS   Did you know of any expert weavers in your community when you were learning to weave?

MW   Ira Retimana, my mother-in-law, was the only one from this area to be involved in weaving the tukutuku[17] panels when the wharenui Te Ikaroa-a-Māui was being constructed in the 1930s.[18] This suggests she was an accomplished weaver in her day but her hands were already crippled with arthritis when she helped me to learn. Whether she ever wove harakeke we will never know, but she knew what to do.[19]

DS   What are the aspects of being a weaver? What do you need to know in order to be excellent?

MW   A good weaver is a very diligent person with respect for their work and with endless patience. She may work on her own or in a group. When working in a group, she respects other people's space. She may use a sheet to work on, enabling her to keep her area tidy and gather up all her own mess at the close of the session. She has her own equipment and does not borrow from others and keeps it all together in a kete or bag. A karakia may start a session but not always, depending on the religion of those present.[20] She keeps her work clean and does not eat where her work is, and always weaves when she is not tired. She always does her best. Mistakes are not glossed over with a laugh to the others. They are diligently dealt with at all times. If done correctly she attains an air of authority and is known as tough. Her answer to that is that your work is a reflection of your teacher. One could be asked who taught you, and if the work is of poor quality one may hear it said 'she is not much of a teacher', not that student is slovenly or won't listen.

DS   In 2006 you wrote: 'As a Pākehā, I was privileged to have been taught in the traditional way.' (White 2006: 28) What does this mean?

MW   What I mean about being taught in the traditional way was that we learnt in groups, ate together, laughed together, were respectful of each

Margaret White, *Muka Kete*, 1999. Muka and kererū feathers with cotton tāniko border. 185 × 230 × 35 mm; 98 mm long handles (7.3 × 9 × 1.4 in.; 3.8 in. long handles). Courtesy of the collection of Anna-Marie White, Nelson, New Zealand. Photograph by Craig Potton, 2013.

other's space, gathered our harakeke by being kind to the bushes and cutting it properly, and disposing of the leftovers under the bush. We never ate where we worked, and we mostly wove outside in the warm sun.

DS   In 1993 you completed the He Konae Aronui course at the Open Polytechnic. Tell me about that.

MW   In 1993 my life had changed. I had left home and had a stroke and shifted in with a learned person whose wife had died and who promised to nurse me back to health. That took two years and during that time I saw an advertisement for this course. I applied and was accepted. I did not say I was a Pākehā. I wanted to learn kete whakairo. Instead, I learnt the rudiments of marae protocol, carving, kōwhaiwhai and weaving.[21] I became the first person in New Zealand to complete the course. I received some very scathing comments from people who I thought were my friends, and was told that the last thing I could do now was to teach Māori women to weave.

This course, and the influence of the person I stayed with, gave my future a new direction. I became confident enough to go to marae and sit in the wharenui, not the kitchen. I started to sing to accompany the many speeches my partner made all over the place. I started craft classes for women whose lives had changed because the local freezing works had closed. It turned out they were mostly Māori. But they didn't want to learn weaving from me. I could teach anything else, but they didn't want to learn weaving tikanga or any of that from a Pākehā.[22]

DS   Why not? What did they object to?

MW   I could not and still can't explain why any students of mine would object to me teaching tikanga or weaving in my early classes, except to say that none of those students as far as I know ever went on to learn from anyone else. It was how they were, not really interested in any of that stuff. They may have been afraid I would show up their ignorance, but that was never my intention.

I was asked to teach tāniko weaving at New Plymouth Girls High School.[23] It was hard going but I persevered. When the kaiako had learnt the technique herself, I was told I wasn't needed anymore.[24] The Māori girls did not want to learn from me and the Japanese girls did not want to learn at all. I was then asked to teach at Sacred Heart College, also in New Plymouth. The classes were so successful I was in trouble with the teachers because some girls were bunking classes to attend.

I was asked to attend a Parents' Evening at the school. I heard one father say to the Te Reo teacher, 'What do you think you are doing employing a Pākehā to teach raranga? She is not to instruct my daughter.' I was promptly told not to come back the same evening. Lovely!

DS   So being Pākehā has affected your encounter with customary Māori weaving?

MW   I never let the fact that I was Pākehā affect anything Māori that I did. I have heard it remarked that I am more Māori than many Māori. That is not my own opinion, but I am definitely different because of what I have learnt.

I formed a close association with a group of Māori women about my age. We started off having breakfast together. A lot of weaving took place. One summer we met all day every day for ten weeks. I was the tutor. It was such fun. We laughed, wove kete, ate together and made a bit of progress. One person who made mistakes would say, 'I'll do the lunch', and drop her work in my lap as she went past. If it might take longer to fix, she would offer to do the dishes as well. Nothing was ever said. If she prepared the harakeke and I wove, we could make five kete in a day and then she would give them all away. We never sold anything and I still don't. I shifted house and began teaching weaving at my place. That was interesting. There was always this feeling of 'I don't want to learn from a Pākehā' going on. I thought if I stayed in my own home it might change. Some people came and sat alongside others who would learn from me and copied off them. I didn't like that but tolerated it for a while. By then I had some rules, which worked for me. For example,

I would say, 'You will make twenty of these kono which you learnt today before you move on.' Those who listened became proficient, some better than me. If I said left, they did right, and if I said anything they would say, 'Just checking if you know what you are doing.' One person older than me who became proficient used to say a European taught her, and I would say, 'I don't come from Europe, I am a New Zealander.'

DS   You've written that 'it has been my obligation as a teacher to uphold, not only the technique of weaving, but the social, cultural and ritual aspects of the craft.' (White 2006: 28) What does this mean?

MW   I feel obligated as a teacher to uphold all aspects of weaving as a craft because I have high standards and hope to pass them on as a teacher. I have learnt everything I can and experienced both the good and the bad. As a teacher it is important to me to be able to explain why something is as it is, including working out the maths associated with the craft. When students understand why, they became more interested in becoming better. I always say, if questioned, that if their work is inferior it reflects on the teacher. Most respond by laughing or making a derogatory remark.

DS   You describe yourself as having a very strict code that you follow. Where did this code come from and what would happen if you didn't follow it?

MW   My rules were what I learnt from experience, and if they worked for me they would for others. Work early in the morning, when your mind is fresh. Don't work at night, as you will become tired and make mistakes. Fix your mistakes. It is a slur on your teacher's reputation if you don't, especially if she is a Pākehā. Don't weave if you are menstruating, since you are not at your best. Pick a nice warm day, as your work will be flexible. Don't pick harakeke in the wind and rain, as it becomes very rigid. My strict code of weaving comes entirely from experience. I listen to my body clock. Imagine weaving five hundred stitches and the next day discovering there is a mistake on

number four. I would have to undo my work and fix it. It would happen if I was tired and trying to do too much. I have not, and don't intend to, sell any of my work. I do however give some of it as an appreciation for something someone has done, especially for me. Only once has someone given me their first piece of work, which was a custom sometimes rigidly enforced long ago.

DS   So these rules are based on practical considerations, rather than questions of tapu.[25] But then they are like tapu, and I suppose tapu always has a function, and no doubt protects weavers from doing a poor job. Do you believe in tapu?

MW   Yes, my rules are based on practical considerations learnt over a period of time. I think tapu is respect. It's not about protecting anyone from anything, which is what tapu is supposed to do. It is a learnt behaviour. I don't believe in tapu as it is generally thought of, as something to be afraid of, as I believe that by being diligent and doing your very best and being respectful, there is nothing to fear. Some use tapu as a form of control over others to boost their own mana.[26] The only time I might talk about tapu is when the subject of women menstruating is brought up. My explanation of that is that one may not be feeling at one's best during that time, so weaving should be left alone. I prefer to teach older women past that stage. They have the time and the right attitude to begin to weave.

DS   What weaving projects have you completed? How do they relate to customary models?

MW   I have completed many weaving projects. The kete I make are usually the same, which have almost disappeared here, replaced by the plastic bag. I refer to them as traditional Ātiawa kete in a pae pattern.[27] Basic weaving is one thread over and the next one under, just like darning. Pae is two over and two under. I do not do coloured work. I did in the early days, when we cooked up the purple lead out of pencils or put nine packets of Dylon dye in the copper and boiled it up. My hands prefer to work with green harakeke and I like the traditional style.

Korowai woven by Margaret White and worn by her daughters outside Whai Tara Nui a Ngarue, Ōwae Marae. Back, from left to right: Joanne wearing *Te Wairua o te Moana*, Mawhaturia wearing *Te Awaroa*; front, from left to right: Linda wearing *Matauranga*, Anna-Marie wearing *Millennium*. Photograph by Fiona Clark, 2007.

It took five years to weave korowai for my four daughters.[28] My shoulders do not like the hard work of preparing muka, so they are made from linen flax or cotton threads. The korowai called *Millennium* was a project to celebrate the new century and the year 2000. It is finely woven from linen flax and decorated with rows of māwhitiwhiti pattern, emu and kererū feathers. The tāniko border is a copy of a belt pattern I found in my mother-in-law's drawing book. Māwhitiwhiti consists of a group of manipulated threads, similar but not the same as some European patterns. The difference is that it cannot be done on a Pākehā loom. There are several versions of it and the name is found in Diggeress Te Kanawa's book, which is where I learnt it. She and her mother, Rangimarie Hetet, give it a prominent place in their weaving. *Te Awaroa*, the old name of the Waitara River and also

my grandson's name, was completed in 2003. It has blocks of māwhitiwhiti pattern and mostly pheasant feathers, and is edged with black ostrich feathers that shimmer in the breeze. *Mātauranga*,[29] with its poutama pattern,[30] created from māwhitiwhiti and mostly pheasant feathers, symbolizes education, was finished in 2004. *Te Wairua o te Moana*[31] is white and blue with a variation of the niho pattern up and down like the waves.[32] It features peacock and white ostrich feathers, and was completed in 2005.

I made a rāpaki from the pieces left over from my kete.[33] That took two years to complete, 2007 and 2008. I went to Canterbury Museum in Christchurch and saw a backpack on display and made one of those, and donated it to them in 2002.[34] As well, I have made numerous feather kete, some with muka.

Inside of rāpaki woven by Margaret White in 2008. Photograph by Fiona Clark, 2013.

Rāpaki woven by Margaret White in 2008,
worn by Tāne Pue-Skellern. Photograph by
Fiona Clark, 2013.

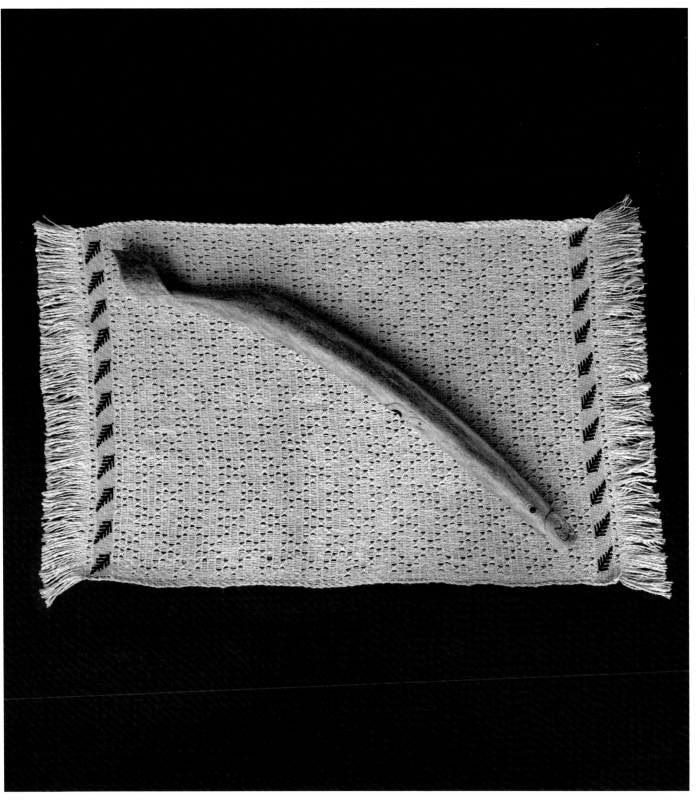

Margaret White, *Mat*, 2010. Linen flax with
māwhitiwhiti pattern and fern pattern tāniko
border. 780 × 479 mm (30.7 × 18.5 in.).
Atop: Putorino (flute) carved by Brian Flintoff.
Pilot whale bone. 685 × 440 × 145 mm (27 ×
17.3 × 5.7 in.). Photograph by Craig Potton, 2013.
Courtesy of the collection of Richard Nunns.

Can Pākehā make customary Māori art?

Margaret White, *Māori 'Backpack'*, 2002. Harakeke (flax) with supplejack supports. 77 cm diameter × 33 cm diameter (opening), 18 cm high (30 in. diameter × 13 in. diameter (opening), 7 in. high). Image courtesy of Canterbury Museum.

Incidentally, I learnt that work from Digeress Te Kanawa's book. She was a very sharing person. I like to think I use traditional techniques, not anything of a contemporary nature as regards style and colours.

I made a traditional Māori kete for Hamish Keith.[35] Hamish said he feels like a 'cultural amputee' if he doesn't have his kete with him at all times. That was surely a compliment and an appreciated one. I made a mat from linen flax for Richard Nunns to lay his musical instruments on at his concerts.[36] He has taken it as far as the Faroe Islands and all across Europe, and he says it is greatly admired everywhere. It is definitely not traditional. The pattern is māwhitiwhiti with fern fronds woven in black on the ends, so there is a Māori element there. Innovative perhaps!

DS   Why do you favour traditional techniques?

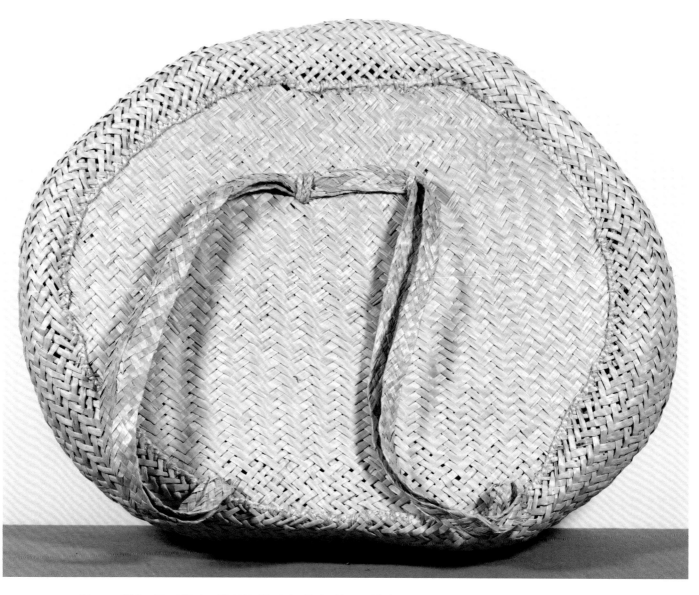

Margaret White, *Māori 'Backpack'*, 2002. Harakeke (flax) with supplejack supports. 77 cm diameter × 18 cm high (30 in. diameter × 7 in. high). Image courtesy of Canterbury Museum.

MW It is an attitude I have about taking the time to do good work. Of course there is excellent contemporary work but I haven't seen enough of it to colour my thinking. I hate half-made objects turned into art because the maker can't be bothered to finish something or runs out of time. Good weaving takes good preparation and time. It is not about getting it finished quickly. I am inspired by traditional weaving well done, and sometimes, but not always, very old.

It is good in my opinion to try and emulate such practice.

DS How would you describe your identity?

MW I identify myself as a New Zealander, getting old now and not so productive. By following my own rules I have kept my hands free from aching joints, as well as preserving my body. It is important to rest. I have seen weavers' bodies pack up because they weave all year round, usually for money. I don't mind being called a Pākehā but I prefer to be a New Zealander because I was born and have lived all my life here. I object to being called a European however.[37] Some Europeans are very arrogant and I'm not like that.

DS   Do you think of what you make as customary Māori weaving?[38]

MW   I believe that some of my work is customary weaving, particularly my kete. I use customary Māori techniques for some of my work but the threads are not. I don't know what other people think about my weaving except that it can be described as 'awesome' – but definitely a Pākehā made it. A Pākehā can never be a Māori weaver, but a Pākehā can accomplish Māori weaving techniques.

Being Pākehā and doing customary Māori art should not be a problem. My mother once said to me in an angry voice, when I dared to say 'Māori ways of doing things colour my thinking', that 'You can try as hard as you like but you will never be a Māori. 'You cannot even pretend to be a Māori when you are weaving, nor should one want to. Being sloppy, wearing no shoes and talking roughly to fit in does not work either. Some would try that. Pākehā can make customary Māori art. No need for karakia, tapu and the like, but respect for the work in hand.

In my opinion Pākehā do not belong in Māori groups, in weaving classes or in Te Reo classes. A little knowledge becomes a problem. Pākehā want to take over, suggest a better way of doing things, talk too much, often ignorantly. I have always been embarrassed by those who know it all, do it their way.

While that attitude exists, it makes it hard for those of us who are happy to be there but always at the side. On the other hand, Māori in my group who are too lazy to do good work will say, 'I'm just a dumb Māori.' I get very upset at that comment.

DS   You've described what you do as 'dabbling in another culture'. (White, 2006: 29) What issues does this raise for you? How do you deal with them?

MW   I do feel I dabble in another culture. Other people remind you who you are not, even if that was never your intention. I have many instances of that. There is a lot of jealousy among good weavers. It is almost as if by keeping the numbers small they create an elitist group.

DS   Have you ever encountered any resistance to your weaving activities? If so, what form did this take?

MW   I have tried to keep a low profile to avoid any resistance to my weaving activities. It is easier nowadays. No one is interested in learning from me like they used to, because you can get a ticket now, which enables one to become a teacher and get paid. What I do is help students to gain their levels with sensible advice explaining why something goes where, but that is not as often as it was either. Now it is all about getting the students through, cutting corners, lowering the standards, making contemporary work, which is often making something that we used to call half pie. I don't like it. If that is moving on, it is a shame, even if it means the world is changing and one must adapt. Traditional weaving is hard. One learns patience and can become skilful because of that.

NOTES

1. Pākehā is a Māori word for New Zealanders of European descent. The term has also taken on political overtones, and suggests someone who is willing to take responsibility for the effects of colonialism, to engage with Māori politics and culture, and to challenge the ongoing effects of settler privilege in Aotearoa. Margaret's decision to introduce herself in Māori, in a format that mirrors the ceremony of mihimihi, when you say who you are by describing your ancestors, is a good example of Pākehā cultural practice.

2. Māori is the name for indigenous New Zealanders, or tangata whenua, literally people of the land. It originally meant normal, and came into use as the challenges of colonialism demanded a pan-tribal identity.

3. A shellfish also known as abalone; the iridescent shell has been extensively used by Māori and Pākehā artists and craftspeople.

4. A communal, sacred complex made up of various buildings.

5. Pā is an old-fashioned word for marae that originally described a fortified settlement.

6. House.

7. The Māori language.

8. Woven basket.

9. Female elders.

10. Trouble, bother.

11. A woven basket or platter.

12. Food cooked with heated stones in an earth oven.

13. An advanced form of weaving kete with fancy patterns, with no corners to turn, which are started above the cast-on or first row.

14. Diggeress Te Kanawa (1992), *Weaving a Kakahu*, Wellington: Bridget Williams Books in association with Aotearoa Moananui a Kiwa Weavers.

15. Sydney Moko Mead (1952), *Taniko Weaving: How to Make Belts and Other Useful Articles*, Wellington: Reed.

16. Mick Pendergrast (1987), *Te Aho Tapu: The Sacred Thread*, Auckland: Reed Methuen.

17. Panels used in the meeting house, constructed of rods and battens with different coloured threads creating patterns.

18. Meeting house, literally big house.

19. Flax.

20. Prayer, or incantation.

21. Painted patterns used on the rafters of the meeting house.

22. Cultural practice, custom.

23. A customary Māori weaving technique related to twining; also a term that describes textiles made in this way.

24. Teacher.

25. Sacred, ritual restrictions, rules and prohibitions.

26. Integrity, charisma, prestige.

27. A Māori iwi (tribe) from the Taranaki and Wellington regions.

28. A form of cloak distinguished by its flax tassels.

29. Knowledge, wisdom.

30. A 'stepped' pattern that represents growth and striving.

31. The spirit of the ocean.

32. Sometimes called niho taniwha (teeth of the monster), a triangular pattern that resembles teeth.

33. A garment that can be worn on the waist or shoulders.

34. See Michael M. Trotter (1987), 'A Prehistoric Backpack from Inland Canterbury', *Records of the Canterbury Museum*, vol. 10, May: 9–24.

35. A Pākehā cultural commentator with a long history of involvement in the visual arts, and very active in the 1980s when key elements of Pākehā identity were being formed.

36. A Pākehā musician who specializes in customary Māori music and instruments.

37. This reflects a dimension of Pākehā identity, in which the term is intended to represent the idea that Pākehā are the descendants of European settlers, but whose values and behaviour have been transformed by living in Aotearoa. Pākehā are, precisely, not European, or British.

38. The term 'customary' is used in preference to 'traditional', since it does not imply a static, unchanging practice in opposition to modernity, but rather changing practices that maintain complex and direct relationships to the past, and adapt past models to address current problems.

BIBLIOGRAPHY

Davidson, A. (2005), 'The Far North Award and Waka Huia: Margaret White', *Creative Fibre*, vol. 8, no. 3, December: 24–25.

White, M. (2006), 'Māori Weaving in New Zealand', *The Wheel: Ashford's Fibrecraft Magazine* 18: 28–29.

Chapter six

Crafting difference: art, cloth and the African diasporas

Christine Checinska

Christine Checinska wrote her PhD at Goldsmiths College, University of London, on the genealogy and impact of the creolized aesthetic of the Empire Windrush generation, and is currently a postdoctoral fellow at the University of East London. She shares with many contributors to this book a personal experience of her subject matter, writing movingly about memories of her own upbringing in England as a child of Jamaican parents who 'became West Indian shortly after arriving in Britain', and a wariness at 'advocating an African diaspora essentialism'. Instead she reminds us that 'there was never a singular West African culture from which diasporic cultural expression could grow'. Her contribution here focuses on the use of stitch by two male artists, Ernest Dükü and Nick Cave, and refers to kente cloth, the same textile that is the focus of the short story 'The End of Skill' found in chapter four.

'Africa and its diasporas' is the term Checinska settles on to discuss the complex identities occupied by those with cultural and national connections to Africa, as well as a lived reality outside Africa. Embroidery and the act of stitching are presented as creative acts that offer a way to hold together disparate parts, textile structures that are compared to the narrative voice constructed in postcolonial life-writing. 'Aesthetics moves beyond theory and abstract philosophizing,' she writes, 'approaching instead a way of looking and becoming'. This interest in moving beyond the theoretical to action appears throughout this book, perhaps most closely echoed in Françoise Dupré's writing in chapter seven on her collaborative-participatory practice.

Jessica Hemmings

THIS PAGE AND OPPOSITE
Hyacinth Shaw, embroidered table cloth.
Image courtesy of Christine Checinska.

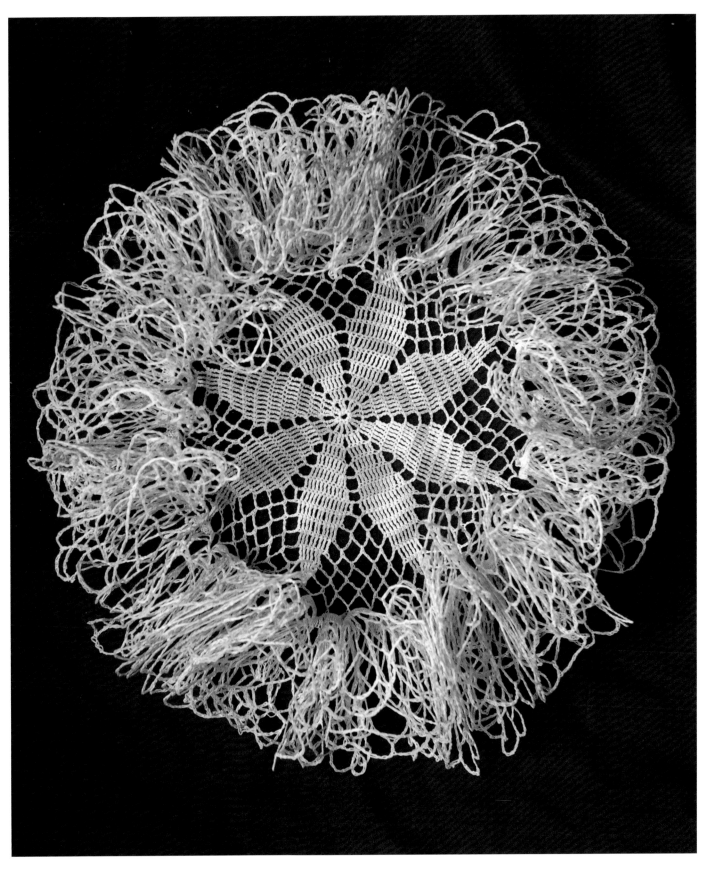

Maker unknown. *Yellow Ruffle*, circa mid–1960s. Crochet with cotton embroidery thread. Photograph by Vanley Burke. Courtesy of the collection of Vanley Burke.

Artists Ernest Dükü and Nick Cave employ stitch
– to wrap, bind, appliqué, embroider – in their
practices. Each happens to have a connection to the
African diaspora. But this does not define them. And
it is not the first thing that catches the eye.

The title for this chapter is borrowed from
bell hooks's article 'An Aesthetic of Blackness:
Strange and Oppositional'. (hooks 2007: 315) It
begins with a reflection on the home in which hooks
grew up, the home that shaped her aesthetic and
taught her who and how to be:

> This is the story of a house. It has
> been lived in by many people. Our
> grandmother, Baba, made this house a
> living space. She was certain that the way
> we lived was shaped by objects, the way
> we looked at them, the way they were
> placed around us. She was certain we
> were shaped by space. (hooks 2007: 315)

What hooks writes is the story of a house, but it
is also the story of relationships, of intimacy, of
remembering. It is the story of the inscription of
the hooks family history through everyday objects
and spaces. Her grandmother Baba, a quilt-maker,
teaches hooks to see; to find beauty in the everyday.
She also teaches her how to recognize herself.
Aesthetics moves beyond theory and abstract
philosophizing, approaching instead a way of looking
and becoming.

Here I wish to explore the relationship between
postcolonial life-writing, fractured diasporic narratives
and stitching.[1] Craft has historically occupied a
central position in ethnography, where it has been
used as a marker of otherness. Considering the
presence of stitch within the gallery and domestic
space, this chapter embraces the notion of 'thinking
through textiles' (Maharaj 2001) to posit the idea
of stitching, or working by hand, as both a means of
thinking about oneself and one's place in the world,
and a means of thinking at a conceptual level beyond
oneself. The act of stitching is seen as an aesthetic,
conceptual and subversive strategy. It is, at one level,
a means of suturing the fractured diasporic narrative,
transcribing histories that would otherwise be hidden,

and crafting difference. At another, it is a process of
continual 'doing and undoing' that allows the mind to
wander and wonder.

The need to write one's own history is central
to postcolonial life-writing. In contrast to the
canonical Western autobiography, the postcolonial
genre voices the plural self, characteristic of the 'in-
between' diaspora mode of being. (Bhabha 1994: 2)
Issues around self-representation and fragmented
identities marked by cultural and historical
dislocation are central to postcolonial theory itself.
Frantz Fanon, for example, wrote of a 'third-person
consciousness' (Fanon 1986: 110), which resulted
in the mind through the rupture of colonization.
He noted the shattering of horizons and psychologies
that occurred with the confrontation between
what he termed the 'civilized' and the 'primitive'.
(Fanon 1986: 14)

According to Fanon, in the white world the
'Negro' developed a negating consciousness of the
body, one which fixed him or her in a disadvantaged
position shaped by feelings of inferiority, inadequacy
and uncertainty. Colonial discourse depends on
this notion of 'fixity', which renders the individual
and their history invisible. (Bhabha 1994: 75)
This masking of individuality was similarly pivotal
to the system of enslavement in the Americas.
Indeed the fracturing of the African diaspora
narrative begins with enslavement. Through slavery's
dehumanization, the enslaved were rendered without
agency, without culture, without history. 'Culturally
unmade', they became social non-persons. (Spillers
1987: 64–81)

Hortense Spillers' phrase 'suspended in the
oceanic' conveys an impression of the nothingness
and nowhere-ness of slavery's Middle Passage.
(Spillers 1987: 64–81) Without diminishing the
horror of the Middle Passage, I want to suggest
that the limbo of the Middle Passage could be seen
as a creative void in the psychological sense, as
an intermediate space between one sense of being
and another. As with Bhabha's 'in-between space',
this facilitated strategies of selfhood that provided
an impetus for new signs of identity. Ideas and
experiences of nation-ness and cultural value were
shaken and renegotiated. Such patterns of 'between-
ness' are repeated with subsequent migrations.

(Bhabha 1994: 63) In the aftermath of slavery, it is as though loss and innovation sit together. Dislocation and doublings of consciousness open the possibility of creativity. Where Fanon calls upon the creative spirit to resist the colonization of the mind by reconstituting the self through violence (Fanon 1964: 27–75), W.E.B. Du Bois, writing of slavery and emancipation, points to renewal through cultural expression. (Du Bois 1994: 155–165) Applying their findings to crafting, I would suggest that stitching offers a way of suturing the rupture of movement, piecing one sense of being to another, simultaneously subverting a sense of unbelonging and an assumed 'historylessness'. (Bhabha 1994: 96)

Cultural expression – the visual arts, dance, the written word, song, textile crafts – provided displaced West Africans with a connection to home, a tangible way of remembering, of writing themselves into the history of their new homelands. Embracing the creative spirit was seen as a tool with which to challenge social hierarchies based on race. Some argue that African-American aesthetics are founded on certain West African cultural retentions.[2] At first glance this parallels the development of creolized culture in Jamaica, my family's cultural home. Kamau Braithwaite for example, suggests that 'unity is submarine'; cultural connections flow back and forth beneath the sea with the movement and migration of African peoples. (Braithwaite 1974: 64) I agree to an extent, however I am not advocating an African diaspora essentialism. Furthermore I would argue that there was never a singular West African culture from which diasporic cultural expressions could grow. I am mindful of the trap of over-racializing the motivations and practices of African diaspora artists. Kobena Mercer has written of the 'burden of representation' that falls on our shoulders. (Mercer 1994: 233–259)

Bhabha also states that the representation of difference should not rely on the fiction of 'pre-given ethnic or cultural traits'. (Bhabha 1994: 2) He urges us to look beyond narratives of origin and initial subjectivities and to focus instead on that which is produced in voicing cultural differences. As he suggests, negotiating our way within the 'in-between' spaces allows us to look again at the idea of nation and community. (Bhabha 1994:

1–2) I would extend this to the idea of the African diaspora itself. Bhabha's writings constantly raise questions that promote an understanding of cultures as complex intersections of multiple histories, places and positions. Hence cultural identity, shaped by both similarities and differences, becomes unstable, paradoxical and changing. The aim then of this chapter, and arguably this book, is not to define the use of cloth within the African diaspora as a whole, but to raise awareness of diverse perspectives within it. The intention is to map out a selection of art practices generated by a range of artists and makers, each using textile crafts to tell individual stories and explore individual concerns, while sharing a viewpoint that is informed by being in the diaspora.

Stuart Hall once drew a parallel between the 'diasporic view' and the knight's move in chess, likening his own methodological approach to critical theory as a stepping forward or back and to the side. By this he meant that his view was that of one who has been displaced, one who is the same but not quite. This is all too often considered to be the view from the margin to the centre. However, it emerges from within the 'in-between' space that we in the diaspora inhabit. (Bhabha 1994: 1–2) The 'diasporic view' as a mode of critical thinking and looking feeds on flux; it holds the tension between the multiple perspectives that are created by the cross-cultural entanglements that migration and displacement produces; it thrives on continual translation and reinscription.

There is a point of convergence with Sarat Maharaj's 'thinking through textiles', a concept that is comfortable with 'openended-ness' and 'undecideability'. (Maharaj 2001) The repetitive action involved in the making of textiles – for example, in the case of embroidery, the stitching, unstitching and re-stitching – echoes the thinking process. Indeed there is a meditative quality to creative making and to the attentive looking that precedes Hall's critical thinking noted above; the constant in-out of needle and thread, the shifting gaze forwards, then backwards, then to the side. Such making and looking involves repetition and revision and allows us to explore ideas and concepts in flux. As Maharaj suggests, the process of making textiles promotes a way of thinking beyond fixed limits, one that resists the closure that occurs when we attempt to transcribe concepts through writing. The possibility of multiple viewpoints and interpretations are reduced. Layers of potential meaning are emptied out. 'Crafting', in the sense of creative making and attentive looking, hinges on meticulous reworking and relooking, finessing and fine-tuning. There is a sense of ongoing work and questioning. In this schema stitching becomes a way of concentrating on and asking questions about a particular topic.

The artists featured in this chapter force us to revisit the everyday things usually found in domestic settings; we have to step forwards, backwards and to the side to begin to unravel the layered meanings enmeshed within their stitch work. In Dükü and Cave's hands, needle and thread become a tool to transform the familiar into the unfamiliar via a process of translation and reinscription. Our familiarity with the materials, in particular the sisal used by Dükü and crochet doilies used by Cave, draws us in but then the 'openended-ness', the 'undecideability' of the finished piece unsettles us. It is the possibility of multiple interpretations that holds our attention.

THE DOMESTIC SPACE

In the domestic space, stitching offers agency. Through craft's potential to empower its makers, the experiences of displacement, unbelonging and invisibility are momentarily transgressed. Quilting can be likened to a spiritual process of renewal (hooks 2007: 327), the constant in-out of needle and thread taking on an almost meditative quality, as new ways of thinking about oneself and one's place in the world are stitched together. These concepts find expression through fragments of my personal reflections as a child of Jamaican migrants who travelled to England from Jamaica in the mid-1950s. hooks has drawn parallels between such fragmented memories and the 're-used fabrics in a crazy quilt, contained and kept for the right moment'. (hooks 2007: 326)

Like many West Indian homes in Britain in the 1960s and 1970s, the house I grew up in was dressed in homemade, handcrafted or hand-embellished textiles. Like many Jamaicans, my parents became West Indian shortly after arriving in Britain. Like many children of West Indian parents, my sister and I learnt how to be, how to recognize ourselves, behind net-curtained Victorian windows that allowed us to watch the hustle and bustle outside while keeping us all from view. The front room was left largely unoccupied, a monument to Englishness and Jamaican-ness, respectability and reputation, exhibiting a sanctity and purity that brought together spirituality and morality. Most of the actual living was done either in the 'telly room', the 'dining hall' or the kitchen.

Naturally, the focal point of the telly room was the black and white television set, as wide as it was deep, with its wood surround and chunky ivory-coloured buttons that made a clunking sound when you pressed them to change the channels. The television always sat on a specially designated 'telly table' which, though it stood on casters, never moved from the corner of the room. The telly table was dressed with a white cloth, hand-embroidered by my mother and carefully set at an angle, so each point hung down between the centre of each pair of table legs. The telly itself was bedecked with a cloud of orange mesh that had been pinched and gathered, stitched to a cotton base and fashioned into a rectangular runner. Inside the runner sat a trailing houseplant, from memory a geranium cultivated by my father. Almost every other surface was adorned with a crochet doily; starched ones, multi-layered ones, space-dyed ones in an array of colours, from optic white to bright pink. These doilies acted as cloth frames or lace plinths on which cherished objects were displayed. They were the 'undergarments', the white petticoats that gave shape and structure to the domestic interior.

Reflecting on her childhood, my mother remembered my great grandmother, Joanie Gooden, dressing the mahogany *chis* situated in her bedroom with a white lace runner. The *chis* was an important piece of furniture. As my mother recalled, inside its locked draws sat important documents and receipts as well as the best linen, such as a decorative white tablecloth. As far as she was concerned, the furniture in her living room had to be dressed with white lace and crochet doilies because that was the way things were done in the house in which she grew up. This outlook reveals concerns regarding respectability, grooming and the right way of doing things that she undoubtedly learned growing up in a pre-independent colonial Jamaica.

The family home in the countryside, or 'in country' to use the Jamaican vernacular, was dressed by the Gooden women. My mother recalled Granny Joanie buying calico in the village shop, cutting it to just the right length, blanket stitching around the edge and drawing on floral patterns with a pencil to create a border. My mother and her sisters would then embroider over the pencil design using different coloured threads. She saw the contemporary covering of furniture with runners and doilies as a continuation of a West Indian tradition handed down over the generations.

Today my mother's embroidered telly table cloth is draped over an old kitchen stool in the corner of my bedroom. In its early years, this stool sat underneath the everyday Formica table that was used in the kitchen at the old house when we were children. Chipped and worn, too rickety to sit on, the stool has now become a nightstand. My mother's tablecloth is folded lengthways and placed over the seat to hide the faded floral fabric that my father had used to replace the original PVC covering, which had become dirty and torn with use. It is the first thing I see in the morning as I wake up. It has been the first thing I've seen in the morning for the last three years.

So my stitching began 'as a way of remembering the past and imagining the future'. (Herman 2006: 216)

THE GALLERY SPACE

Traditionally, men would have created most of the everyday West African textiles. When the enslaved Africans were brought to the Americas, their work was allocated according to a Western patriarchal framework that dictated women take up these skills. What inspires me within a contemporary art context are those male artists who embrace a discipline that has previously been associated with women as a marker of a somewhat narrowly defined femininity. Considering male stitchery, I am reminded of Janis

Jefferies' British Crafts Council show: 'Boys who Sew' (5 February 2004 to 25 March 2005). Jefferies troubled our understandings of art, textile crafts and fashion by juxtaposing the work of seven male artists who use textile crafts to explore issues around gender, sexuality, race and cultural identity. The artists discussed here are similarly accidental textile artists; artists who use textiles as a tool with which to think, explore and challenge, without necessarily exhibiting a self-conscious agenda to raise the profile of textiles.

This chapter considers the work of Ernest Dükü, an Ivoirian living in Paris, and Nick Cave, an African-American. Both were invited to respond to a series of questions about the relationship between their creative process, use of textiles and personal narratives. Each voice is presented in monologue form, mirroring the self-representation key to postcolonial life-writing. Honouring the individual artists in this way also highlights the diversity and differences within the African diaspora. Indeed these particular artists were chosen precisely because they have very different thoughts on being in the diaspora, different attitudes towards their cultural identities and differing responses to the ways in which this does, or does not, inform their practices.

ERNEST DÜKÜ

Ernest Dükü migrated to Paris in the 1970s. His multimedia bound and stitched 'tableaux', or 'sculpture-paintings', see an eclectic mix of writings, signs and mark-makings deployed creatively across large constructions of multi-layered felted material. These inscriptions or 'sign-words' narrate his personal story whilst recording interwoven histories in a wider sense. His practice embraces influences from his remembered Ivoirian home alongside his interest in ancient writing systems, the spiritual realm and the many cultures that inhabit his adopted European homeland. He is particularly attracted to Caribbean, Ethiopian and Islamic cultures, referring to his practice as a 'dialogue of matters, cultures and sideways glances'. (Dükü, cited by Nooter Roberts 2011: 73)

He uses these influences to speak about the 'threshold' between the past, the present and

Ernest Dükü, *A Question of Writing* (detail), 1999. Painting, mixed media. © Ernest Dükü.

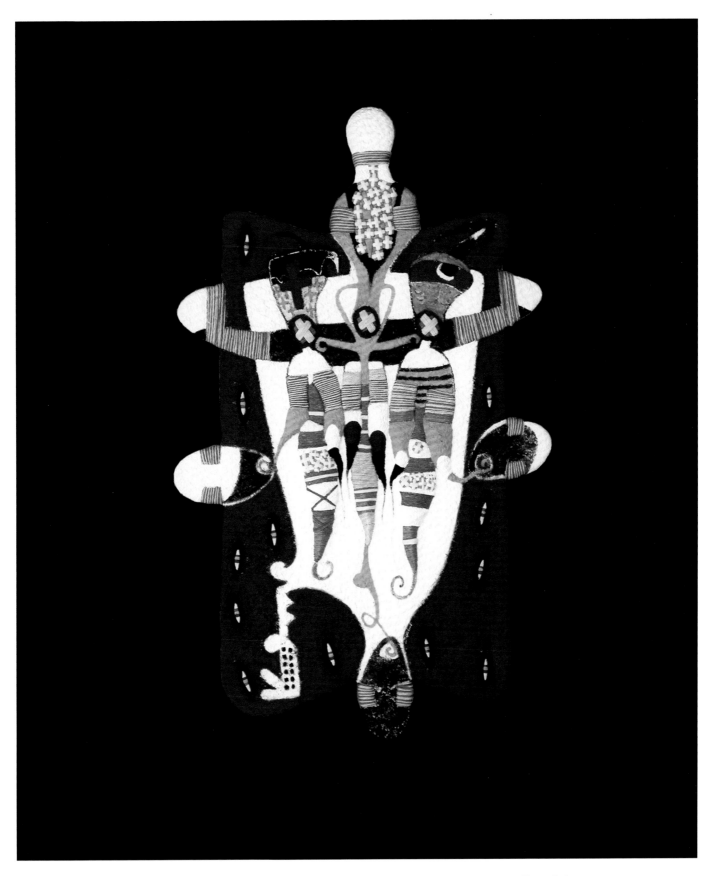

Ernest Dükü, *Yaoday Anan Ya code @ just like that*, 2012. Painting, mixed media. 47 × 42 × 4 cm (12 × 16 × 2 in.). © Ernest Dükü.

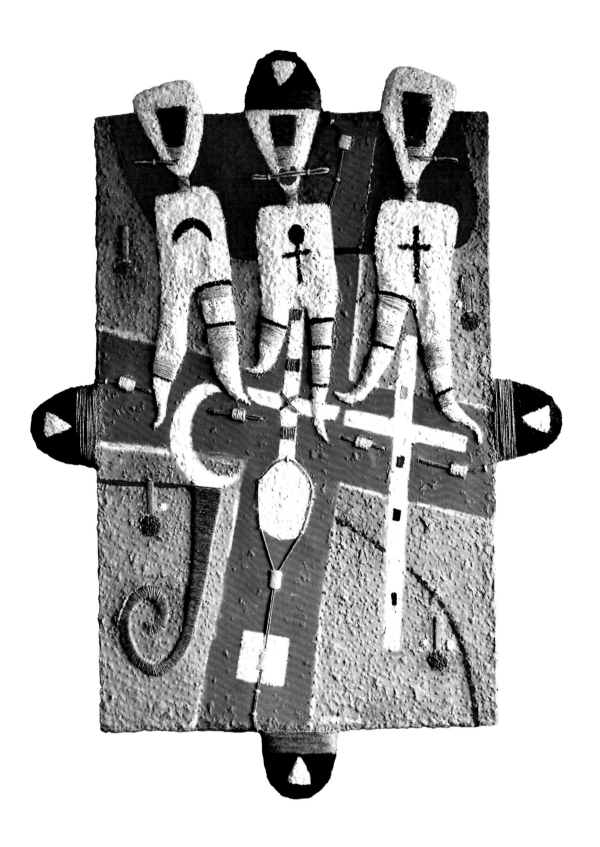

Ernest Dükü, *Le berceau KA Ô LIN*, 2002. Painting, mixed media. 150 × 130 × 5 cm (59 × 51 × 2 in.). © Ernest Dükü.

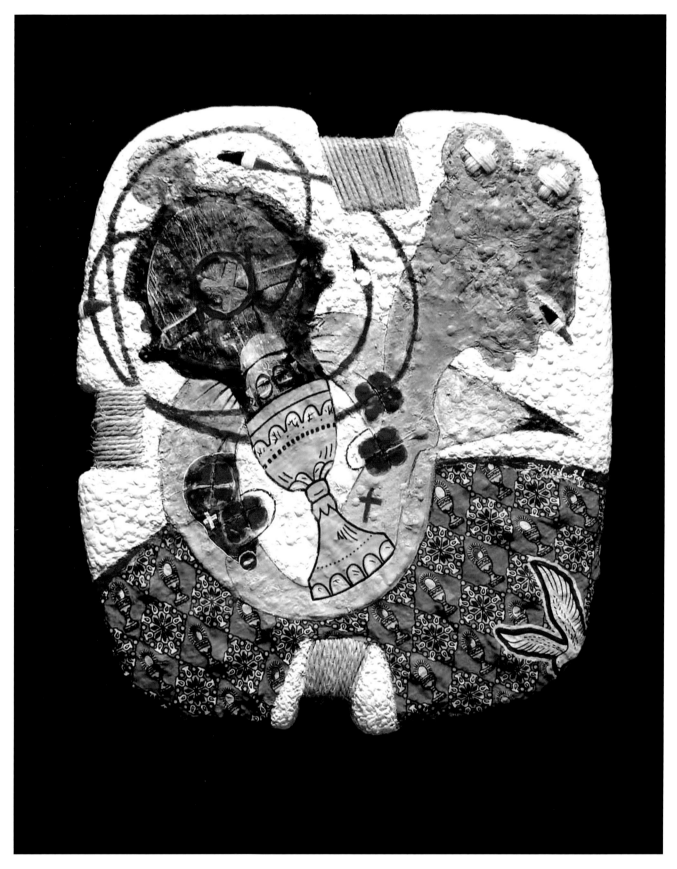

Ernest Dükü, *Y voir Net @ amalagokatiolo shuffle Neech O,* 2012. Painting, mixed media. 47 × 42 × 4 cm (21 × 16 × 2 in.). © Ernest Dükü.

the future, and between the spiritual and secular realms. He has said that working in Paris released a 'multicultural spirit' in his practice, which is underpinned by Ivoirian ancestral knowledge. In effect his sculpture-paintings ask: 'Who are we? Where are we going? Where do we come from?' (Dükü, cited by Nooter Roberts 2011: 71)

The symbols that Dükü deploys take inspiration from Ashanti sculpture, murals and woven cloth such as kente. He uses a weaving technique with ropes and threads, drawing a link between the rhythmic process of weaving and the creative process of writing, of formulating words and sentences. Weaving is key since 'the weavers delivered the words of the ancestral myths'. He also uses a form of *nzassa* (a Baule, Akan term for patchwork) to piece together materials such as cardboard, thread, pastels, acrylic paint, wax and coffee. (Nooter Roberts 2011: 71)

Dükü uses a deliberately restricted colour palette of mostly white, red and black. Drawing on West African spirituality, white refers to the kaolin used in traditional masquerade ceremonies. Black means ending and regeneration. Red symbolizes knowledge. (Dükü, cited by Nooter Roberts 2011: 71) But he also uses the contemporary symbols present in everyday life in Paris such as road signs and traffic lights. This creates a hybridized aesthetic that appropriates and reinscribes the signifying matter around him, challenging the notion of authenticity. Authenticity is questioned further since the kaolin used to create the white spaces discolours as the chemicals within it react with the air. The viewer is left wondering whether this is an artefact from the past or contemporary? Dükü explains in his monologue:

African textiles, the symbolic system of signs, writings, graphemes constitutes the petrol of my research. I study the ancestral tradition of the art of weaving, which translated the world starting from graphic symbols ... to question societies' relation with [the] cosmos ...

My interest in the art of textiles began with my parents, by training with directions and on the significance of the symbols. More specifically with my mother. She especially

taught me that the art of weaving transmitted messages by these symbols, like written forms, [to] serve societies, to tell [about] the world. My curiosity [has] always been to try to understand how the old societies used ... this practice to communicate, translate their myths and facts.

The texts that compose the titles of works are built following the example signs and the 'image symbols' ... Titles ... form the 'word bags' [that] come to function, for the spectator, like codes to be deciphered. By 'word bags' I express association, the combination of the words, and the various languages [that] create a title ... While proceeding thus, I seek to establish a mode of communication for a meeting of the languages and symbols that offer the transgression of borders, meaning that the various symbolic systems mix to open the doors of universal, unknown borders.

My work and my approach are the expression of an art that tries to scan and to carry out a reflection on memory. I treat memory questions which contribute to the dialogue between cultures. The combination of current art enables me to build a singular approach [aligned] to the globalization of artistic practices. This work is characterized by a transborder approach. Indeed, I nourish myself with principal matrices, such [as] old African art in general [Art Parietal] and Egyptian old art. These references signify the historical anchoring of my artistic practice. The Akan universe of the signs, the myths and traditions are useful to me as another point of reference to question the world.

[Migration] enabled me [to create artwork that explores issues around geographical place] The consciousness to go towards other cultures has create[d] the need for ... me to offer it [my culture] in exchange, in dialogue with the other ... My work is influenced by my origins, certainly related to the Ivory Coast, place of my birth, but also by those more total [origins], of the African traditions.

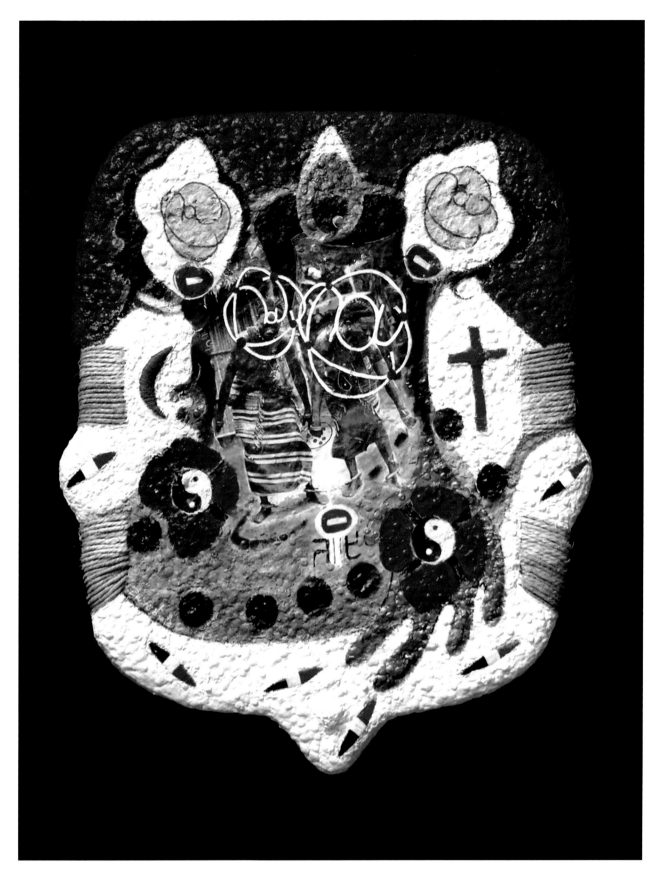

Ernest Dükü, *Yaoday Anan Ya code @ just like that*, 2012. Painting, mixed media. 47 × 42 × 4 cm (21 × 16 × 2 in.). © Ernest Dükü.

Nick Cave, *Holy Holy Holy*, 2009. Mixed media including wood and vintage salt and pepper shakers. 32 × 192 × 20 cm (13 × 76 × 8 in.). Photograph by James Prinz Photography. Courtesy of the artist and Jack Shainman Gallery, New York.

My current environment and the lived [experience] which results from this, challenges me on the question of the safeguarding of the memory, and the reasons to nourish it. Indeed, thanks to the environment of my childhood, where I … became aware of its artistic wealth. I try to take part in the diffusion of this ancestral knowledge by confronting it with other artistic forms of expression. I practise an art of junctions, by scanning the places of convergences of interpretation of symbols through time and the divergences of interpretations related to geographical place.

As in creations and African thought where one … cohabit[s] parallel universes, I investigate the question of visible and the invisible … Symbolically paintings offer a mark of research towards new visual horizons, other worlds. The cosmic and cosmological reality questions … our intrinsic relation to the world which surrounds us. The vision of art must be established beyond simple geographical locations, even if … any [every] artist has a geographic origin. His art carries the traces of this origin for him [to] make it possible to sign its singularity.

To be registered in the 'African diaspora' is for me a means to carry these values and to give direction to their historical memory. It is Africa that I carry in me, which comes to clash with other cultural realities. Thus I define my position of contemporary artist. This one translated my artistic concerns with ideas and reflections nourished by an African culture, which questions our time. [Faced with] the complexity of the world and the questions inherent in this situation, the problems related to this diaspora help me in the development of my works. The African context nourishes my artistic approach.

NICK CAVE

There is something of the Anancy in Nick Cave. His uniquely seductive and deceptively playful pieces pay no attention to the boundaries between fine and applied art, high and low culture, gendered and racial identity, let alone fashion, textiles and craft. Instead their drama and sheer tactility arrests you. The bits-and-pieces nature of his wearable sculptures or *Soundsuits* springs to life through movement. Each suit is meticulously sewn together from found materials like crochet doilies, buttons, beads, artificial flowers, funeral wreaths, bric-a-brac, vintage toys and scraps of fabrics. Cave's use of cast-offs and under-represented craft practices, such as crochet, is a powerful metaphor for those whom society discards.

Nick Cave, *Soundsuit*, 2005. Mixed media including knit and crocheted fabric, embroidery and sequins. Photograph by James Prinz Photography. Courtesy of the artist and Jack Shainman Gallery, New York.

Cave takes an improvisational approach to making – choosing not to sketch things out, preferring instead to allow each *Soundsuit* to evolve on its own. The pieces morph again when worn. As in ceremonial masquerade, the body is completely masked. This provides a powerful means of self-reflection, self-expression and liberation from the perspective of the wearer. For the viewer, the *Soundsuits* inspire new ways of thinking about themselves, others, their environments. By hiding gender, race and class, Cave forces us to look without judgement. The wearing, performance and viewing of the suit thus becomes a transformative act.

But there is much more to Cave than his visually show-stopping *Soundsuits*. His practice encompasses two genres: 'suits' and found-object sculptures. Cave creates dangerously, both genres working in a hybrid space where there is familiarity yet unfamiliarity; there is a familiarity to the objects selected but they become unfamiliar through his interventions. His aim, as he explains in the monologue below, is to use his practice as a 'vehicle for change':

It starts with an object. I think that the object is an instigator. Can it provide a different meaning? That's the negotiation. Then I decide if it goes on the wall, on the body and so on. There's always a pulse within an object. We have to continue to nurture, continue to be out in the world recognizing, feeling, responding to things. It's like, what's the origin of the object? What's its original function? Is that significant? How and why is the function relevant? Should I reconsider it?

Sometimes when I collect, I'm looking for techniques, for domestic processes that are becoming obsolete … they [women] would do their crafts in the time before their significant others' return. They would do their crafts [as a way of] honouring the

Nick Cave, *Soundsuit,* 2012. Mixed media including mannequin, fabric, hot pads, vintage toys, toy box and hooked rug. 356 × 102 × 81 cm (140 × 40 × 32 in.). Photograph by James Prinz Photography. Courtesy of the artist and Jack Shainman Gallery, New York.

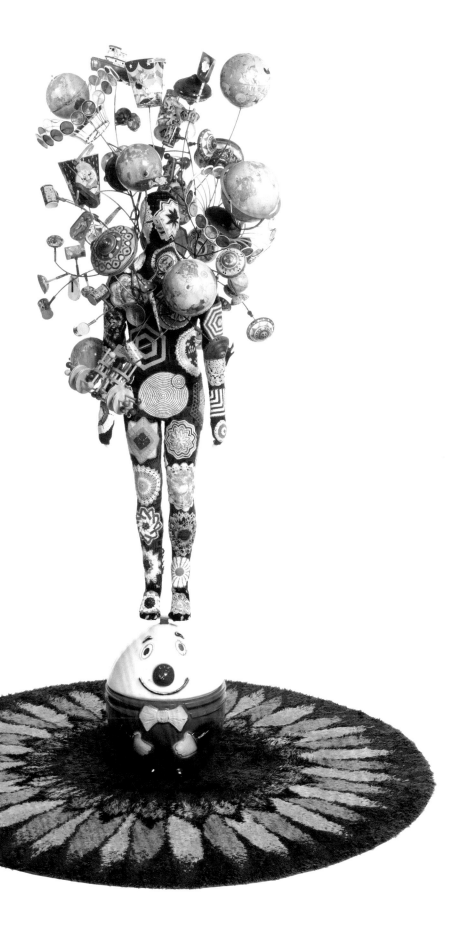

Nick Cave, *Soundsuit*, 2008. Mixed
media including knit and crocheted
fabric and vintage metal toys. 239 × 89
× 89 cm (94 × 35 × 35 in.). Photograph
by James Prinz Photography. Courtesy
of the artist and Jack Shainman Gallery,
New York.

home, celebrating the home, adorning the home. It was a way of being useful, keeping busy and finding contentment. So [in my work] the doily becomes a medallion, a way of honouring that task of handwork. What interests me is memory and time, past and present come together, the domestic property that the object conveys. I'm scouting for materials that are pivotal to the history of craft.

The critical decision is where and how we negotiate positioning these elements within the body of work. It is not about the segregation between art and craft ... Some of us push those boundaries. I find the media to suit the idea; the work has to sustain the idea; 'What's going to be the best material to support this idea?'

Through our sight we first feel. It's about being open to our experiences. Sometimes I have no idea why I buy things. Something has to draw you; what does it [the object] want to be? I don't draw anything. I'm basing it all on impulse. I may write a few things down, but it [the work] could take a different direction in the middle of the process. I have to pay attention to the moment. What has helped me has been just to be quiet.

In the studio my work is one thing. It becomes something else when other people respond. I'm not one-dimensional. It [the work] might be about movement, about sculpture, about putting it on the wall ... I want my work to have potential ... I want to be open to broader possibilities.

We can talk about masquerade, but what are we hiding behind? What is actually behind the masquerade? Everybody wants to tie it into cultural identity, to historical cultural identities, but the masquerade is the seducer, the unfamiliar. Thinking about 'why am I attracted to it?', people start to dissect, then they reach a point where it is too dark for them. People have opinions about things but they are afraid of confrontation. It's all there in the form, in the materials. But I am not going to force

you to confront it. So how do we make our work talk in this broad perspective? How can I seduce you to come along on this journey? [By] allowing the work to expand, allowing for multiple layers of readings.

I'm an artist with a social conscience. I am a messenger. Art is my religion ... it's about 'how did you become purposeful in your life? How can I be an instigator in the community realm? How can I inspire?'

For me, my work stands alone. Bringing a body to it, we create an experience. I like to hear the responses. At the end [of collaborative community projects] we have a testimony. It's so extraordinary because everyone's voice can be heard. It's so amazing! You may find that you go home and have the courage to leave your job and do something else! You are affected! I am affected! It is an out-of-body experience – you've become empowered to be yourself.

I don't think that I am culturally identified by race. I feel I'm incredibly happy and fully embrace my identity and the history that is attached. I keep my work broad ... Who am I in the world? I am an individual. I am not shaped to be one thing as opposed to many things. People don't allow you to broaden your identity. I think it's detrimental.

No work is ever finished to me. The curiosity continues. There is not a completeness.

CRAFTING DIFFERENCE

The relationship between postcolonial life-writing, fractured diasporic narratives and stitching is borne out in wrapping and binding and the intricate stitch and appliqué of scraps of cloth and bric-a-brac of Dükü and Cave's work. In hooks's memories of home, autobiographical references are pieced together to trace personal histories that connect to wider African-American social and cultural histories; my reflection on my mother's stitchery suggests cloth's ability to connect us to another moment in time, allowing

162

Nick Cave, *Soundsuit*, 2009.
Mixed media including fabric
and hair. 246 × 66 × 51 cm
(97 × 26 × 20 in.). Photograph
by James Prinz Photography.
Courtesy of the artist and Jack
Shainman Gallery, New York.

Nick Cave, *Soundsuit*, 2009. Mixed
media including fabric, wire, twigs
and found basket. 241 × 81 × 104 cm
(95 × 32 × 41 in.). Photograph by
James Prinz Photography. Courtesy of
the artist and Jack Shainman Gallery,
New York.

remembrance to act as a catalyst for renewal; in Dükü's hybrid tableaux, assumptions about who we are and where we are from are unravelled; in Cave's cut-and-mix assemblages, our quickness to render people and things obsolete confronts us.

These works operate at the threshold between the past, the present and the future. But as Bhabha observes:

> Such art does not merely recall the past as social cause or aesthetic precedent, it renews the past, refiguring it as a contingent 'in-between space' that innovates and interrupts the performance of the present. The 'past-present' becomes part of a necessity, not the nostalgia, of living. (Bhabha 1994: 7)

Whilst there may be traces of memory or earlier traditions, these are reconfigured as they come together in specific contemporary situations. Where craft once played a central role in ethnography, marking an otherness fixed in an imaginary bygone time, it now becomes a way of thinking as found in the domestic works of my childhood discussed in this chapter, and a subversive strategy exemplified by Dükü and Cave.

In the domestic examples stitching is primarily a means of thinking about oneself and one's place in the world by mapping the past. However Cave's determination for the layers of meaning behind and within his work to be unearthed regardless of his and the viewers' cultural, racial or gendered backgrounds, highlights the idea of stitching as a method of conceptual thinking that is not solely tied to the redefinition of self through personal history. Discussing the ongoing references to masquerade in his practice he states:

> We can talk about masquerade, but what are we hiding behind? What is actually behind the masquerade? Everybody wants to tie it into cultural identity, to historical cultural identities, but the masquerade is the seducer, the unfamiliar …

Masquerade is a tool that Cave uses to catch the viewers' attention, as opposed to a device

through which a real or imagined cultural past is remembered or honoured. In fact his research into this vernacular art form extends well beyond West Africa, creating a cross-cultural resonance. What interests him is the role that masquerade performs at a global human level, and the way such rituals allow us to connect to the power within that, when coupled with transcendence, creates an altered state of consciousness.

In contrast Dükü actively marries the two ways of thinking through stitch at a conceptual level and at a personal level. He writes:

> The vision of art must be established beyond simple geographical locations, even if … any [every] artist has a geographic origin. His art carries the traces of this origin for him [to] make it possible to sign its singularity.

Yet,

> My work is influenced by my origins, certainly related to the Ivory Coast, place of my birth, but also by those more total [origins], of the African traditions … The African context nourishes my artistic approach.

Such weaving of the past into the present circumvents an assumed 'historylessness'. (Bhabha 1994: 96) However as Bhabha notes, such practices also resist nostalgia. These works are not bound by romantic notions of the past or by a misguided longing for a 'pure' pre-colonial culture that never actually existed.

Just as the authors of postcolonial life-writing do not disavow the influence of Western culture, instead writing from the space between cultures, these artists take a 'transborder approach', to cite Dükü. He goes on, 'It is Africa that I carry in me, which comes to clash with other cultural realities.'

This 'transborder approach' characteristically crosses historical, cultural and geographical boundaries; it is the 'art of junctions'. As the artists suggest, complex cultural collisions and exchanges take place with migration and occupation of the 'in-between' space. (Bhabha 1994: 20). These entanglements become enmeshed in creative practice

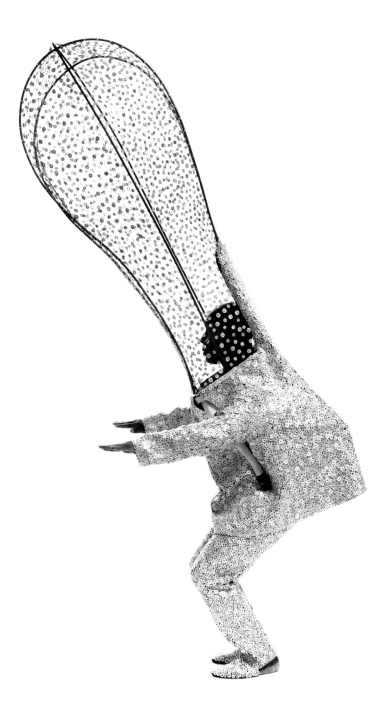

Nick Cave, *Soundsuit,* 2012. Mixed media including fabric, buttons and bentwood chair. 300 × 61 × 71 cm (118 × 24 × 28 in.). Photograph by James Prinz Photography. Courtesy of the artist and Jack Shainman Gallery, New York.

whether language-based, in the case of life-writing, or stitch-based in the case of these artworks. As in postcolonial life-writing, migration is not a negating experience. Instead it is an open-ended outlook that appears comfortable with undecideability. It echoes Maharaj's concept of 'thinking through textiles', which suggests that the process of making textiles promotes a way of thinking beyond fixed limits, one that resists the closure that occurs when we transcribe concepts through conventional writing.

Just as identities are in a constant state of flux, never reaching completion, 'thinking through textiles' involves an ongoing process of thinking and rethinking, which in turn mimics the repetitive doing, undoing and redoing of stitch. Cave's use of textiles and found objects supports this: 'No work is ever finished to me. The curiosity continues. There is not a completeness.'

The power of postcolonial life-writing lies in its ability to represent/re-present the cultural, racial and social histories of those who often remain absent from received histories in the West. As in the written text, the artistic practices shared here mesh together intricate personal narratives and historical legacies, alongside concepts and concerns that relate to the wider circuit of ideas at a global level. There is a lightness in approach that never becomes overtly didactic. Stitch, as an aesthetic, subversive and conceptual strategy, draws the viewer in, enabling new meanings and associations to be made, whilst allowing the fissures in personal and received history to be temporarily sutured. The impetus is a creative spark that celebrates the hybridity, entanglements and transformations that come with movement and migration as cultures clash and coalesce. What inspires is the artists' refusal to be defined by the idea of the African diaspora that empties their work of its complexity or closes down broader readings.

To be in the diaspora may involve fracturing – of one's perception of self, of one's sense of belonging, of the notion of historical continuity – but it also involves setting up a metaphorical home in the 'in-between' space of possibility. (Bhabha 1994: 20) To be in the diaspora is to live in a world in which new knowledge and ways of seeing challenge 'fixity' (Bhabha 1994: 75), and can be spun into a yarn of their own.

AFRICAN DIASPORAS

Dükü and Cave's responses cover a striking
range of work infused by specific cultural,
geographical and conceptual considerations.
These are many-layered pieces that can be read
at different levels. I have chosen to focus on
issues connected to the postcolonial, to cultural
history, to identity politics. Writing this chapter
I have become increasingly aware of the need
to think more in terms of African 'diasporas',
by this I mean to emphasize the plural, to
resist reduction and the inevitable restricted
reading of the works. What this chapter offers
is a snapshot in time of particular viewpoints
that sit within what might be defined as African
diaspora contemporary art, or should I say the
contemporary art of 'Africa and its diasporas'?
(Silva 2013: 4)

Nick Cave, *Soundsuit*, 2013.
Mixed media including
fabric, buttons, antique sifter
and wire. 213 × 76 × 64 cm
(84 × 30 × 25 in.). Photograph
by James Prinz Photography.
Courtesy of the artist and Jack
Shainman Gallery, New York.

NOTES

1. Postcolonial life-writing has been defined as a form of autobiography that resists the Western patriarchal model, giving voice to decentred migrant subjectivities, to those whom the West relegates to its periphery. Aligned to postcolonial fiction and poetry, it is characterized by the use of vernacular language structures, metaphors and culturally specific discursive traditions. Stylistically, both language and form are hybridized, drawing on the cultural expressions of both the former colonizer and colonized. In this context, autobiography moves beyond the chronicling of one's personal history, and instead becomes a political strategy or vehicle for change. (Moore-Gilbert 2009: xi–xxvi)

2. Majors and Mancini Billson, in their analysis of coolness and African-American male dress, identify a number of interrelated aspects of West African culture that they suggest have influenced African-American aesthetics and cloth-based cultural expression. Some examples include 'expressive individualism' – the cultivation of a distinctive personality and tendency toward spontaneous, personal expression; 'harmony' – the notion that humankind and nature are harmoniously conjoined; 'movement' – an emphasis on the interweaving of movement, rhythm and percussiveness. (Majors and Mancini-Billson 1992: 56–57) Thompson notes such alleged retentions as the propensity to access everything aesthetically and the use of assemblage or *bricolage* in creative making. (Farris Thompson 1984) Ross, in an overview of John Michael Vlach and Maude Wahlman's writings alerts us to the influence of kente cloth on African-American strip quilting. (Ross 2012: 129)

BIBLIOGRAPHY

Bhabha, H.K. (1994), *The Location of Culture*, London: Routledge.

Braithwaite, K. (1974), *Contradictory Omens: Cultural Diversity and Integration*, Mona, Jamaica: Savacou Publications.

Bucknor, M.A. (2005), 'Rooting and Routing Canadian-Caribbean Writing', in *the Journal of West Indian Literature*, vol. 14, nos. 1 and 2: November 2005, Kingston, Jamaica: The Department of Literatures in English, the University of the West Indies, i–xliii.

Cave, N. (2013), telephone interview with Christine Checinska.

Douglass, F. (1995), *Narrative of the Life of Frederick Douglass*, New York: Dover Publications.

Du Bois, W.E.B. (1994), *The Souls of Black Folk*, New York: Dover Thrift Editions.

Dükü, E. (2013), email interview with Christine Checinska.

Fanon, F. (1986), *Black Skin, White Masks*, London: Pluto Press.

Fanon, F. (1963), *The Wretched of the Earth*, London: Penguin Books.

Gates Jr., H.L. (1988), *The Signifying Monkey: A Theory of Afro-American Literary Criticism*, New York: Oxford University Press.

Herman, B.L. (2006), 'Architectural Definitions', in P. Arnett, J. Cubbs and E.W. Metcalf Jr. (eds), *Gee's Bend: The Architecture of the Quilt*, Atlanta: Tinwood Books.

hooks, b. (2007), 'An Aesthetic of Blackness: Strange and Oppositional' in J. Livingstone and J. Ploof, *The Object of Labour*, Cambridge: MIT Press, 315–333.

Maharaj, S. (2001) 'Textile Art – Who Are You?' in J. Jefferies (ed.), *Re-inventing Textiles*, Winchester: Telos Art Publishing, 7–11.

Majors, R. and Mancini Billson, J. (1992), *Cool Pose: The Dilemmas of Black Manhood in America*, New York: Lexington Books.

Mercer, K. (1994), 'Black Art and the Burden of Representation', in *Welcome to the Jungle*, London: Routledge, 233–259.

Moore-Gilbert, B. (2009), *Postcolonial Life-writing: Culture, Politics and Self-Representation*, Oxford: Routledge.

Nooter Roberts, M. (2011), 'Ernest Dükü: Writing Identities', in *African Arts*, vol. 44, no. 1, Los Angeles: UCLA James S. Coleman African Studies Centre, 68–73.

Rael, A. (2013), 'Nick Cave "Sojourn" Exhibit At Denver Art Museum Explores The Sensory With Flea Market Items', in the *Huffington Post*, <http://www.huffingtonpost.com/2013/06/08/nick-cave-sojourn-denver-art-museum_n_3398345.html > [Accessed 12 June 2013].

Ross, D.H. (2012), 'Kente and its Image outside of Ghana', in C. Harper (ed.), *Textiles: Critical and Primary Sources*, vol. 4, London: Berg, 150–187.

Showalter. E. (2012), 'Piecing and Writing', in C. Harper (ed.), *Textiles: Critical and Primary Sources*, vol. 4, London: Berg, 203–220.

Silva, B. (ed.) (2013), *N. Paradoxa, Africa and its Diasporas*, vol. 31, London: KT Press.

Spillers, H. (1987), 'Mama's Baby, Papa's Maybe: An American Grammar Book', in *Diacritics*, vol. 12, no. 2, *Culture and Countermemory: The American Connection*, Baltimore: The Johns Hopkins University Press, 64–81.

Thompson, R.F. (1984), *Flash of the Spirit*, New York: Vintage Books.

ACKNOWLEDGEMENTS

I would like to thank the artists Ernest Dükü and Nick Cave for their generosity in giving their time. I also thank Andrew Stephenson.

Chapter seven

From Brixton to Mostar: social practice through textiles

Françoise Dupré

London-based French-born artist Françoise Dupré discusses her collaborative-participatory practice and the suitability of textiles for her work in this chapter. Writing in 'pieces', Dupré explains that three framed sections – Brixton, Whitechapel and Mostar – 'zoom into the stuff of making' providing three geographically discrete points of focus in her writing. Her chosen material of large plastic carrier bags are the same materials used by Zimbabwean artist Dan Halter and discussed in chapter three; both artists adopt these materials for the narratives of migration and movement that they communicate.

Alternative textual structures are present throughout *Cultural Threads*, from the use of interview transcripts to preserve a sense of dialogue and conversation so central to the research underpinning this book, to the monologue preserved by Christine Checinksa as a record of the artist's engagement and response to the author's inquiry. The textual structure Dupré explores here is yet another example of the desire to ensure the voice of the maker – the artist as author in this case – is as articulate as the communication of their visual practice. This is of particular importance to Dupré's practice, which often takes the form of workshops with local communities and her interest in our 'becoming cosmopolitan'.

Jessica Hemmings

Françoise Dupré, *Étoile (Star)*, 2007–2012. Site specific installation at The Gallery @ Idea Store Whitechapel, London, 2012. Stitched and pinned woven and printed polythene, PVC, pins, plastic bottle tops, hair clips. 200 × 1000 × 3 cm (78 × 393 × 11 in.). © Françoise Dupré.

Imagining ourselves at home in the world, where our homes are not fixed objects but processes of material and conceptual engagement with other people and different places, is the first step toward becoming cosmopolitan. (Meskimmon 2010: 8)

On the bus journey through South East London to my studio, many tongues are spoken. Mother tongues, father tongues, official tongues. On the bus, I hear a multiplicity of conversations and news is relayed. I imagine stories of migrations that knot individuals and communities together across the world. Pasts, presents and futures fold and unfold. Space and time collide. The bus becomes a portal for imagination and connectivity. Travelling with women in traditional African dresses, niqab or the latest street fashion I am connected to the world. I am at home, becoming cosmopolitan.

Textiles, too, travel across the globe, through time and space, connecting people and places. Indeed it is the combination of textiles' cultural specificity and transnationalism, its mixture of history and contemporality, that have been instrumental in my choice of this medium for context and art making. Located in the studio as well as in social and public spaces, my cross-disciplinary practice combines fine art and textiles and uses individual and collaborative approaches. This text is an opportunity to reflect upon and discuss why and how these aspects that underpin my practice have come together and matter to me. As a French-born, London-based woman artist, I engage with our cosmopolitan world and attempt to make sense of belonging to multiple cultures. My practice is an integral part of this ongoing renegotiation and process of becoming. I practise feminist ethics and aesthetics and my social and cultural engagement has continuously evolved since the early 1980s when I graduated from art school.

For this chapter, I shall unpack aspects of my textiles-based art practice and discuss strategies and approaches that I have adopted in different times and spaces. My main intention is to argue for a critical repositioning of textiles in a multicultural and cross-disciplinary social (art) practice.[1] The strategic use of textiles in socially and politically engaged art practices is not new, as I shall demonstrate first, when I reflect upon my experience and involvement with Brixton Art Gallery and the role of textiles as medium and context in women's struggle and liberation in the 1980s. The late Rozsika Parker in her 2010 preface to *The Subversive Stitch: Embroidery and the Making of the Feminine*, first published in 1984, writes that 'Feminist artists were part of a thriving political movement, whereas today's embroiderers, most notably Tracey Emin, are working in a very different time.' (2010: xv) Yet Parker clearly argues that there are nevertheless artists who have continued with the 'historical association between embroideries, collectivity and political protest'. (2010: xvii) Indeed, I believe that the legacy of 1980s feminist artists working in textiles and multicultural contexts is more than ever relevant today when migrant individuals and communities are confronted by xenophobia and racism. How can we, today, live together as multicultural subjects and think 'a generative utopian thought – a world without foreigners' where otherness is accepted and understood? (Kristeva 1993: 36) These are issues that have continuously motivated my art making and writing, and that I shall attempt to articulate here.

This text will take readers on a journey from Brixton to Mostar, via Whitechapel. The text is not constructed as a linear, evolutionary and chronological narrative. It is a montage, a fitting approach to my subject in an effort to resist singularity of thought. The format aims to emphasize the interconnectivity and multidimensional aspects of my practice and its critical and theoretical underpinning. Cross-disciplinarity and social practice are discussed in the main text in three separate sections to allow for fuller discussions. Three framed texts: Brixton, Whitechapel and Mostar, puncture the flow and rhythm of the main text, to zoom into the stuff of making, experiencing and thinking in different spaces and times. Hovering above and looping throughout is textiles.

BRIXTON

Trained in sculpture at Camberwell College of Arts in the early 1980s, I learnt about the formal quality of materials and making as meaning. Here meaning was to be considered within the pure and self-contained language of sculpture where emotion, as well as social and cultural references, remained out of bounds. Educated in post-1968 France, I found this concept of art extremely difficult to comprehend because I could not envisage making art without cultural contexts and social conscience. I struggled, rebelled and went on to develop multi-stranded art-making activities based in the studio and among Brixton's communities. In June 1983 I was part of a local group of artists who co-founded Brixton Art Gallery and Brixton Artists Collective.[2] The gallery was a collective and multicultural experimentation in art. Artists challenged established rules and conventions and understood art as a transformative and empowering force for change.[3] Unlike most art galleries, Brixton Art Gallery showed textiles and clay works in its exhibitions. These exhibitions contributed to the growing debate about the gendered and hierarchical differentiation between fine art and craft or decorative/applied arts.[4] In multicultural Brixton Art Gallery, textiles were not chosen by self-obsessed individual artists as a calculated avant-garde artistic tool to antagonize the bourgeoisie and shock the art establishment. Textiles were used and exhibited for their social and world connections.

In 1986, collective member Teri Bullen in collaboration with the Zamani Soweto Sisters Council and the Maggie Magaba Trust curated an unforgettable exhibition *Soweto: The Patchwork of our Lives* (24 May to 14 June 1986). I remember meeting these remarkable women, listening to their stories of life under apartheid and seeing their stories translated through stitch in their quilts. The opening night of *Soweto: The Patchwork of our Lives* was truly memorable. It brought together the South African community in exile in London and included a speech by writer and activist Ellen Kuzowayo. At the opening, African textiles were worn with pride. The Zamani Sisters were dressmakers, and textiles provided economic independence and self-respect. Using quilting and patchwork techniques, the Zamani Sisters also created wall-hanging pieces, translating traditional designs as well as telling their stories of struggle. Their textile collages were inspired by an early visit in 1980 to a Chilean refugee group in London where they saw Chilean patchworks that depicted life under the Pinochet dictatorship.

Women's Work, the women artists' group based at Brixton Art Gallery, paid homage to the use of textiles in past and ongoing political and emancipatory struggles with the making and display of collaborative textile banners.[5] For each of the Women's Work exhibitions, artists created textile squares that were stitched together to create and display exhibition banners. The banners were contexts for individual stories, feminist slogans as well as stitched records of local struggles such as the occupation of the South London Hospital for Women in Clapham South[6]

Textiles make up a broad and complex discipline that includes a wide range of techniques and processes. Further on in this essay, when discussing textiles, I shall refer mostly to stitching and looping, the techniques I use.[7] At Brixton Art Gallery, exhibitions curated by Women's Work and Black Women in View (the Black Women Artists' group based at Brixton Art Gallery) included embroideries, appliqué, weaving and prints. Cloth was also used as sculptural material and a cultural signifier in performances and installations. Textiles were therefore chosen as a tool and context for creativity, imagination and resistance, inspiring and enabling women to transform their lives. Women's Work banners, Zamani Sisters' quilts, and Chilean patchworks actively contributed to women's struggles that were part of wider international political networks like the Anti-Apartheid movement.[8] At Brixton Art Gallery, feminist artists strategically employed textiles as a medium because of their universal association with women's everyday work and for their connection, through time and space, with social and community struggles.

CROSS-DISCIPLINARITY

Though the history of modern art, there is a long-standing tradition of using non-fine art materials and processes to question and reject existing elitist modes of cultural production. The emancipatory and revolutionary quality of cross-disciplinary practice has long been argued for and acknowledged. From the early twentieth century, cross-disciplinary practice has been favoured by artists who wish to challenge authorship and elitism, and engage with other cultural and social contexts. However, a cross-disciplinary practice is not by essence political. It is the artist who makes her practice political. Nevertheless, by shifting across disciplines, the artist finds herself in a hybrid, in-between position that does not fit well with artistic norms. In *La transversalité et le seuil* Caroline Renard argues that cross-disciplinarity is a zone without a territory, in-transit, a threshold.[9] Referencing Walter Benjamin's concept of the threshold, Renard defines it as a space of variation, of difference and becoming.[10] For this reason, cross-disciplinarity provides a potentially subversive context, predisposed to engagement with differences and otherness.

Furthermore a cross-disciplinary approach that combines textiles and art gains an extra dimension in a threshold condition because in patriarchal society, textiles are associated with the feminine and women's marginalized position. From a feminist perspective, an art practice that crosses with textiles becomes political because textiles, and specifically the act of stitching, offer far more than disciplinary cross-fertilization. In Western societies, textiles are the site of the feminine. Here, the feminine is to be understood not as a form of repression but a form of resistance: a performative and transformative site for political struggle and becoming.[11] Indeed women, who have 'the luck and responsibility of being boundary-subjects' (Kristeva 1993: 35), have the privileged position to open up dialogues with history, subjectivity and others, and understand and promote the idea of a 'polyvalent society'. (Kristeva 1993: 35) Choosing cosmopolitanism means choosing 'a transnational or international position situated at the crossing of boundaries.' (Kristeva 1993: 16)

A zone without territory, common to women and others and to cross-disciplinarity between art and textiles is therefore fertile ground for the exploration and development of one's cosmopolitan subjectivity. This is nevertheless a predisposition that is not performative in itself. To engage with multiple cultures, women's lives, social and community struggles, to open dialogues with the world, the artist needs, I believe, to develop transformative art-making approaches to create socially meaningful art objects. Next, I shall demonstrate that this is possible with social practice through textiles.

WHITECHAPEL: CRAFTING THE EVERYDAY

I buy my art materials in markets where I search for large bags, the totes with long handles and a zip.[12] Made from woven polythene, some bags have woven stripe patterns while others have digitally printed designs, texts or photographs. They are used for daily shopping or carrying goods and belongings across continents. Mass produced in China, available in markets across the world, these bags are a constant reminder that textiles are global. Back in the studio I cut and stitch and create new patterns using appliqué techniques. The same techniques and materials are also used when working with women's groups. Inspired by quilts and stitched motifs from England to Gujarat, Balkan architectural and textile designs, Ottoman and Islamic geometric patterns, French floral textile designs, ornate ironwork, I create site-specific wall installations for art and non-art spaces.

Françoise Dupré, *Étoile (Star)*, 2007–2012. Detail of central motif, wall installation. Stitched and pinned woven and printed polythene, PVC, pins, plastic bottle tops. © Françoise Dupré and FXP Photography, London.

Étoile (Star) was developed and installed at The Gallery @ Idea Store Whitechapel in 2012.[13] Whitechapel is a distinct area of East London with a strong working class history and a long tradition of migration from Irish, French Huguenots and Eastern European Jewish immigrants to today's Bangladeshi communities. The installation, a ten-metre long all-over geometric pattern, was created by assembling and pinning individually stitched forms that had been cut out of market bags and tablecloths from Brixton and Petticoat Lane in London, as well as Paris, Brisbane and Morant Bay, Jamaica. For the duration of the exhibition, the installation became a portal into other cultural spaces and times, connecting with Whitechapel library's multicultural context and users.

The term crafting implies an ongoing activity and a space that continues to be activated by the installation and viewers whose imagination takes them through 'snapshots of public and private moments', local and world contexts. (Alfoldy & Helland 2008: 4) My exploration and experimentation with decorative and repetitive patterns is informed by the understanding of the transformative role of crafts and ornament, in our experience of space and the notion of the 'crafting of space'. (Alfoldy & Helland 2008: 2) Crafted objects placed in interior and exterior architectural spaces contribute to and alter our understanding and experience of these spaces. 'Spaces are necessary to craft; craft is fundamental to space.' (Alfoldy & Helland 2008: 3) This implies the possibility for craft to disrupt spaces, through spatial interventions and temporary installations. On the top floor of the Whitechapel library, *Étoile (Star)*, with its highly decorative patterns, subtly disrupted the functional design of the building designed by architect David Adjaye. *Étoile (Star)* activated the space and became a site of spatial imagination, a space with a 'multiplicity of trajectories' and narratives; a space

of resistance against globalization and for different and multiple futures. (Massey 2006: 5) Doreen Massey argues that globalization is making a world that is in the process of turning space into time. Globalization (of capitalism) aims to flatten our differences and futures into a single evolutionary model of progress. Massey argues for an alternative approach to space and a conceptualization of time and space that do not define space as a surface in which we are placed and where the 'trajectories of others can be immobilised'. (2006: 8) For Massey, space needs to continue to exist, as the product of interactions from the global to the intimate, a sphere of 'contemporaneous plurality' and possibilities. (2006: 9)

Françoise Dupré, *Crafting* (detail), 2010. Wall and door installation, woven polythene, plastic tubing, black irrigation pipe, galvanized wire, cable ties.
© Françoise Dupré and FXP Photography, London.

OPPOSITE Françoise Dupré,
Tiger, 2011. From the *Screens
(Flowers)* series, hanging panel.
Stitched woven and printed
polythene. 60 × 90 cm (23 ×
37 in.). © Françoise Dupré.

RIGHT Françoise Dupré,
Stripes and Flowers, 2012. One
of six panels, wall hanging
installation. Commissioned
for the new Royal London
Hospital, Antenatal
Department, Whitechapel,
London, by Vital Arts (Barts
and The London NHS Trust).
Woven and printed polythene
from carrier bags, webbing,
thread, pins on MDF boards.
45 × 129 × 3 cm (17 × 50 ×
1 in.). © Françoise Dupré and
FXP Photography, London.

OPPOSITE Françoise Dupré, *Sunflowers*,
2011. From the *Screens (Flowers)* series, hanging
panel. Stitched woven and printed polythene.
60 × 90 cm (23 × 37 in.). © Françoise Dupré.

ABOVE Françoise Dupré, *Flowers and Star*, 2011.
From the *Screens (Flowers)* series, hanging panel. Stitched
woven and printed polythene. 60 × 90 cm (23 × 37 in.).
© Françoise Dupré.

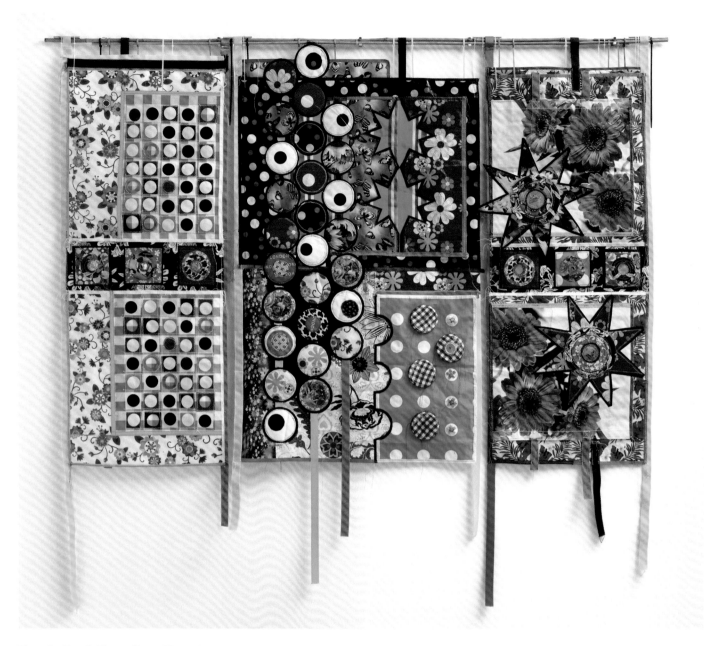

Françoise Dupré, *Flowers (Bonne Mamans)*,
2012. Wall hanging installation. Commissioned
for the new Royal London Hospital, Antenatal
Department, Whitechapel, London, by Vital Arts
(Barts and The London NHS Trust). Woven
and printed polythene from carrier bags, webbing,
thread, quilting pins, bamboo canes, cable
ties, clips, PVC mirrors. 176 × 195 × 6 cm
(69 × 76 × 2 in.). © Françoise Dupré and FXP
Photography, London.

SOCIAL (ART) PRACTICE

Social practice is the most recent term used to describe a wide range of participatory practices that have been developed since the 1960s. They include: socially engaged art, littoral art, interventionist art, participatory art, collaboration art, contextual art, community-based art, dialogical art.[14] The term social practice does not include the word art, let alone textiles! I have therefore added (art) to this section's heading, to indicate that the context of the practice is aesthetic as well as social. Indeed, with social practice, there are two challenging and tightly related issues: the status of the handmade or handcrafted art object and the nature of the artist-participant relationship. Here, I use the term art object to mean any physical and tangible art form or temporary installation that involves materiality, handmaking and crafting. Today, social

practice is a highly debated area of research and practice but I have been troubled by predominant thinking that privileges dialogues, communication and intersubjective connections over the haptic and aesthetic experience. I believe these concerns are pertinent to address here, when the artist is seeking to generate conditions for critical and transformative dialogues between aesthetics, locational identities and cosmopolitanism. I shall argue therefore, in the following sections, for the relocation of the art object in social practice, and demonstrate that social practice and crafting are not incompatible. On the contrary, I intend to demonstrate that social practice through textiles is the perfect approach with which to critically engage with our cosmopolitan subjectivity.

MOSTAR: OUVRAGE [uvra:ž]

OUVRAGE [uvra:ž] was a self-initiated art project developed with Jasmina Zvonić, the director of the French Cultural Centre in Mostar, Bosnia and Herzegovina.[15] The project took place during a five-week residency at the French Cultural Centre in the summer of 2009. Its outcome was a textiles-based temporary installation exhibited in the Ćejvan Ćehaja Hamam. The installation was developed and realized in the context of a series of workshops and using a collaborative-participatory approach.[16] OUVRAGE [uvra:ž] was made with Novi Pogled, a Mostar-based women's association that supports breast cancer survivors and campaigns for better breast cancer treatment and awareness. Other participants were friends of the French Cultural Centre, art students from Mostar, Birmingham (England) and Cluj-Napoca (Romania). Mostar's participants came from the Croatian and Bosniak communities.

While OUVRAGE [uvra:ž] engaged with participants' multiple cultural identities, social

contexts and histories, the installation was not about a representation of participants' lives and experiences. It was not a 'symbolic practice' (Helguera 2011: 5) and it was not craftivism.[17] This was particularly relevant for Novi Pogled who, through the project, wanted to be perceived as active and creative subjects rather than as victims of cancer. It is important to note that the aim of OUVRAGE [uvra:ž] was not therapeutic either, though participants' memories and life experiences were shared through the project's workshops and social events. Besides the intersubjective engagement between participants and artist, it is therefore the emphasis on the haptic experience and creation of an art object with a strong materiality that is of central concern here.

The installation was created using looping (French, or spool, knitting, and crochet), stitching (appliqué and embroidery), construction and assemblage techniques. A wide range of materials, bought in the UK and Mostar, were used including

Françoise Dupré, *OUVRAGE [uvra:ž]*, 2009. Project workshop at the French Cultural Centre, Mostar. © Françoise Dupré.

woven polythene (market bags), felt fabric, yarns, wire and PVC tubing. The performative and transformative nature of looping and stitching and their contribution to identity formation – the process of becoming – were instrumental in delivering the project's aim: to celebrate women's creativity, cultural diversity and commonality through crafting. Traditional stitches in Bosnia and Herzegovina can provide strong clues when identifying ethnic communities' social as well as geographic origins. A trained eye examining a woman's long shirt from the National Museum of Bosnia and Herzegovina's collection of nineteenth and early twentieth-century textiles can easily ascertain the wearer's identity, faith, social status and rural or urban origin.[18] In the *OUVRAGE [uvra:ž]* installation, one also finds, reconfigured, culturally specific stitches and designs. For example, the orange diamond-shaped appliqué pieces, inspired

by Ottoman rugs and embroidery stitching, used in Catholic textile imagery. However, in its entirety, *OUVRAGE [uvra:ž]* celebrates what participants have always had in common and shared: their love of crafting, stitching and the handmade.

While walking in Mostar, one's spatial experience of the city is made of sharp contrasts, travelling back and forth in time. The Balkans' contrasting and rich cultures and multiple histories are there for all to see and experience through the city's streets and architecture: Ottoman, Austro-Hungarian, Communist Yugoslavia and postwar Bosnia and Herzegovina. Yet there is continuity through the crafting of interior and exterior architectural spaces. While crafting celebrates differences, it also becomes a tool for spatial imagination, enabling us to cross over historical, cultural and religious boundaries and bring together the private and public spaces of daily life activities.

Françoise Dupré, *OUVRAGE*
[uvra:ž], 2009. Project workshop at
the French Cultural Centre, Mostar.
© Françoise Dupré.

Françoise Dupré, *OUVRAGE [uvra:ž]*, 2009. Installation at the Ćejvan Ćehaja Hamam, Mostar. Stitched woven and printed polythene, wool, wire, tapes, plastic (bags, bottle and tubing), bamboo canes, crochet and French (spool) knitting. 250 × 360 × 50 cm (98 × 141 × 19 in.) © Françoise Dupré and photographer Ada Muntean.

Participants' designs and stitching were instrumental in providing the installation with its individual, collective and cultural specificity. Here, stitching and looping were used as sculptural mediums to create a temporary aesthetic space, a site of spatial imagination, where Mostar's vernacular architectural and decorative patterns and designs were reconfigured to create a culturally hybrid installation that connected the city's multiple trajectories. This was an undertaking that was not lost on participants and viewers, in the context of a city and country's enormously complex past and present.[19]

OUVRAGE [uvra:ž] provided a context for participants to articulate their rich and multiple cultural histories and identities. A context that went far beyond the reductive image of war victims, cancer patients and displaced refugees. Through *OUVRAGE [uvra:ž]*, multiple trajectories were opened, in time and space, connecting together European, Islamic and Bosnian textiles, design and architecture.

SOCIAL PRACTICE
THROUGH TEXTILES

Art making happens anywhere. The everyday is full of 'wonders' without names which one needs to be 'prepared to see' (de Certeau 1990: XIII).[20] However, to engage with individuals, communities, cultures and places, the artist needs more than predisposition. An art practice centred around the involvement of others requires different approaches to art making than one developed around and for a single author. For more than a century, cross-disciplinarity, in its many forms, has allowed artists to break away from traditional restrictive artistic models, and provided fertile ground for collaborations between artists and non-art specialists. At Brixton Art Gallery, women artists chose cross-disciplinarity as well as collaborative and participatory approaches to develop feminist strategies that challenged a phallocentric art world. From my experience and work in Brixton, I learned that inclusiveness and openness, inherent to critical collaboration and participation, allow for a plurality of makers and multiple making contexts far beyond the realm of art galleries, studios and art schools. Here, the everyday is transformed yet not transcended, and its materiality is used 'to realize the possibility of change'. (Meskimmon 2011: 49)

For Pablo Helguera, who favours the term socially engaged practice above social practice, a socially engaged practice is not a practice that represents social or political issues on a symbolic level, but a practice that is 'a hybrid, multi-disciplinary activity that exists somewhere between art and non-art'. (2011: 8) Indeed, it is this resistance to fixity, the ongoing negotiation between the social and art, the in-between position of socially engaged practice that makes such practice relevant and appropriate for artists and communities to engage in creative dialogues between multiple cultures. Where art ends and life starts might not be the right question to ask here because it is the permeability of art and life, the constant 'linkages' between art and life, that give the practice its constantly shifting position. (Rancière 2002: 151) Socially engaged practice 'brings together, engage[s]

and even critique[s] a particular group of people'[21] (Helguera 2011: 8), it involves 'the co-presence of bodies in real time'. (Kester 2011: 114) Here we are located in the real and actual society where the emancipatory potential of cross-disciplinarity is not for the artist alone but for all involved.

While it is tremendously liberating to think about a practice that is never fixed or resolved, one ought to question whether or not social practice necessitates getting rid of the art object altogether! At the very least, it is time to rethink the art object in social practice. In dialogical art, exchanges and dialogues between participants are considered to be more important than the aesthetic experience of the art object. Nevertheless, it is not very useful to oppose dialogical art to object-based art practices. Indeed, Kester, advocating dialogical exchanges, acknowledges neglecting the 'significance of visual or sensory experience'. (2004: 12) Indeed, 'to consider collaboration through craft is to recognize that making involves dialogues'. (Ravetz, Kettle & Felcey 2013: 8) Crafting and dialogues are therefore far from incompatible; they are bound together. In a drive to get rid of the single author, it is tempting to throw away the art object at the same time. It might be rather more useful to consider different kinds of art objects and adopt other attitudes and approaches to making in social practice.[22]

Textiles-based art practices of collaboration and social engagement in the 1980s, discussed first in this text, are helpful and offer us relevant models. Stitching used for making quilts, banners and patchworks contributed to women's empowerment and changed lives. Kester, in his discussion of Dialogue Collective's project with Adivasi tribal and peasant communities in central India, discusses Dialogue's 'recognition of the contingency of the crafted object' in its complex and ongoing engagement with the communities. (2011: 90) Craft here is understood as an evolving 'cultural practice'. (Kester 2011: 90) It is not fixed by tradition to the past, neither is it 'an antidote to modernity'. (Adamson 2013: XV)

Françoise Dupré, making *Fujaan*, 2005. Collaborative French (spool) knitting project realized for the Crafts Council England with the London based Somali Women's Group Back To Basics with group leader and surface pattern designer Rakhia Ismail for *Knit 2 Together: Concepts in Knitting* 2005 touring exhibition. Mixed media including French (spool) knitting, wire, yarn. © Françoise Dupré.

With *OUVRAGE [uvra:ž]*, participants were invited to bring examples of their own handmade work, share making skills (stitching, looping), re-translate stitches using other kinds of yarns, fabric, tools and scale and reconfigure traditional architectural designs and textile patterns. Through the workshops, artist and participants were able to think about textiles in different ways beyond, yet starting from, cultural tradition and the familiar. The collaborative-participatory approach allowed craft knowledge to open up. Knowledge was shared, skills were unlearned, relearned, passed on and adapted, 'know how' was exchanged and new relationships were made between participants and with the artist.

While expertise and considerable knowledge and understanding of materials, complex techniques and technologies are required for the making of stitched and looped works in studios, it is also possible for hand stitching and looping to be rapidly adapted and used by a wide range of makers in social and collaborative-participatory art contexts. Indeed it is the 'underlying plasticity

Françoise Dupré, *Spiral*, 2007. French (spool) knitting by patients and staff during the artist residency at John Radcliffe Hospital, Oxford, England, 2007. Part of *Joie de Faire (The Making of Stuff)*. Alexandra Reinhardt Memorial Award 2006–07. Wool, wire, 94 × 96 × 3 cm (37 × 37 × 1 in.). © Françoise Dupré and FXP Photography, London.

of craft' that has been instrumental for my choice of textiles for collaborative-participatory projects. (Kester 2011: 91) For example, French (spool) knitting, a simple and quick technique to learn, is a 'powerful starting point' for group activities and an ideal context for dialogues and social engagement between participants and artist. (Ravetz, Kettle & Felcey 2013: 5) The technique allows for a wide contribution from participants and can be easily adapted in response to a project's social context and cultural specificity. French knitting's versatility was

instrumental in the development of my previous projects *Fujaan, Exotic MK* and *Joie de Faire (The Making of Stuff)*.

Underpinning my approach is the notion that a project's final outcome is never pre-designed but is the result of participants' and my engagement through making in the context of workshops. This is made possible by the strategic use of techniques and materials that have a high transformative ability. Here taking risks is possible because stitching and looping allow for improvisation, imagination and multiple cultural trajectories as shown in *OUVRAGE [uvra:ž]*. 'The openness of craft to the contingent and the unknown' makes textiles a powerful medium and a context for collaboration and participation. (Ravetz, Kettle & Felcey 2013: 3)

Besides the propensity of textiles to physically adapt and change, the sociability of textiles is also relevant here. In the first section, I reminded readers that textiles are a site of the feminine that is transformative and empowering. I demonstrated that with the making of Women's Work banners, the women artists' group was tapping into the 'subversive history' of stitching. (Turney 2009: 203) As demonstrated with *OUVRAGE [uvra:ž]*, textiles can be a powerful context for social agency that tapped into this 'act of sociability'. (Turney 2009: 203) *OUVRAGE [uvra:ž]* brought together women from a wide range of social, cultural and ethnic backgrounds. However, participants had in common 'a mutual and visceral attraction to stuff', the 'necessary conditions for collaboration through craft'. (Ravetz, Kettle & Felcey 2013: 5) These commonalities were highly significant in the context of Mostar and visually present in the installation. The project went far beyond the symbolic and convivial to engage with the potential for change and the reconfiguration of the social and cultural self and collective.

Central to *OUVRAGE [uvra:ž]* was the making of a tangible art object in the form of a textiles-based temporary installation. Although the installation was exhibited in public and cultural spaces, I do not consider the installation a conventional art object, but rather a transformative site, integral to social practice. Indeed, Kester argues that while there is, in dialogical art, 'dematerialization of the conventional art object (as painting, sculpture, etc.) this does not mean that materiality as such is suspended in the aesthetic configuration of the work'. (2011: 139) There is no 'denial of materiality but its rearticulation'. (Kester 2011: 139) It is therefore this re-positioning of materiality and the presence of the haptic experience through crafting that allows for the materialization

of a social art object. While the collaborative-participatory approach frees textiles from its familiar context, textiles, in turn, gives social practice its generative quality and multiplicity of becoming, and the ability to 'transform, rather than merely transmit, meaning and value'. (Kester 2011: 139)

CONCLUSION

Re-examining the legacy and relevance of 1980s textiles-based art practices has been extremely relevant and valuable when considering the role of textiles, as medium and context, in today's multicultural and cross-disciplinary social practice. A cross-disciplinary approach that combines art and textiles is a highly charged radical site for engagement with the feminine, otherness and difference. Understanding space as the product of interactions between global and local, individuals and communities, times and possibilities, allows us to think about crafting as a spatial site. This spatial site is a creative site for disruptive yet generative interventions, haptic and visual experiences that activate our imagination and understanding of the self and others as cosmopolitan subjects. Located in multiple cultural and social contexts, textiles-based installations can become portals for the imagination and offer multiple trajectories and futures.

From Brixton to Mostar via Whitechapel, textiles' plasticity and sociability are well suited for contemporary collaborative and participatory art practices. Textiles' capacity for transformation, adaptation, their generative and powerful context, make them an ideal medium and context for an art practice that is actively involved with others, in the ongoing reconfiguration of our cosmopolitan subjectivity. Through textiles, social practice, with its unique yet unfixed position between the aesthetic and the social, can articulate and engage with our multiple cultural and spatial experiences, our becoming cosmopolitan.

Françoise Dupré, *Exotic MK*, 2009. Collaborative-participatory
project commissioned by Milton Keynes Gallery's Offsite Education
Programme, Milton Keynes Shopping Centre, England. French (spool)
knitting, crochet, Lycra fabric, wool, metallic yarn, wire, plastic bottle
tops, pins, cake boards, dowels, PVC mirrors, sequins, flat elastic,
woven polythene, felt. 300 × 140 × 260 cm (118 × 55 × 102 in.).
© Françoise Dupré.

NOTES

1. Here I used the term 'multicultural' (Hall 2000) as an adjective. A multicultural society is a society where its culturally different parts are considered equal, and people aim to build a common life together. It is this definition that I have adopted in my text, though I am aware that the term is rarely used today because of its association with multiculturalism, a term that has been highly contested by a wide spectrum of politicians and thinkers.

2. For a detailed history of Brixton Art Gallery and its exhibitions for the period 1983–1986, visit Brixton Artists Collective member Andrew Hurman's website: http://brixton50.co.uk/ Visual documentations of *Women's Work* and *Black Women in View* exhibitions are available at Women's Art Library, Special Collections Goldsmiths, University of London. Brixton Art Gallery and Brixton Artists Collective were revisited in 2011 with the project *Brixton Calling!*, an archiving and community project based at 198 Contemporary Arts and Learning, London in collaboration with Tate Britain, Tate Archive and Women's Art Library. Archive materials, ephemera and records gathered during *Brixton Calling!* were deposited at Tate Archive (TGA 201211), Women's Art Library, Hall Carpenter Archive (LSE) and Lambeth Archives. For more information about *Brixton Calling!*, visit http://www.axisweb.org/p/ francoisedupre/

3. Brixton Art Gallery was part of a growing network of galleries and temporary exhibition spaces that grew and thrived through the 1980s in the UK. These were organizations that dared to exhibit and campaign for artists and communities excluded from mainstream British culture. In London, they included: the Africa Centre, Battersea Arts Centre, Black Cultural Archives, Black Art Gallery, Camerawork, Creation for Liberation, the Docklands Community Poster Project, Drill Hall, 198 Gallery, October Gallery, Pentonville Gallery, Riverside Studios, Sankofa, Black Audio Film Collective, Women Artists' Slide Library, to name a few.

4. In 1981, Griselda Pollock and Rozsika Parker published *Old Mistresses: Women, Art and Ideology*. In 1984, Rozsika Parker published *The Subversive Stitch: Embroidery and the Making of the Feminine*. By the time the exhibition *Women and Textiles Today*, curated by Pennina Barnett and Beth Bytheway, opened in 1988 in Manchester, Brixton Art Gallery had shown textiles in at least a dozen exhibitions.

5. For example: Trade Union Banners, Suffragette Banners, Greenham Common Women's Peace Camp, where textiles decorated the base fence.

6. Following its closure in July 1984 by Thatcher's government, the South London Hospital for Women was occupied until March 1985. Women's Work supported the occupation and led workshops out of which the lens-based cooperative Cinestra (1985–1992) was founded.

7. In the context of my practice, I understand the term craft to mean the application of know-how, 'making something well through hand skills'. (Adamson 2013: 24) Craft here transcends all disciplines and exists in all disciplines. Crafts, on the other hand, is a term that is used to describe specific activities associated with specific materials, processes and techniques, traditionally identified as glass, ceramics, wood, textiles.

8. Chilean patchworks were exhibited at Brixton Art Gallery in the *Latin American Arts Exhibition*, an exhibition of work by artists associated with the Latin American Cultural Centre (13 July to 3 August 1985).

9. *Cross-disciplinarity and threshold* (my translation) pp. 163–177 in *Arts, transversalités et questions politiques* (Coëllier and Dieuzayde 2011). Caroline Renard's discussion around cross-disciplinarity centres around the crossing over of art and cinema. I have found it inspiring and useful in my attempt to argue for art and textiles' cross-disciplinarity.

10. Walter Benjamin's concept of threshold, and rites of passage, can be found in *The Arcades Project*, pp. 494.

11. Inspired by Professor Griselda Pollock's keynote speech at *The Subversive Stitch Revisited: The Politics of Cloth*, 29–30 November 2013, V&A, London. Conference curated by Jennifer Harris, Pennina Barnett and Althea Greenan.

12. Market bags are also called 'Ghana-must-go', a phrase that was used by Nigerians in the 1980s as a statement against the influx of refugees from Ghana. In French the totes are called *cabas*. The red and white tartan motif is visually similar to the gingham pattern on Tati's shopping bags. Tati is a low price store in Barbès in the multicultural eighteenth arrondissement of Paris, where I spent my childhood.

13. *Étoile (Star)*, solo exhibition, 3 August to 2 September 2012, The Gallery @ Idea Store Whitechapel, London 321 Whitechapel Road, London E1 1BU, England, UK.

14. Claire Bishop in *Artificial Hells, Participatory Art and the Politics of Spectatorship* unpacks the numerous approaches that artists have employed in the development of participatory art though the twentieth and twenty-first centuries. Bishop favours the term participatory art since it implies the involvement of many people while for her, engagement can be an individual activity and context. For her, social engagement is always present even when an artist is not political. I personally do not like the term Participatory Art because of its association with conviviality and relational aesthetics and 'spectatorship'. (Bishop 2012: 277) For a full discussion on relational aesthetics and my collaborative-participatory approach, read my commissioned essay *Making Stuff* for AXIS Dialogues 2008, relocated as a PDF in Project B: *sebilj* on http://www.axisweb. org/p/francoisedupre/

15. *OUVRAGE [uvra:ž]* (2009) was realized within the context of my recent BCU, BIAD research project *here and there* (2003–2011), *OUVRAGE [uvra:ž]* followed *Project B* (2007–2008), realized in collaboration with artist Myfanwy Johns, architect Sabima Fazlic and the charity organization Bosnian Cultural Centre-Midlands (BCCM). *Project B* included research visits to Sarajevo and Mostar in 2008. For more information about *here and there* projects, *Project B* and *OUVRAGE [uvra:ž]* visit http://www.mkgallery.org/exhibitions/ Dupre_Exotic_MK/ and http://www. axisweb.org/p/francoisedupre/

16. I use the double term collaborative-participatory to describe my approach because I believe that when used alone,

the terms are not adequate. The terms are often confused and used inappropriately and this is an ethical issue. Collaboration is an approach where individuals are equally involved in managerial as well as conceptual and creative matters. This is a highly demanding role not always possible for participants. In my projects, participants are invited and encouraged to become involved in decision making, designs and development of the installation right up to its public viewing. These activities generate a collaborative element through participant engagement.

17. Here, craft activities were not used as a vehicle or medium for mass political protest.

18. While on a research visit to Sarajevo in 2008, I had the opportunity to see *Which is my shirt? Long shirt in BiH in 19th and 20th centuries*. The exhibition was held at the National Museum of Bosnia and Herzegovina.

19. The French Cultural Centre and the Ćejvan Ćehaja Hamam, the restored sixteenth-century classical Ottoman hamam, are located near Mostar's famous bridge, the Stari Most (Old Bridge). The bridge, destroyed in 1993 during the bitter fighting between the Bosniak and Croatian communities was reopened in 2004. It remains a strong symbol for reconciliation.

20. My translation from French, quoted by Luce Giard in her introduction to de Certeau, Michel (1990) *L'invention du quotidien vol. 1 Arts de faire*, Paris: Gallimard.

21. My collaborative-participatory practice does not aim to be a social critique, nor create tension within a community nor between communities. For Claire Bishop, antagonism, favoured in the classic avant-garde and revolutionary model of art, is instrumental in participation because it prevents collusion with dominant culture and loss of artistic autonomy. Indeed Bishop is very dismissive of artists' collective projects that favour consensus, collaboration and ethics. For her these projects lack artistic rigour and belong more to the social sphere than the art sphere. While Bishop advocates an oppositional mode in participatory art, where tension is needed between artistic and social critiques, I believe that an antagonistic approach can be unethical

and have serious negative impacts on vulnerable communities. I prefer to adopt creative and constructive approaches rather than follow the traditional modernist 'orthopedic aesthetic' model which needs to provoke discomfort and unsettle viewers, and where art and viewers are in conflict. (Kester 2011: 35)

22. I have been concerned with the task of repositioning textiles within an art practice that is socially engaged. But the challenge is also for the art establishment, critics and art historians, who, when faced with participatory-collaborative projects that combine art, textiles and multicultural communities, simply dismiss these projects. With any ethical and social-political project, it is expected that the aesthetic integrity of the produced artwork will automatically be diminished and compromised. These are simplistic expectations, following hierarchical differentiation between fine art and craft or decorative/applied arts, and founded on lack of knowledge and prejudices against non-art trained individuals, working class and migrant communities who have nevertheless, like artists, strong desires to create beautiful things, to make things well, to exchange know-how. Social practice through textiles does not need to compromise aesthetic quality. The challenge remains for these 'new modes of aesthetic experience and new frameworks for thinking through the haptic and verbal exchanges that unfold in the process of collaboration' to be more widely acknowledged and understood. (Kester 2011: 113)

BIBLIOGRAPHY

Adamson, G. (2013), *The Invention of Craft*, London: Bloomsbury.

Alfoldy, S. & Helland, J. (eds) (2008), *Craft, Space and Interior Design, 1855–2005*, Aldershot: Ashgate.

Araeen, R. (2000), 'A New Beginning: Beyond Postcolonial Cultural Theory and Identity Politics', *Third Text*, 50, Spring: 3–20.

Benjamin, W. (1999), *The Arcades Project*, Cambridge, Mass.: Belknap Press.

Benjamin, W. (2008), *The Work of Art in the Age of Mechanical Reproduction*, London: Penguin Great Ideas.

Benjamin, W. (1974), 'The Author as Producer', in *Understanding Brecht*, New York: Verso.

Bishop, C. (2012), *Artificial Hells, Participatory Art and the Politics of Spectatorship*, London: Verso.

Coëllier, S. and Dieuzayde, L. (2011), *Arts, transversalités et questions politiques*, Aix-en-Provence: Université de Provence.

de Certeau, M. (1990), *L'invention du quotidien vol I. Arts de faire*, Paris: Gallimard.

Hall, S. (2000), 'The Multicultural Question' <http://www.slashdocs.com/wsktp/the-multicultural-question-by-stuart-hall-the-political-economy-research-centre-annual-lecture-2000.html> [Accessed 2 December 2013].

Helguera, P. (2011), *Education for Socially Engaged Art*, New York: Jorge Pinto Books.

Kester, G. K. (2011), *The One and the Many*, Durham and London: Duke University Press.

Kester, G. K. (2004), *Conversation Pieces: Community and Communication in Modern Art*, Oakland: University of California Press.

Kristeva, J. (1993), *What of Tomorrow's Nation*, New York: Columbia University Press.

Massey, D. (2005), *For Space*. London: Sage.

Meskimmon, M. (2011), *Contemporary Art and the Cosmopolitan Imagination*, London: Routledge.

Parker, R. (2010), *The Subversive Stitch: Embroidery and the Making of the Feminine*, London: I.B. Tauris.

Rancière, J. (2002), 'The Aesthetic Revolution and its Outcomes: Emplotments of Autonomy and Heteronomy', *New Left Review* 14, March–April:133–151.

Ravetz, A., Kettle, A. and Felcey, H. (2013), *Collaboration Through Craft*, London: Bloomsbury.

Turney, J. (2009), *The Culture of Knitting*, Oxford and New York: Berg.

Chapter eight

A post-slavery reading of cotton: Lubaina Himid in conversation with Sabine Broeck and Alice Schmid

Tanzanian-born Lubaina Himid is an artist, writer and curator. Over the past thirty years Himid's creative practice has addressed the legacies of colonialism and historical representations of the African diaspora. Today Himid works across a variety of media, often in response to objects held in museum archives. One of her many areas of textile research is the kanga, explored in *Kangas From the Lost Sample Book* (2012), also discussed by Mr Somebody and Mr Nobody in chapter one. In conversation with German academic Sabine Broeck and her research assistant Alice Schmid, here Himid discusses the place of beauty in her practice, the reality that creating art is work and the challenges confronting art that deals with the subject of slavery. As Himid explains in this interview, '*Cotton.com, The Dinner Service, Naming the Money*, any of those large-scale installations … made up of a hundred pieces: none of it was a labour of love. Making work is not a pleasurable thing … The point about making a hundred was absolutely to try to imagine what it's really like to work … To have to work until the job's done.'

Jessica Hemmings

SABINE BROECK AND ALICE SCHMID:
Could there be such a thing as a particularly postcolonial craft? What would that imply about colonial craft? Is it political, or could it be an aesthetic feature?

LUBAINA HIMID: I think that it would have to be a political feature. I can't see that you could lump something together and call it particularly that; there could easily be a way of doing things or a way of thinking about ideas that would thread through pieces of work. When I think of the artists that I work with, you know, we were pursuing many of the same sorts of ideas, but each was so utterly different from the others. I can't see that it's anything to do with how it looks.

SB / AS   If one attends to the wordplay in crafting the postcolonial, it entails quite some power for the making of craft, or the act of crafting, to create, or at least creatively impact on, a specific cultural, political and social moment: that of the postcolonial. Does this mean in turn maybe that this moment, of the postcolonial, has turned out to be particularly welcoming to craft, as opposed to being made into 'Art' (capital A)? Or is that one of those dubious binaries, which artists such as yourself, and others, want to undercut?

LH   For a younger artist than me, this kind of dividing art and craft doesn't make any sense. If crafting is the care in the making, and art is the care in the thinking – they still blur. But the postcolonial as welcoming to craft? How would that show itself?

Lubaina Himid, *Naming the Money*, 2003. Composite image first exhibited at the Hatton Gallery, Newcastle, England (17 January to 13 March 2004). Photograph by Denise Swanson.

A post-slavery reading of cotton

SB / AS   Maybe because of the material, the materiality that we associate with colonialism, like particular materials, cotton or sugar, for example.

LH   Yes, but when I make work, I just know what the material to make it with is. I don't think the crafting of it through to the end. Sometimes you need to come at the idea with materials from the left field. I make with very little thought about the materials with which I'm making.

SB / AS   So you don't start with the idea of cotton, for example, or a particular material, you start with the idea and then you know which material to take?

LH   That's it absolutely. I ask: How could I make the idea seductive, or how can I make the idea playful, or how can I make the idea work in this place, or this site, or with these museum objects? It will always be like that. That's not to say everyone works that way, but that really is how I work.

SB / AS   The radiance of your work has puzzled us: it so recklessly risks the beautiful. Would you want to insist on a momentum, an urgency of beauty implied by your work?

LH   Well, it's interesting this idea of beauty. When you say my work 'risks the beautiful', does this mean that it is beautiful but it tries to throw this beauty away? It is beautiful, because I'm trying to lure you towards it, to imply that I'm addressing particular issues, inviting you to a dialogue, but a brain dialogue. You as the viewer are supposed to act on that dialogue, so it's beautiful only so that you don't come into the room and go out again. So you come into the room and want to play or want to talk … It's never been designed to be beautiful so that you admire it … I'm not going to make something that's harmonious. There is a sort of unease, a dis-ease in the work, which is why I would dispute the beauty in the work. It's not beauty in the sense of harmony. It might be beauty in the sense of seduction, but not of a fabulous vista that disappears. It definitely is not that sort of beauty. But it is the glimpse of say, orange with turquoise, which might make you go a bit nearer the work than if it was grey and brown.

SB / AS   I was wondering what would be the function of such visual beauty in relation to your kinds of subjects, like slavery, colonial monumentalism, or the black diasporic experience?

LH   Well, if you really want to make work about this subject there is no point in making purposefully ugly work – whatever that means – because the subject is already ugly. You could never be as ugly as the subject itself. You could never be as ugly as the hold of a ship, or branding, or rape, or blood-stained bodies, so you couldn't achieve that. If you're going to talk about it and change it, you have to use some other manner or means. I would dispute the notion of beauty. It's rather an ability to know how to make people stop long enough near the work to either see themselves in it, or to see something in it that reminds them of something that they do know. But it isn't the beauty of a nineteenth-century painting. And, so I don't feel any difficulty making work like that, because I want you to talk about the subjects within it.

SB / AS   Would you say that there is a movement among contemporary black diaspora artists (if one might be allowed the categorization for a minute) to work through, and with, beauty, with allure, with pleasantness, as opposed to rather more explicit politically framed kinds of realism, which might call this a dangerous indulgence?

LH   I thought about Ellen Gallagher or Chris Ofili when you asked this question, but I don't think these particular contemporary black diaspora artists are dealing with facile beauty either, or harmony or pleasantness. There is this kind of beauty on the one hand, seduction on the other hand, and a kind of unease in the middle. It's an engagement and discussion with an audience and then a disrupting of that. It is certainly far from a more obviously 'political' kind of aesthetic, as for example in past forms of social realism. Much of the time in the art gallery you are addressing an audience that you haven't necessarily made the work for.

Lubaina Himid, *Naming the Money (dog trainers)* (detail), 2003. Paint, collage, wood, sound. First exhibited at the Hatton Gallery, Newcastle, England.

Lubaina Himid, *Naming the
Money (dog trainers)* (detail)
2003. Paint, collage, wood,
sound. First exhibited at the
Hatton Gallery, Newcastle,
England.

In British art galleries the proportion of African or African-Caribbean audiences are much smaller than European white audiences. Very often when you have lots of African [or] African-Caribbean viewers of the work, they are small children who have come to experience an art gallery with their school. So a lot of the time you're trying to talk to an audience about what action they might take as white Europeans with this work. This is a bit of a challenge, because when you're making it – when I'm making it – I'm talking to the black women that I know. There's a necessity to make work that will stop people in their tracks and allow them to feel that they can have a conversation.

SB / AS   What about the aspect of love, as in labour of love, in the production of, say, *Cotton. com*, which must have been a haunted love, railed by Cotton (capital C) that haunts on the side of the viewer? We have had a feeling of sensuous affection for your work, and the immediate desire to touch it, to get closer to its colours, its dimensionality, boldness and wit. And then that affection gets stuck in one's throat, because of the distance one feels to the object or topic in question, as in cotton. Have viewers, but also your students at Central Lancashire, problematized similar questions with you? What kind of debates have you had about this after *Cotton.com*, and *Naming the Money*, but also *The Dinner Service* exhibition, and the *Jelly Moulds*?

LH   *Cotton.com*, *The Dinner Service*, *Naming the Money*, any of those large-scale installations, if you like, are made up of a hundred pieces: none of it was a labour of love. Making work is not a pleasurable thing. It's torturous. The point about making a hundred was absolutely to try to imagine what it's like to really work. You know, to really work. To have to work until the job's done. With all those projects I was trying to imagine what it's like to be inside the place where the task is more enormous than you can bear – than you think you can cope with – and to try to generate, in the making, a sense of being overwhelmed by the enormity of it all, and the impossibility of it all. In a sense I needed to punish myself, in a way, if I was going to understand how you survive beyond

enslavement, even if your body doesn't survive beyond enslavement. If your people survived beyond it, you have to understand what it's like to be in it, and to try and make the work be the place where you come up with strategies for getting beyond it. It was a method of keeping going. I didn't want to get run over by a bus until I had finished the task.

SB / AS   We've got these questions that are to do with *Cotton.com* and its basis in that particular material, that particular textile. Why make cotton beautiful?

LH   Well, I didn't think I was making it beautiful. I was trying to make an installation that was overwhelming, and would give the viewer a sense of unease and displacement. When the work was shown, it was shown in the gallery that used to be a showroom for fabric, and the square paintings, a hundred of them, kind of started at the ground and went up the wall and into nooks and crannies, and you had to strain your body, really, to be able to see them. And you couldn't see them all at once. The text that went with them was behind you. So all the time you were looking at the work the text was behind you. You've got those hundred patterns in black and white – they were either black squares with white patterns, or white backgrounds with black patterns, and you couldn't ever keep your eye still. I wanted there to be a kind of drifting, or a kind of dizziness, or as if … maybe you felt a bit sick, or as if maybe your glasses weren't at the right prescription … so, it's much more [than beauty]. Maybe the beauty you might feel if you were on a boat, looking out at water … it is beautiful, but if you think about how deep that water is, or you think about the kind of blinding light of the sun on it, or if you think about being underwater then it suddenly isn't beautiful anymore. That's what I'm trying to do.

SB / AS   If somebody made the argument that the harrowing beauty of your work could be said to 'save cotton' – is that a risk you have run? Or have you devised means to insist on a post-slavery contextualization. If so, how did that work?

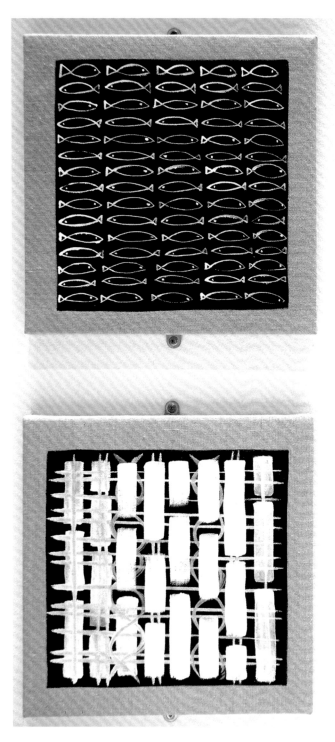

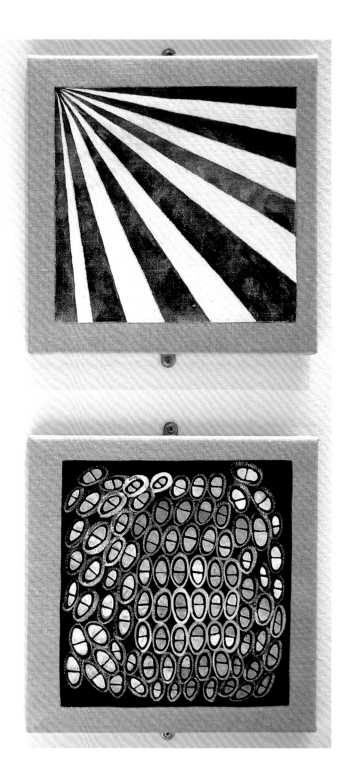

Lubaina Himid, *Cotton.com* (detail),
2002. Acrylic on canvas. Installation
at the Fabrications exhibition, CUBE
Manchester, England (11 September
to 2 November 2002).

Lubaina Himid, *Cotton.com* (detail), 2002. Acrylic on canvas. Installation at the Fabrications exhibition, CUBE Manchester, England.

A post-slavery reading of cotton

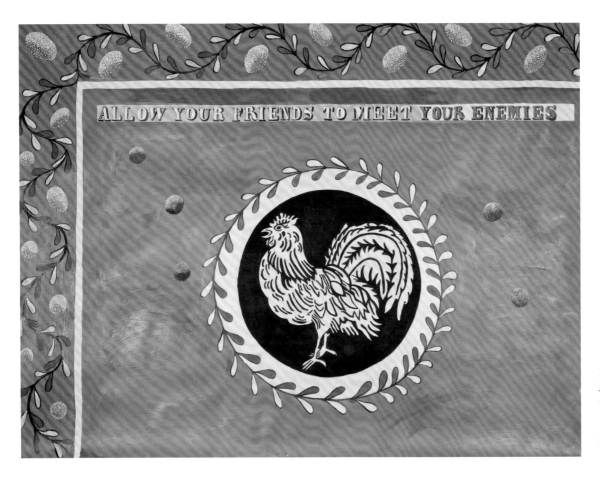

Lubaina Himid, *Kangas from the Lost Sample Book: Allow Your Friends to Meet Your Enemies*, 2011–2012. Acrylic on paper. Photograph by Denise Swanson.

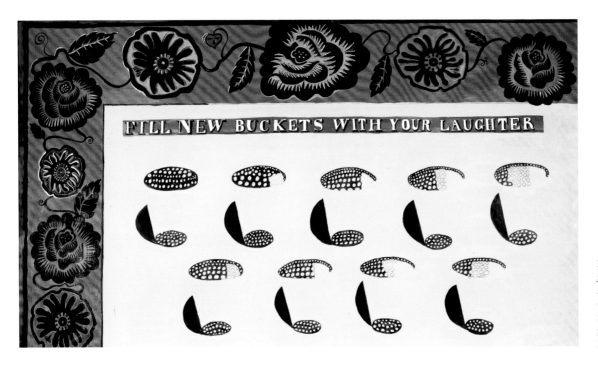

Lubaina Himid, *Kangas from the Lost Sample Book: Fill New Buckets with Your Laughter*, 2011–2012. Acrylic on paper. Photograph by Denise Swanson.

LH   I certainly never set out to save it, to redeem it from its past. I don't think it does save cotton. It certainly puts the money involved, gained from that trade, right at the centre of the piece. But yes, if it does save cotton then in a sense it hasn't worked. If you do come out from being in a room with that piece and you can only think about how beautiful it is, and how you want to touch it, and how … how lovely it is, then it hasn't really worked.

I think that probably depends upon where you see it. It was in a very awkward place in the gallery it was made for, at the bottom of the stairs, and then it sort of shot up the wall right next to those stairs. I've shown it where it's been at the end of a long gallery space; a hundred paintings in a perfect grid, with the text running through it. The showing of it needs to be a little more thought through … it was quite thought through the first time, but then after that, I just wanted to make it work in the space. Maybe that means that the conversations people had might have been a bit too easy.

SB / AS   How have people responded to the very strong textile quality, the tactility, and the materiality of your work with cotton?

LH   I found that fabric pattern, or even motif and text, and those conversations about how fabric speaks, are really some of the most successful things about the work. *Naming the Money* is not really about the fabric, except that all the people are dressed in quite particular ways and they've obviously been very careful about the clothes that they have chosen to wear, so that their clothes are saying something.

This preoccupation probably comes from two things: my mother used to be a textile designer, so pattern and cloth were always part of our conversations. We were always talking about what people were wearing and where they had probably bought their clothes. She could tell how long they'd had a summer dress because she'd know that those colours, or those patterns were last year's model, or the year before, or that they'd bought it new. Those were everyday conversations. In the photographs of my Zanzibari family, most of the women who live there were always dressed in kangas,

these are clothes that are two pieces of fabric with the same pattern and the same text, so I have always been very caught up in the fact that clothing and fabric are speaking a language.

This weaving of words and the weaving of cloth, the printing of text, the printing of pattern, seemed to be at the centre of what I do. So the response is very strong because it's part of people's everyday. Even if they're audiences that go about in jeans and a t-shirt, the t-shirt has probably got some text written on it – you know, some rock concert or some funny text or whatever they've chosen to wear that morning. They've chosen to wear a tartan jacket or chosen to wear a red jumper, and they've understood – even if they haven't understood in the front of their brain – that textile is a language and that you can speak to people without speaking. You're using clothes and fabric to say something about yourself.

SB / AS   In *Kangas from the Lost Sample Book*, however, you choose to use paper over textile?

LH   What I tried to achieve was a connection to the materiality of the sample book. So what they were supposed to be were kangas from the lost sample book – they were samples, not actually kangas. I was making reference to kangas, obviously, but I was also making reference to the sample books – hundreds and thousands of which were thrown out and put into skips and into dustbins when the Manchester print studios came to the end of their lives in the 1960s. So many of the designs that were actually created for these West and East African textiles in the studios of Manchester were lost. The evidence of that creativity, along with all the paisleys and stripes and the rest of it, was thrown away in these sample books. Because I made the work for the Whitworth [Art Gallery] in Manchester, using some kangas from my collection and some from theirs, I was making a kind of Manchester-specific reference to those lost sample books to acknowledge the loss. Also, I felt I could convey the power of the designs better on paper than going into the print room to print kangas directly. I couldn't have achieved the intended effect that well with printed cloth.

**SB / AS   Do you see differences between
Cotton.com and your later work with textile?**

LH   Yes, I do. *Cotton.com* is undoubtedly firmly
rooted in the questions I ask about slavery, about
being enslaved, about how to deal with that, survive
that, strategize for resistance. The later textile work is
much more rooted in what it's like to be an African
woman in another place, a place that is our home
today. The later work is much less about forced
displacement, about commodification, than it is about
simply trying to belong. Or about trying to connect
to a given locale, or – as a diasporic artist – trying to
be two people, in two places at once; and much less
about past enslavement.

**SB / AS   Coming back to the 'crafting': there are
so many layers of crafting, and so many different
'crafts' in the very word cotton and what it
evokes, in the (post)enslavement colonial history
of cotton, in the black labour and white profit of
the making of cotton, in the travelling of cotton
through time and space.**

**How is it that you arrived at making *Cotton.com*,
at 'crafting' such a condensed abstraction? Does
this imply that the memory of enslavement,
and its ongoing urgency for today's societies
should best be crafted into a memorable form,
instead of into images that always run the risk of
arousing the abolitionist empathy that Marcus
Wood has criticized as pornographic?**

LH   Yes, I think that's key. My whole practice is
about how to talk about this without just plainly re-
showing it; as I said earlier, you cannot paint anything
uglier than rape or branding. I've never been able
to see the point of putting work like that into an art
gallery. Twenty-five African people, African-Caribbean
people, come in – why would you want those people
to re-experience that in such a way? Why would you
want any one of these communities to be observed
experiencing something like that in a public place?
I think that pornographic is absolutely the right phrase
for that kind of work, it simply re-presents the horror
and then expects that horror, in this facile way, to be
made impossible for the future. It simply repeats it.

There are people who are going to get some kind
of, perhaps not pleasure from it, but some kind of
desire to keep looking at it, and for it to be shown
again and again. You as a viewer have within you all
sorts of understandings about pain and all sorts of
understandings about your body, and you don't need
a painting to hand violence to you on a plate. You have
to be able to engage with a piece of art and imagine
yourself in it, without that kind of prodding.

**SB / AS   So you would agree with Wood's
notion of empathy as being to some extent
pornographic in itself? So that seeing a picture
of a whipped body and imagining that it must
have been terrible, and trying to sort of feel this
pain, which is inaccessible, becomes a mere
titillation of the viewer?**

LH   Yes. Those paintings of African enslaved women
hung up in a tree being whipped, in British abolitionist
cartoons to make people feel the tragedy of it – that
is exactly the same thing as the 1960s and 1970s idea
of putting starving Africans on the television with
flies all around them, so we would feel terribly sorry
for them, and give money. Yes, I think you would feel
terribly sorry and you would give your money. It's not
that it doesn't work; it's just that it gives no dignity, no
humanity, no intelligence to the black person in the
image. It might work as an effective pressure to make
people give money, but showing those images did not
give the onlooker any idea of what it meant to be that
person. We are more than our tragedy, and more than
our pain. We're still somebody's daughter, somebody's
friend and somebody's lover, somebody with a life.
This kind of empathy takes away your somebody-
ness. If you condense experience into an aesthetic,
even abstracted form, the viewer must relate to it
cognitively, and perhaps feel differently vis-à-vis the
subject of that piece of art.

**SB / AS   What has always appealed to us about
your work starting with *A Thin Black Line* and
Naming the Money is this brazen turn to crafting
in the margins, as it were, to supplement (as in:
add to and in the process, alter) the substance
(topically and materially) of the objects you
engage with.**

Lubaina Himid, *Jelly Mould Pavilions*, 2009–10. Acrylic on Victorian ceramic jelly moulds. Installation at Sudley House, Liverpool, England (27 March to 6 June 2010).

Would you say there is a turn in your work away from the mode of visualized abstraction in *Cotton.com* to later work, and why might this be so? Is there an affective interest in jelly moulds, that you chose not to show for cotton? Do you see a productive tension in your work between abstraction and concreteness of objects? Like moving from the condensation of *Cotton.com* to the tender look at concrete and, as it were, 'found' detail, 'found' material, in the newspaper project, but also the jelly moulds? Is this a move from abstraction to another mode, and which one would that be?

LH   The ideas I'm trying to explore are not special. They're ordinary. They're about our lives now, how we are as people now, today in this space; using found objects, found things like newspapers, or dishes, to jolt the memory of a viewer. All the work is to remind you of what you already know, or already feel. I'm not ever really telling you something you don't know. I'm reminding you of something that you know already. Sometimes the problem of painting on canvas is that it seems like a special thing that belongs in a grand place, that is for other people, not for the average person. It's a beautiful way of working, but sometimes if you want to make connections to communities, then you need to use a found thing because I want to say 'if

Lubaina Himid, *Jelly Mould Pavilions* (detail), 2009–10. Acrylic on Victorian ceramic jelly moulds. Installation at Sudley House, Liverpool, England.

I made it, then you could have made it', and 'if you made it then how would you do it?', and 'why did I make it like that?' Whereas if it's a painting then you might say: 'Oh, I could never do that, I don't do art.' And that's not the sort of conversation I want to have with my audiences. I want to say, 'we're the same people, and there's a chance here for us to have some conversations, be playful with what I've done … come amongst it – it's not separate from your shopping, or different from your music-making, or that activity you do with your friends on Tuesdays, it's the same thing.'

I do show much more in museums, in places where it is possible to interrupt the reading of objects, rather than in an art gallery where they want to present an object as itself, to be read as itself. I guess that's why my work shifted from one kind of material to another: I want to see if I can make it funnier or whether I can make it less durable, or whether I can make it more playful, or whether I can make it more precious. For example, with *Kangas from the Lost Sample Book*, these were pieces of paper in frames, but I was trying to get across that this was something not just about the now and the everyday, but something lost, something thrown away, or something gone. 'Things thrown away and lost' is very much the average experience for many people.

If you make work for long enough, you come round again. So yes, for some of the things that I did in *The Dinner Service* or the *Jelly Moulds*, I was using particular objects, over-painting them, painting a history, painting another one on the top, making you think about the period that those objects had come from, and telling the story that isn't being told in a plain jelly mould or in those particular dinner plates. *Jelly Pavilions* for Liverpool is very different from *Cotton.com* in terms of its layering, and abstraction. It was less serious, it was a much more jokey, ironical piece, and it's the same with *The Dinner Service*, it's much less serious – there are vomiting toffs, and figures taken from British cartoons of the time. It's completely different from *Cotton.com*, where there was much more a desire to convey this sense of being enslaved, a sense of unease and danger.

With *The Dinner Service*, the fact that black people's figures and faces were painted on the tureens and the jugs meant that there was a sense of embodiment.

What I'm doing now is sort of moving back to some of the things I was trying to do with *Cotton.com*, in that I'm making a series of shelves, very plain wooden shelves, but they're hung at a height so that only by leaning against the wall can you look up and see patterns; the whole shelf is painted with patterns. A combination of toiles de Jouy and kanga patterns; a kind of crashing of European pattern and the history of European pattern, colliding with African pattern.

Some of those things that you might experience when *Cotton.com* was hung how it should be, where it was awkward to look at, that looking up and feeling dizzy, that trying to get back far enough, then not being able to see it all at once, is revisited in this new work. It will be difficult again to see the work without placing your body in an awkward place, and there is this coming together, this colliding of a European pattern and an African pattern. I've come around to pattern, I guess. I moved away from it, and I've found it again.

SB / AS   I'd also like to ask you about the relationship between visual material and text in your work. What is the function of writing in pieces such as *Cotton.com* and *Naming the Money*? Was this ever met with resistance by viewers who protest about 'being told what to think'?

LH   I don't care in the slightest about any kind of resistance. Text doesn't tell the audience what to think, but it does tell you, the audience, what the artist thinks. That's what I'm doing, I'm telling you what I think, and I'm hoping that you think some of the same, but probably something different. At least we can have some kind of a conversation.

Quite often when I've put text in work as I have in the text and image works in *Plan B*, for instance, or as I have in *Naming the Money* written on the back of the cut-outs, I'm giving you two pieces of art at once. So that if you are the sort of person who wants to read, then you have the chance to make your own picture with the words that I've given you. I see the texts as a chance to speak to the viewer twice, but it is an offer – some people don't want to read, so they don't have

Lubaina Himid, *Jelly Mould Pavilions* (detail), 2009–10. Acrylic on Victorian ceramic jelly moulds. Installation at Jacksons Art Shop, Liverpool, England (27 March to 6 June 2010).

to read, they can just engage with the picture. Some people can't read because they never learnt to read, and some people can't read English. So the text is an extra painting if you want it – if you can read it. It is telling you what I think, rather than telling you what you should think.

SB / AS   Your work has been used as part of gallery education programmes. What is your opinion of the use of your work in this context?

LH   I make a piece of work and then it has its own life and its own use. I am happy if there are groups of people in art galleries who feel they can use a piece of my work to bring out discussions they want to have with either young people, or people who come on educational days. If it can be used in that way then

that is more than fine. So many of the pieces of work were made as political tools – so if they're used in that way then that's probably better than if they were in their own white space alone with no label, with people simply admiring them for their loveliness. That would be kind of sad, and useless.

There are plenty of artists who are deeply insulted by being used in education programmes. They just happen to be Africans or African-Americans, and they want to make work about whatever they want to make work about. To have it categorized, packaged, as in 'they made it this way because they are black' is insulting for them. The discussions around my work are supposed to revolve around the politics of representation, and the politics of what it's like to function in this dysfunctional setting that is our postcolonial world.

SB / AS How does postcolonial thinking, particularly about hybrid cultural identities and contemporary migration, inform recent textile practice?

LH My work is part of all those discussions. I have been trying to represent one part of myself – the African part of myself – and have it speak to the English part of myself, by using pattern and by using textiles. The very essence of it, especially when I'm using patterns, or if I think about the use of textiles, is the question of how to reconcile the different impacts from the two cultures. These are hybrid pieces of work. Quite often they're made from several parts that do communicate, but historically they were not always meant to come into conversation. They have entangled histories, but those histories are not really always talked about so as to see the connections.

I am of both those worlds. My mother is English and my father came from Zanzibar to England to University College, met my mother who was at art school at the Royal College of Art. They went back to Zanzibar, which was a British protectorate at the time, and very soon after I was born, [my] father died from malaria, and so my mother came home and brought me with her. I am completely enmeshed in that kind of individual and collective conversation – in that challenge of being neither one thing nor the other, but being both things.

SB / AS Does contemporary textile practice engage with the themes of postcolonial thinking more frequently than other craft disciplines; if so, can the physical portability of the textile explain the connection?

LH Interesting question. Personally, one of my passions is ceramics, whether it's tiles or the use of found ceramics, and painting on top of them – the only reason I am painting on top of them is because I don't know how to make ceramic pieces of the same quality. If I knew how to do it, if I'd spent the years honing that craft, I would have done it.

But to your question: I think one can have really interesting conversations with and about textiles and the way they thread, if you like, through the everyday. The same sorts of conversations you can have about ceramics – if you take that broad notion of ceramics, everyday ceramics from tiles and bricks to plates and jugs. For me, textiles are one perfect medium to make visual metaphors for all the things I'm interested in, like a kind of wrapping oneself in the textile, which can make a connection with the body, with all stages of life, really.

I'm not somebody who weaves. I'm not somebody who even works with fabric. I make work *about* fabric, which I think is an important difference. I am at one remove from making the textile. I didn't make those kanga paintings into kangas, so I don't deal with the fabric itself … I re-imagine the fabric, really.

SB / AS Does the longstanding relationship between textile scholarship and feminist thinking help explain the particular interest of contemporary textile practitioners with ideas of the postcolonial?

LH I would think so. North American and European feminists were almost totally responsible for women artists being able to bring anything into the art gallery, and to be able to have discussions about the mundane in the art gallery. The way that they did it was very often with the stuff of the everyday, which was often made of textiles, whether it was clothes or other things. They broke down so many barriers and allowed a different way of showing and different conversations about what could be art and what was craft, blurring the edges of it, using textiles so many times to do it. Performative artist weavers [contributed] – quite often designers who had turned themselves into artists – there were also graphic designers or textile designers, not always trained as fine artists. There's an inextricable link between feminist art practice, textiles and the opening up of the art gallery to allow many, many more people in as artists. This couldn't have been done without them. So this opening then in turn also enabled access for postcolonial issues.

Chapter nine

Contemporary textile imagery in Southern Africa: a question of ownership

Sarah Rhodes

9

Sarah Rhodes is a designer, jeweller and PhD candidate at Central Saint Martins, London. She has lived for several years in Botswana and writes here about a number of development initiatives based in Southern Africa over the past thirty years. Even when the best of intentions are in place, development initiatives often struggle to establish longevity. In this chapter Rhodes discusses the use of printed textile design by several San communities who have faced multiple displacements in their history, but who have also shown remarkable affinities in visual style even when separated by time and space. Rhodes considers the authenticity and ownership of work made by development initiatives, citing numerous examples of instances where the work of indigenous artists – including commissions by British Airways in the late 1990s – have received scant financial remuneration. Rhodes shares with Kevin Murray, the author of chapter ten, an interest in how design and craft can be fostered with greater respect for the ethics of production. This chapter concludes with discussion of a hearteningly positive example, the Art-i-San project, a rare instance of a development project that provides royalties to the displaced San artists who contribute textile designs sold as products and by the metre. Based on Namibian San communities' designs, the Art-i-San project produces printed textiles in Cape Town, South Africa and is now entering its second decade of work.

Jessica Hemmings

Cg'ose Ntcöx'o, *Animals & Trees.* Photograph by Kuru Art Project, 1998. © Maude Brown for Kuru Development Trust Art Project.

Utopia was the optimistically titled range of multicoloured aeroplane tail fin designs for the British Airways (BA) image rebrand in 1997. Unfortunately it was a short-lived ideal, but the airline's concept of connecting different communities in the world through symbolic imagery is reflected in the current rise of designers seeking inspiration from cultures beyond their own. Prompted by the increase in popularity of the handmade combined with a quest for authenticity in art and design, this interest in adopted cultural references can be seen as a backlash against commercial globalization. Image appropriation from indigenous artists such as Australian Aborigines has been widely documented. (Burns Coleman 2005) The most well-known case occurred in the 1970s when Aboriginal artist Wandjuk Marika asked the Australian government to investigate the use of indigenous designs on tourist art, which led to the recognition of copyright for indigenous work. (Myers 2004: 1–16) However, in relation to Southern African San groups, most intellectual property rights discussion has centred on the *hoodia* plant commercialization[1] and repatriation of San cultural objects from international museums.[2]

With the current rise of nostalgic iconography, the way indigenous San images are used in contemporary textile production should be questioned. As South African academic Marian Sauthoff explains, issues that have been stressed in many postcolonial contexts have, as yet, to receive serious consideration in South African design, including the ethics and politics of cultural appropriation, representations of previously marginalized groups and the recuperation of indigenous histories. (2004: 41) This chapter explores issues of indigenous cultural depiction and intellectual property rights within Southern African textile design. It examines the way in which Art-i-San, a textile project initiated with San communities from Namibia, began, developed and continues to run, presenting it as a positive case study.

Newell and Sorrell, the London-based graphic design agency behind the BA rebrand, were unusual at the time in their approach to the new BA livery because, not only were the selected artists and designers from diverse countries, they were also from a wide range of visual practices including painters,

calligraphers, weavers, textile artists, printers, ceramicists and sculptors.[3] Newell and Sorrell sought permission to reproduce the designs, credited the artists (their signature was included on the tail fin) and bought the copyright by paying for the work. One of these was San artist Cg'ose Ntcöx'o (Cgoise) from the Kuru Art Project in Botswana, whose *Animals and Trees* design of seven jackals resting under trees around a water hole was printed on eight of the planes. This established Cgoise's reputation internationally, opening up other commissions and her participation at a printmaking workshop in the United States, as well as designs for a range of Botswana Postal Service stamps.[4] Unfortunately, BA's now infamous global scope for the designs wasn't such a success with the market, particularly with the late British Prime Minister, Margaret Thatcher, who covered up the model of Cgoise's design with her handkerchief, proclaiming 'we fly the British flag, not those awful things'. (Stone-Lee 2013) The Union flag was reinstated on BA planes in 2001.

In contrast to the exclusive BA tail fin design commission, the diversity of contemporary textiles produced in South Africa is vast. Embroidery, printed fabric, handmade felt and woven cloth are made by a variety of artists ranging from individual designer-makers to community-based, not-for-profit organizations. Just as the BA *Utopia* designs sought to do, the imagery on the textiles references local culture and landscape in one form or another; cultural group iconography (Afrikaner / Ndebele / San / Xhosa / Zulu), flora and fauna or narratives depicting the lives of the people who craft them. This imagery reflects South African post-apartheid nostalgia.

Under apartheid rule, South African artists were isolated in the access they had to the rest of the world, particularly in relation to culture, which was heavily censored. This has led to artists and designers post-independence questioning both personal and cultural identity. The complex nature of a country with eleven national languages and comprising many different cultural groups with images that traverse these groups was secured in national history in 1995 when Nelson Mandela wore a green Springbok rugby jersey, symbolically

BELOW Fabricnation, *Veld*, 2007.
Screen print on cotton. © Jann
Cheifitz for Fabricnation.

ABOVE Fabricnation,
Old Postcards, 2008.
Screen print on cotton.
© Jane Solomon for
Fabricnation.

OPPOSITE Fabricnation,
Umlungu Print, 2010. Rotary
print on cotton. © Jane
Solomon for Fabricnation.

Afrikaner, to the rugby World Cup and the white, Afrikaner, South African team sang *Nkosi Sikelel' iAfrika*, formerly a black resistance song and now part of the national anthem. A new coat of arms was designed incorporating different cultural symbols to integrate the nation and create a sense of national identity for the future. The protea flower, secretary bird and elephant tusks were combined with two Linton stone figures of prehistoric humans (Oosthuizen 2004: 69) alongside the motto '!Ke e: |xarra ||ke' (people who are different come together) written in !Xam, the language of a group of San who no longer exist. (Szalay 2002: 6)

In 1998 the *Proudly South African* campaign began in order to encourage the country to make and buy locally, promoting national pride, patriotism and social cohesion. Subsequently, national imagery has been explored even more through art, design and culture in many different ways, showing prominence internationally from the science fiction dystopia of

Johannesburg in the film *District 9* (Neill Blomkamp, 2009) to the controversial vandalism of Brett Murray's satirical painting of President Zuma, *The Spear* (2012).

This focus on South Africans' constant interrogation of personal, national and cultural identity is reflected in the work of textile designers Design Team from Johannesburg. Their fabric collections are titled *Homegrown*, *Indigenous*, *African Archive* and even more explicitly *Young at Heart Nostalgia*. The designs depict historical photographs from the magazine *Drum*, published in the 1950s and 1960s and the national iconography of the springbok and the protea flower.[5] Echoing this is Cape Town-based Fabricnation's work with *Veld*, *Old Postcards* and *African Royale* showing images that have a printed feel of the historical or antique.[6] Their *Umlungu Print* illustrates the dichotomy of white South African designers questioning their personal history in a many-layered country.

The *Umlungu Print* imagery is also many-layered, depicting a blue tall sails ship with the western goddesses Artemis and Venus in the foreground, in a style referencing traditional sixteenth-century Delft blue ceramic tiles. Jane Solomon, the designer, explains that the boat and goddesses represent her European ancestors and she sees the Greek goddesses as becoming African. *Umlungu* is the isiXhosa word for 'from the sea' and is used to describe white people. As Venus was born from the sea in the myth, Solomon feels the *Umlungu* design connects European myths to an African existence, linking the complex nature of the recognition of her past history with the exploration of her identity in contemporary Southern Africa. (Soloman & Cheifitz 2010)

This postcolonial tension between social inequalities, conflicting cultural values, and negotiating identity through art are explored much less explicitly, but remain visible, in the work of San groups from both South Africa and Namibia.

Historically, the San are a marginalized group of former hunter-gatherers in Southern Africa. Their history has been widely documented and they have been extensively studied (including Bleek & Lloyd 1911, Van Der Post 1958, Winberg 1997, Skotnes 1996, 2007, 2009). Living within several countries, San is a term for different groups of people including the Naro, !Xun, Khwe, !Kung, Khomani, Ju|'hoansi, Hei||omn and others, meaning 'first people' in most cases. (le Roux 2004: 2) The names given to the indigenous peoples of the Kalahari by others are varied and contentious, and include Bushmen, Basarwa, First People of the Kalahari, and Khoekhoen. As Willemien le Roux, the coordinator of a San oral history testimony project in Botswana states, 'San has been accepted by a large number of representatives of several surviving groups of First People as being the least derogatory in meaning and history.' (2004: 2) In practice, most groups prefer to be known as 'Bushmen', as documented by American anthropologist Robert J. Gordon (1999: 185) and reinforced in an interview with Karin le Roux, director of the Namibian non-governmental organization (NGO), Omba Arts Trust. (2013) However, as Omba uses the name 'San' on their

website and the name of their textile range is 'Art-i-San', this term is used for the purpose of this writing.

The majority of San in Southern Africa today live in Namibia, Botswana, South Africa and Angola, not through a nomadic lifestyle as might be assumed, but mainly via resettlement. The !Xun and Khwe were hunter-gatherers living in Angola before the 1960s. However like most San, their lives have changed dramatically over recent years, due in part to their involvement in the Angolan and Namibian wars. In 1974 the South African Defence Force (SADF) began to recruit and train San as trackers in the low intensity war against the South West Africa People's Organization (SWAPO) insurgents, who were fighting for the liberation of South West Africa, or Namibia as it is now known. The SADF army base in the Caprivi area grew even more the following year when San refugees fled across the border from war-torn Angola and the Omega army base was established to provide them with shelter. (Gordon 1999: 185)

When Namibia gained independence in 1990 the SADF were worried about reprisals and resettled the !Xun and Khwe to Schmidtsdrift in the Northern Cape, not far from the mining town of Kimberley. This was essentially a tented refugee camp where the San lived for over ten years while land settlement claims were disputed and eventually reconciled and the groups were moved to the town of Platfontein. This is one of the many documented dispossessions that the San have endured over the years – all of them controversial – ending in displacement and, generally, distress for the San.

The Schmidtsdrift camp was made up of more than 4,500 !Xun and Khwe originally from Namibia and Angola, housed in 1,900 military tents. (Godwin 2000) Peter Godwin, who visited the camp for *National Geographic* magazine in 2000, reported it as 'a cheerless spot that smells of desolation'. (2000) With military pensions provided by the government, a school and health care clinic, paradoxically this was one of the most affluent San communities in Southern Africa. However, these material gains adversely affected the !Xun and Khwe. Godwin observed 'the rampant use of alcohol and marijuana is a sign of the dislocation and loss in Schmidtsdrift, palliatives against a world that has overwhelmed these people'. (2000)

It was in this environment that South African Catharina Scheepers-Meyer set up the !Xun and Khwe San Art and Culture Project in 1993. Scheepers-Meyer had successfully established the Kuru Art Project at D'Kar in the Kalahari, Botswana (from where Cgoise produced her design for the BA tail fin) in 1990. Her motivation came from first-hand experience with the D'Kar San where she observed individuals grow through art making to become respected and, in some cases, recognized internationally as artists.

Beginning with a simple textile exercise, the Kuru Art Project's remit was to provide materials and equipment for the San to express themselves through art. Typically, like many grassroots community-based organizations, the Kuru Development Trust emerged out of the missionary projects from the Dutch Reform Church in 1986. In 1989 the Trust focused its attention on strengthening its cultural identity by organizing a trip to view the San rock art paintings at the Tsodilo Hills in Northern Botswana. The success of this trip resulted in the formation of the Kuru Art Project and the first workshop was held in 1990 with the artists painting on fabric. (Scheepers 1991: 7) The results were exhibited at the Botswana National Art Gallery, who bought two of them for their permanent collection. One of these, *Playing*, was painted by one of Kuru's most well-known artists Coex'ae Qgam (Dada) who described creating it: 'They said we should just take that paint and play. It was at the beginning … I was taking that paint and pouring it in a plate. I was not knowing what I can do, but just taking the brush there and painting whatever I can see. Yes, I like colour.' (Gollifer & Egner 2011: 84)

Scheepers-Meyer believed the San in Schmidtsdrift could also be empowered through the benefits of developing an art intervention. Backed by money from the Officers' Fund from the SADF,

Coex'ae Qgam (Dada), *Playing*, 1991. Permanent collection of the National Art Gallery, Botswana. Photograph by Sarah Rhodes 2013.

Art Workshop, (left from front) Fillipus Shikomba, Simon Hamupolo, Fillemon Sakaria, (right from front) Hendrina Hamukanda, Sem Hamupolo, Abraham Hamupolo, Joseph Lazarus. Okashana, Namibia, 2006. Photograph by Cheryl Rumbak. © Omba Arts Trust & Cheryl Rumbak.

she instigated the project, hoping it would provide a shared social space to foster a positive sense of self and community for all members of the !Xun and Khwe at the camp, regardless of their age or sex. (Rabbethge-Schiller 2006: 18)

The themes for the artwork were generally drawn from the !Xun and Khwe's traditional knowledge and stories: bows and arrows, animals, seeds and pods, musical instruments and other cultural symbols. Unsurprisingly, many of the older men focused on animal hunting, an important traditional San activity and something that was not continued after the relocation because Schmidtsdrift and Platfontein did not have game, or veld food to forage. When documentary writer Marlene Sullivan Winberg recorded the oral stories of the !Kun and Khwe artists, she was surprised that, although the communities had suffered the most profoundly sad dispossession, their art and folk tales were full of inspirational and provocative images. (2001: 8) What she found most remarkable was the way in which the artists communicated through narrative, each choosing to answer her questions with a tale, often using animals as metaphors for human behaviour.

Scheepers-Meyer's initial aim for the !Xun and Khwe to experience the benefit of empowerment from an art project (in the same way that the Kuru Art Project achieved it) incidentally seemed to have a cathartic, almost therapeutic effect, particularly on the men involved in the war who chose to document their traumatic experiences through their art. The artist /Thaalu Bernardo Rumao explains:

The other people don't like me, they push me out because of what I draw. But I must draw what I see in my mind. I saw men kill other men – bushmen, white and black men … I loaded the dead men on the helicopter myself. This is why I just draw this. People don't want it and this makes my heart sore. (Sullivan Winberg 2008: 128)

A stark contrast exists between conflict-influenced titles such as *Vehicle Fright* (1995) and *Two Soldiers* (1995) and the pastoral scenes of *Giraffe and Buck* (1996) and the *Story of the Bees* (1999).

During the 1990s, South African art teacher and Kalk Bay Gallery owner, Cheryl Rumbak, developed and facilitated several art workshops for the !Xun and Khwe at Schmidtsdrift too, this time to make a textile range to sell for profit. The aim was to provide an occupation to bring an income into the camp instead of the observed pattern of the San turning to alcohol through boredom. The workshops started from basic observational drawing exercises. The San drew their hands and still-life objects collected from the bush. While it was the first time some of them had picked up a pencil, their line making was confident and the drawings led on to intricate black and white linocuts. The drawings are flat and two-dimensional, but have a graphic quality to them, making the images instantly recognizable. From the linocuts, produced mainly by the men, Rumbak translated the images into repeat designs, which were then printed onto cotton. She feels these first San workshops produced the 'most brilliant range of textiles, they were unbelievable'. (Rumbak 2013)

With the exception of one design, the textiles are no longer in production as none of the artists from the initial Schmidtsdrift workshop are living today. As Rumbak explains, it was alcohol that was partly responsible for destroying the Schmidtsdrift community; they died through neglect, starvation, tuberculosis, HIV/AIDS and alcoholism. They suffered trauma, were displaced and were bored, recurrent afflictions in displaced communities worldwide. (Rumbak 2013)

Alcohol abuse amongst San communities has been widely written about (including Guenther 1997 and Macdonald & Molamu 1999), and in 2000 Godwin documented that the army doctor at the Schmidtsdrift clinic told him that children as young as twelve were addicted to alcohol. He reported alcohol being prominently displayed in the local store and described it as 'starkly utilitarian, carrying only bottom-of-the-line, top-of-the-alcohol-content brands, such as Diamond Fields Late Harvest, a white wine that comes in a silver foil bag, stripped even of the nicety of a bottle'. (Godwin 2000) In an ironic twist, the South African Breweries funded the workshops in these communities struggling with alcoholism.

Rumbak has one textile design, *Dragonfly*, still in production from the Schmidtsdrift !Xun and Khwe artists. This was a linocut she bought from Julietta Carimbwe, originally from Angola, who was the only woman from the project to produce lino prints. Julietta was relocated from Omega in Namibia to Schmidtsdrift with her husband, Katunga. She was born in Mavinga, Angola and didn't attend formal school, however her grandmother passed on traditions and customs to her. Her two children died from illness in Angola, and the rest of her family died in the conflict in

Julietta Carimbwe, *Dragonfly* design (detail), 2000. Flatbed screen print on linen. Photograph by Cheryl Rumbak. © Omba Art.

Namibia before she was relocated. *My Eland's Heart* records Julietta's words about the art project:

> I want to say that it is my work that sustains my life. When I paint I feel good. I draw just what comes into my mind. I like drawing nature, patterns, animals, trees, seeds …
> (Sullivan Winberg 2001: 114)

Ultimately, the textile project failed to continue mainly because of politics and infighting. Rumbak reports that she couldn't get anyone at the project to agree to release the images to allow her to transform them into designs and subsequently into royalties for the artists. There was no one in authority that understood the process of design and business development that she attempted. Today the lino prints and designs remain unused in Rumbak's archive.

Omba Arts Trust, a Southern African NGO, saw the textiles that Rumbak produced with the !Xun and Khwe at Schmidtsdrift and asked her to work with them in Namibia. This working relationship is typical of Southern African craft organizations. An NGO working at the grassroots level will bring in a consultant (sometimes from overseas) for an intervention funded by a donor, usually a development organization. However, just as the BA tail fin design project was unusual in the way it was implemented, here the longevity of the relationship Omba and Rumbak have developed and maintain is unusual and is, in part, responsible for the Art-i-San textile project's sustained success.

Based in Windhoek, Namibia, the Omba Arts Trust works with over 450 craft producers, 350 of those being Ju/'hoansi, !Kung and Khwe San. Its aim is to support the sustainable livelihoods of marginalized communities through the development, sales and marketing of quality Namibian products, generating 'sustainable income … through paintings, prints and textiles'. (Supporting the San 2013)

Art Workshop, Tusnelda Kamati, 2007. Photograph by Cheryl Rumbak. © Omba Arts Trust & Cheryl Rumbak.

Omba Workshop,
Fillipus Shikomba and
Hillia Haushona, 2010.
Photograph by Karin le
Roux. © Karin le Roux.

In the first phase of the project in 2002, instigated by UNESCO and the NGO Working Group of Indigenous Minorities in Southern Africa (WIMSA), Omba Arts Trust developed a community income project for the San in Ekoka, in the remote Ohangwena region on the Namibia-Angola border. Ekoka is a resettlement area for approximately 270 San and, typical of such resettlement areas, has a complicated structure established along linguistic lines. The Ongongolo live on one side, the Kwagga on the other and the Kwanyama, the dominant tribe of the Ohangwena region, encircle both.

Invited by Omba, Rumbak travelled to the San communities in Namibia three times in 2002 to work in collaboration with them to facilitate art workshops. As with the !Xun and Khwe in Schmidtsdrift, they began with observational and still-life drawing. The San worked with themes such as veld plants or animals and they produced lino prints, drawings and oil paintings. Rumbak identified San who had an affinity with either printing or painting and developed this further. She felt that they enjoyed the work, focussed and worked hard. Each time she returned to the community, the same artists would attend the workshops as well as others. She found this consistency from a group who usually live a subsistence lifestyle surprising, but encouraging.

Rumbak feels that it is the workshop structure that brought everyone together. She began with drawing skills, asking participants to find things in their surroundings that they found interesting and to draw them. This developed into more complex observation and life drawing and then into oil painting. She found that because the men traditionally carve wooden objects, they really enjoyed wood and lino cutting and immediately had an affinity with it. The women loved colour and tended to want to paint more, working with strong colour palettes.

However, the San artists developed their own imagery. Rumbak would offer up a theme or subject matter in a workshop and see how the San developed it. One of the most memorable was a discussion of the meanings of words and the seven cycles of life. This needs to be framed in the context of working through translators, as Rumbak's English was translated into Kwanyama, however these discussions were rich with inspiration. So, for example, they spoke about three translations of the cycle of life, from birth to adulthood, which facilitated their drawing.

For the casual viewer, the lino prints, paintings and drawings may seem overly simplistic and stylized, much as Thatcher must have thought when she put her handkerchief over the model of Cgoise's British Airways tail fin design of *Animals and Trees*. However, the most remarkable aspect of the work is that the images produced in Rumbak's Schmidtsdrift workshops in the 1990s, the artwork consistently produced by San groups at the Kuru Art Project, as well as the work from the Omba Arts Trust San, show visual affinity. This is regardless of the fact that they were made by different groups, who spoke in varying dialects and who had experienced different lives in separate countries and worked with assorted outside facilitators. Even more interesting is the fact that the images also have a resonance with the vast number of drawings and watercolours produced by six !Xam San artists recorded by early philologists Wilhelm Bleek and Lucy Lloyd between 1875 and 1881 in Cape Town. Historians assume that the drawings, watercolours and small clay figures produced by the !Xam were made at Bleek and Lloyd's instigation. (Szalay 2002: 6) Whatever their origin, it is interesting to note their resemblance to the later, contemporary San works.

These threads of a common imagery between disparate San communities who are both temporally and geographically distant can also be drawn together with narrative. *My Eland's Heart*, the title of Sullivan Winberg's account of the !Xun and Khwe artists from Schmidtsdrift is taken from

a story told to her by artist Manuel Masseka who was born in Angola in 1946. He served in the Portuguese army before working for the SADF in Namibia for twenty years and recounted an allegory to Sullivan Winberg of two friends hunting an eland and the consequences for their families and lives. The eland, an antelope from Eastern and Southern Africa and highly regarded by the San, is a recurring theme throughout their oral narrative and art traditions and, although South African archaeologist John Parkington cautions against generalities (a 'pan-San' theme) in expressive culture, he nevertheless concludes that the San cultural beliefs are widespread, long lasting and capable of being employed in a variety of contexts. (Skotnes 1996: 281–289)

Rumbak reported on the differences between the materials and equipment used by male and female San artists, and anthropologist Mathias Guenther, who lived and worked with the Kuru Development Trust for many years, notes other gendered differences amongst San contemporary art, too. He feels that the women's art (predominantly painting) tends to be more abstract and less representational in style. Resonating with the white South African female designers from Fabricnation and Design Team, he reports artworks with images that 'are themselves innocent of politics, but instead, depict nostalgic veld-set scenes of a somewhat other-worldly past, become political in an environment that draws such scenes into an identity discourse'. (2003: 95–100)

The San produce these traditional images side by side with more modern, popular cultural images such as radios, jeans, televisions and watches. Guenther feels that 'by blending in their "hybrid" pictures, old with new, the artists engage the new economic and social order, while also keeping in check its hegemonic impact. By juxtaposing elements of modernity with those of tradition they refer the former back to the latter and thereby embrace the new post-foraging order on their own terms.' (2003: 95–100) Guenther is referring to the San artists, however, this could easily be applied to other South African contemporary textile designers' interrogation of identity in today's South Africa.

Zebra lino print, design produced in Ekoka, Namibia by Abraham Hamupolo, 2006. Photograph by Cheryl Rumbak. © Omba Arts Trust

Art-i-San, *Zebra* print. Flatbed screen print on linen. Photograph by Cheryl Rumbak. © Omba Art and Cheryl Rumbak.

218

The economic benefits of all the San art projects have been variable, however the Art-i-San textile project is unique because it has provided a sustained income for their artists over the last decade. The lino prints are translated into repeat patterns that can be screen-printed as textile designs, which were originally marketed as the Ekoka Textile range, but have recently been rebranded as Art-i-San Textiles.[7] The designs are flatbed screen-printed in Cape Town onto South African cotton, making them a wholly Southern African product and keeping their production local and manageable. The resulting fabrics are sold in two ways: either as finished products such as tablecloths, bags, napkins, cushions, etc. or fabric sold by the metre. This two-pronged marketing strategy also contributes to the success and longevity of the project. Local manufacturing means that production runs can be contracted and expanded quickly to meet market demand. The fact that the fabric is sold by the metre means that colourways can be easily changed to suit fluctuating fashions.

Omba works with a lawyer to set up legal contracts with Rumbak's Cape Town-based company, which markets, sells and distributes the work in conjunction with them. Each artist earns either a fee from selling their artwork or royalties when the Art-i-San textiles are sold. Omba pays the artists a lump sum once or twice a year and, for several of them, this figure is quite substantial. Omba, in turn, earns a small percentage to cover their administration and organization costs. Omba and le Roux continue to work with the Ekoka artists, introducing San from other resettlement areas in Ohangwena and Omaheke in Namibia to the textile project and Rumbak launched a new Art-i-San textile design at the annual Design Indaba in Cape Town in 2013.

One of the unexpected benefits from this profitable relationship has been to the San's way of life. With the aim of providing independent living to the San, some of whom still live in domestic servitude (a contentious practice which goes back more than 250 years), the Namibian Ministry of Lands and a local NGO have been working to provide agricultural benefits to the San, supporting them to develop fields for crop growing. Le Roux notes that the San artists who receive Art-i-San royalties generally have much better fields and crops and puts this down to their income from art; with this they are able to hire people to work in their fields and yield better results. (2013)

By employing a lawyer to draw up a legal contract with Rumbak, Omba is securing the intellectual property rights for the Art-i-San artists. However, this is unusual in the typical development model of outside designer interventions with grassroots indigenous groups. As Sauthoff explains: 'Cultural groups, particularly developing rural communities and those with little economic or political leverage, generally have no control over the trivialization of indigenous forms or the re-valorization of historically charged symbols for mainstream consumption.' (2004: 41)

Sauthoff speaks of contemporary South African design circles not questioning who holds the rights to cultural material, its appropriation and dissemination. This was made explicit in the late 1990s when a South African interior design company used a design by Kuru artist Thamae Kaashe without his permission for the carpets of the refurbished first class lounge at Johannesburg International Airport (renamed O.R. Tambo International Airport in 2006). The Kuru Art Project approached the company, who apologized and subsequently paid fees for the rights to reproduce the image. (Brown 2013)

While there are valid questions about power relations concerning the stakeholders in these projects, particularly when an outside-funded agency such as an NGO is involved, this chapter seeks to frame the positive benefits of a commercial relationship where each entity – in Art-i-San's case, the San artists, the NGO facilitator and the marketing retailer – have a vested interest and work together to ensure the success and sustainability of their partnership. This is in distinct contrast to the interior design company who used Kaashe's artwork for their own use at Johannesburg International Airport.

The image, culture and traditions of the San communities of Namibia, Botswana and South Africa continue to be appropriated by designers, particularly within graphic communication and advertising. This appropriation reinforces stereotypes, as Buntman

Omba Workshop, Josephine Naufila, 2010. Photograph by Karin le Roux. © Karin le Roux.

Art-i-San fabrics, 2010.
Flatbed screen print
on cotton and linen.
Photograph by Cheryl
Rumbak. © Omba Art.

Art-i-San fabrics, 2013.
Flatbed screen print
on cotton and linen.
Photograph by Sarah
Rhodes, 2013.

Sofa covered with
Art-i-San textile, 2010.
Photograph by Cheryl
Rumbak. © Omba Art
& Cheryl Rumbak.

Carpet in the first class lounge at Johannesburg International Airport using Thamae Kaashe's design. Photograph by Kuru Art Project, 1998. © Maude Brown for Kuru Development Trust Art Project.

describes, when interrogating the use of San visual imagery: 'where the "silenced" Bushman people remain subjected, being expropriated and exploited: a cultural and social "other"'. (1996: 33–34) She describes the San as epitomizing the liminal state between the old and new South Africa, echoing Monto Masako, an artist from the Schmidtsdrift art project, who describes them as 'in-between people'. (Sullivan Winberg 2001: 81)

Although the BA tail fins credited the individual artists who were commissioned for the *Utopia* designs, their financial remuneration was minimal. Cgoise was given a one-off payment, even though her design was used widely on tickets, luggage tags, upholstery and Heathrow Airport buses. (Griswold 2011) While there are further discussions needed around the complex topics of NGO interventions, hegemonic power relations and legacy, the Art-i-San project continues to supply a steady income to a group of marginalized San from Namibia through the production of art and textiles.

NOTES

1. In 2001 the South African Council for Scientific and Industrial Research (CSIR) acknowledged the San's prior intellectual property rights after they patented the *hoodia* plant as a weight loss drug. A series of historic legal agreements have now been reached between the San and companies who are developing it for commercial purposes. <http://www.protimos.org/what-we-do/iprs-and-biodiversity/san-ipr-project/background/> [Accessed 1 July 2013].

2. South Africa museums removed the controversial 'Bushmen' diorama displays in 2001 and the remains of Sara Baartman (referred to as 'the Hottentot Venus') were repatriated from the Musée de l'Homme in Paris to South Africa in 2002. (le Roux, 2004: 58) <http://news.nationalgeographic.co.uk/news/2001/06/0606_wiremuseums.html> [Accessed 1 July 2013].

3. Including Poland, South Africa, The Netherlands, Australia, Saudi Arabia, Botswana, Egypt and more.

4. Cg'ose Ntcöx'o (Cgoise) (born 1950, died 2013) <http://www.kuruart.com/profile.php?Id=3> [Accessed 1 July 2013].

5. *Drum* Magazine was launched in the newly established Apartheid era 1950s and reflected the dynamic changes that were taking place among the new urban black and South African – African, Indian and Coloured – communities. <http://www.sahistory.org.za/topic/drum-magazine> [Accessed 1 July 2013].

6. Fabricnation was established in 2007 by designers Jane Solomon and Jann Cheifitz who are inspired by the African textile tradition, rendered in a modern urban context with its blending of diverse sources and influences to create the fabric of a nation. <www.fabricnation.co.za/about> [Accessed 1 July 2013].

7. Ekoka is the name of the village where one of the first workshops was held. In 2010 the Omba Arts Trust rebranded the textile range as Art-i-San Textiles.

BIBLIOGRAPHY

Burns Coleman, E. (2005), *Aboriginal Art, Identity and Appropriation*, Aldershot: Ashgate Publishing.

Bleek, W. & Lloyd L. (2011), *Specimens of Bushman Folklore*, <http://www.sacred-texts.com/afr/sbf/index.htm> [Accessed 1 January 2014].

Brown, M. (2013), email correspondence with Kuru Art Project Coordinator.

Buntman, B. (1996), 'Selling with the San: Representations of Bushman People and Artefacts in South African Print Advertisements', *Visual Anthropology*, vol. 8: 33–54.

Godwin, P. (2000), *Bushmen*, <http://ngm.nationalgeographic.com/ngm/0102/feature6/fulltext.html> [Accessed 18 June 2013].

Gollifer, A. & Egner, J. (2011), *I Don't Know Why I Was Created: Dada, Coex'ae Qgam*, Gaborone, Botswana: Eggsson Books.

Gordon, R.J. (1999), *The Bushman Myth: The Making of a Namibian Underclass*, Boulder: Westview Press.

Griswold, S. (2011), *I Don't Know Why I was Created – Book Review* <http://www.mmegi.bw/indexphp?sid=7&aid=1053&dir=2011/October/Friday28> [Accessed 1 July 2013].

Guenther, M. (1997), 'From Lords of the Desert to Rubbish People: The Colonial and Contemporary State of the Nharo Bushmen', in P. Skotnes (ed.), *Miscast: Negotiating the Presence of the Bushmen*. Cape Town: University of Cape Town Press.

Guenther, M. (2003), 'Contemporary Bushman Art, Identity Politics and the Primitivism Discourse', *Anthropologica*, vol. 45, no. 1: 95–110.

le Roux, K. (2013), interview with author.

le Roux, W. (ed.) (2004), *Voices of the San: Living in Southern Africa Today*, Cape Town: Kwela Books.

Macdonald, D. & Molamu, L. (1999), 'From Pleasure to Pain: A Social History of Basarwa/San Alcohol Use in Botswana', in Peele, S. & Grant M. (eds), *Alcohol and Pleasure: A Health Perspective*. Canadian Anthropological Society: Taylor & Francis, 73–86.

Meyer, C., Mason T. & Brown, P. (1996), *Contemporary San Art of Southern Africa: Kuru Art Project D'Kar, Botswana*. White River: The Artists' Press.

Myers. F. (2004), 'Ontologies of the Image and Economies of Exchange', *American Ethnologist*, vol. 31, no. 1: 1–16.

Oosthuizen, T. (2004), 'In Marketing Across Cultures: Are You Enlightening the World or Are You Speaking in Tongues?' *Design Issues*, vol. 20, no. 2 (Spring): 61–72.

Proudly South African About Us (2013), <http://www.proudlysa.co.za/consumer-site> [Accessed 26 July 2013].

Rabbethge-Schiller, H. (2006), *Memory and Magic: Contemporary Art of the !Xun and Khwe*. Johannesburg: Jacana.

Rumbak, Cheryl (2013), interview with author.

San Bushman Art, <http://www.kalkbaymodern.co.za/cp/10074/san-bushman-art> [Accessed 1 July 2013].

Sauthoff, M. (2004), 'Walking the Tightrope: Comments on Graphic Design in South Africa', *Design Issues*, vol. 20, no. 2 (Spring): 34–50.

Scheepers, C. (1991), *Contemporary Bushman Art of Southern Africa: Kuru Cultural Project of D'Kar*, Namibia: Die Republikein Publishers.

Skotnes, P. (2007), *Claim to the Country: The Archive of Lucy Lloyd and Wilhem Bleek*, Jacana Media (Pty) Ltd.

Skotnes, P. (ed.) (1996), *Miscast: Negotiating the Presence of the Bushmen*, Cape Town: University of Cape Town Press.

Skotnes, P. (2009), *The Unconquerable Spirit: George Stow's History Painting of the San*, Jacana Media (Pty) Ltd.

Skotnes, P. (ed.) (2010), *Rock Art Made in Translation: Framing Images From and of the Landscape*. Johannesburg & Cape Town: Jacana Media (Pty) Ltd.

Soloman, J. & Cheifitz, J. (2010), *Category Error 2*. <http://www.fabricnation.co.za/exhibitions/category-error-2/> [Accessed 18 July 2013].

Stone-Lee, O. (2013), *I Was Handbagged by Mrs Thatcher* <http://www.bbc.co.uk/news/uk-politics-11518330> [Accessed 18 July 2013].

Sullivan Winberg, M. (2001), *My Eland's Heart: A Collection of Stories and Art, !Xun and Khwe San Art and Culture Project*, Claremont, South Africa: David Phillips Publishers.

Supporting the San <www.omba.org.na/success-stories/8-success-stories/22-supporting-the-san> [Accessed 1 July 2013].

Szalay, M. (ed.) (2002), *The Moon as Shoe: Drawings of the San*, Zurich: Verlag Scheidegger & Spiess AG, 6.

Van Der Post, L. (1958), *The Lost World of the Kalahari*, London: Penguin.

Weinberg, P. (1997), *In Search of the San*, Johannesburg: The Porcupine Press.

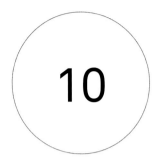

Chapter ten

Social sutra: a platform for ethical textiles in partnerships between Australia and India

Kevin Murray

The final chapter of *Cultural Threads* looks to the future and considers the development of a framework of ethical responsibility for textile and fashion production by Australian designers who work with artisans in India. Australian curator and writer Kevin Murray presents the progress that has been made to ensure ethical production standards are both met and communicated to the consumer, as well as some of the very real challenges that face the development of an ethical code of practice. This chapter draws on Murray's involvement with Sangam: Australia India Design Platform, a recent three-year research project between Australia and India that used workshops, forums and surveys to examine the interests and relationships of producers, developers and consumers of craft.

The project aims to encourage growth in design exchange between Australia and India and has worked to identify common standards for best practice in craft-design partnerships. In this last chapter, Murray takes stock of the present moment and outlines a number of objectives necessary to ensure that the commercial and creative exchange that occurs between postcolonial cultures genuinely moves towards a *post* colonial moment, where the gross imbalances of the colonial past are replaced with models of commerce based on, as Murray puts it, 'mutual respect between the risk of capital and the commitment of labour'.

Jessica Hemmings

While design is much celebrated as a creative practice, writers such as Richard Sennett (2010) have argued for the necessity of craft as a complementary focus on the realization of ideas, not just their invention. The hierarchy between concept and execution, capital and labour, is the subject of much contention in the historic processes of both industrialization and colonization.

In response to the devaluation of labour though industrialization, the English Arts and Crafts Movement sought to celebrate endangered craft traditions. Mahatma Gandhi placed this critique in the service of the independence struggle against what was perceived as colonial exploitation that diminished the role of artisanship. (Brown 2010) By the end of the twentieth century, many Western

designers were travelling to India to collaborate in solidarity with traditional craftspeople. This chapter focuses on a number of Australian designer-makers who have established practices involving Indian artisans. In response to scepticism towards the use of artisan labour, (Scrase 2003) I consider the degree to which these collaborations diverge from the colonial model of value extraction and towards an ethical partnership.

Prior to British colonization, India had been a major source of textiles for the world market. Before Portuguese traders arrived in the early sixteenth century, Gujarati merchants had dominated trade in Southeast Asia. Indian textiles had been traded as far as Africa where they were used as a form of currency. But trade with Europe soon led to a reversal of economic power. From the 1640s, the East India Company had been commissioning print designs for the English market. (Prasannan 2009) With the Battle of Plassey in 1757, the increased authority of colonial rule led to coercion of weavers towards Western interests. (Riello & Roy 2009)

The goods that India supplied to Britain reduced in value from textiles to raw materials, particularly cotton. The rise of technologies such as the mule, invented in the late eighteenth century, led to the mechanization of advanced processing in England. Hand spinning that would have previously taken 50,000 hours was reduced to 300 hours in the 1790s and then 135 with the use of the self-actor in 1825. (Berg 2009) As a result, British textile exports to India increased fifty-fold between 1780 and 1810. (Riello 2009)

The subsequent 'de-industrialization' of India was the subject of much hardship. (Parthasarathi 2011) In the words of Karl Marx, 'English interference having replaced the spinner in Lancashire and the weaver in Bengal, or sweeping away both Hindoo spinner and weaver, dissolved these small semi-barbarian, semi-civilized communities, by blowing up their economical basis.' (Marx 1853) The colonization of India enriched the British Empire at the expense of its artisan population.

Though far from Europe, settler Australia shared the fortunes of the British Empire. Because of its proximity to India, the first settlers in early nineteenth-century Australia were clothed in muslins and other textiles imported directly from India. (Australian National Maritime Museum 2013) With industrialization, this was replaced by clothes made by cheaper mill-produced textiles from centres in Northern England such as Manchester. As a population of largely British origin, Australia had little cause for solidarity with Indian artisans made redundant by technological progress.

The globalization of the later twentieth century saw the movement of factories themselves to countries previously of colonial interest. Textile manufacture was offshored to Asia, particularly China. Following the principle of labour arbitrage, many corporations looked to the countries with lowest wages and standards in order to maximize

profit. While this has led to low prices for Western countries, the stark contrast in lifestyles between producers and consumers is a source of concern. (Stiglitz 2003) The Rana Plaza collapse in Bangladesh on the 24th of April 2013 revealed the dangerous conditions that textile workers have to endure in order to meet the demands of Western companies. (Burke 2013)

This tragedy has prompted some rethinking on globalization. As the wages in China have been increasing, the reverse practice of 'onshoring' has begun to emerge in the Unites States. (Booth 2013) The negative effect of this trend is the denial of livelihood to Asian textile workers, who have decided that it is better to work even in poor conditions than suffer being unwaged. Ameliorative measures such as building codes and minimum wage increases may improve the situation marginally, but they are unlikely to address the divide that separates the West from the Global South. (Amin 2010)

An alternative mode of engagement might be found in the field of 'world craft', where traditional techniques from the Global South are adapted for museums and markets in the West. Craft played a critical role in the cause for independence in India. In the 1919 Amritsar Congress, the Indian National Congress adopted Gandhi's position where hand weaving and spinning were seen as central to the *swadeshi* movement of resistance to Western rule. (McGowan 2009) After independence, this took on an international dimension with the work of Kamaladevi Chattopadhyay, who established the World Crafts Council with the US philanthropist Mrs Vanderbilt Webb in 1963. (Dhamija 2007) More recently, publications like *Hand Eye* cover the myriad of businesses and projects that bring these crafts to the urban Western market. The implied relationship is largely one of solidarity between the artisan and the appreciative collector.

In Australia, given its geographical location, many craftspeople have travelled to Asia in order to increase their appreciation of crafts. The pioneers of New Zealand contemporary jewellery, Alan Preston and Warwick Freeman, both discovered their craft while on the 'hippy trail' through Asia to Europe. In Australia, the first generation of studio potters travelled to Japan, where they could imbibe the reverence for nature that forms the context for serious ceramic practice. And in 1980 Australia took on the Presidency of the World Crafts Council under ceramicist Marea Gazzard.

Many Australian textile artists and designers have been drawn to India. Its craft production capacity is unrivalled. Today, it is estimated that India has up to 200 million artisans ('Craft Economics and Impact Study: volumes 1 & 2' 2011). This has special value for fashion designers, for whom an Indian craft such as embroidery can be a prestige feature in a new range. At this historical moment, it is important to consider the grounds for such exchanges. In what way do they differ from the asymmetrical arrangements put in place during British colonization?

This chapter describes a number of Australians who have developed projects working with textile artisans in India. Their practices will be examined in terms of how they diverge from the 'race to the bottom' of global labour arbitrage. From this experience, the process of platform development that is conducive to partnership will be described. This begins with the development of standards of best practice, and proceeds further to the emergence of e-commerce platforms that claim to make direct links between the producer and consumer. Though consideration will be given to the practitioners' own thoughts on their activity, primarily through interviews, it will be important to look at how the story is then packaged for consumers. The resulting textiles have a role to play not just in beautifying the lives of their owners, but also materializing postcolonial values.

ETHICAL RELATIONSHIPS

Despite the inequity between Asian workers and Western management, offshoring can be justified in terms of relative needs. The standard framework for considering relations between West and East is a developmental one in which the First World leads the way in science and human rights for others to follow. Global justice is thus seen to be a matter of enabling others to catch up with the West, on a singular path of technological and economic change. (Escobar 2010)

This chapter takes its bearings from an alternative consensus approach to developmentalism. While acknowledging the desirability for many of the benefits promised by globalization, these are not presented as universal markers of progress that any country must inevitably follow. Amartya Sen distinguishes between *niti*, the abstract justice encoded in law, and *nyaya*, or realized justice, which concerns the consequences of the law for the actors involved. (Sen 2009) Any universal principle such as development needs to be understood in terms of implications for the local population themselves. This allows consideration of the costs to cultural sustainability in pursuit of certain economic benefits. The ethical relationship is thus one in which there is potential for consensus through informed consent rather than conformity to a universal ideal.

The various practices involving design partnerships with artisans diverge from the industrial model of anonymous labour. The contribution of the artisan is seen as particular to place, in contrast to the rudimentary factory skills that can be easily replaced when cheaper wages are offered elsewhere. The ethical dimension concerns the degree of equality beyond the absolute asymmetry of the master-slave relationship, in which one person's life is in total service to the other. (Hegel 1977) At the other end of the scale are partnerships involving equal benefit, dual agency and mutual respect. An example of this is the relationship between a film director and the lead actor. While this relationship reflects the combination of concept and execution as occurs in craft-design partnerships, the realization of the director's vision is not something to be taken for granted. When considering awards, reviews and advertising, credit between director and lead actor is relatively equally distributed.

When considering such artisan partnerships in the creative arts, I have previously (Murray 2013) distinguished between the developmental, romantic and dialogical models. Developmental partnerships subscribe to a hierarchy that places emphasis on the creative agency of the designer. The romantic model is at the service of the artisan, without consideration of the interests of the designer. Finally, dialogical relationships are characterized by a reciprocal process of ideation

Easton Pearson, Spring/Summer
2013 Collection, Rebel Coat.
Cotton, hand embroidered with
glass and plastic beads. 102 ×
73 cm (40 × 29 in.). © Easton
Pearson 2013.

Social sutra: a platform for ethical textiles in partnerships between Australia and India

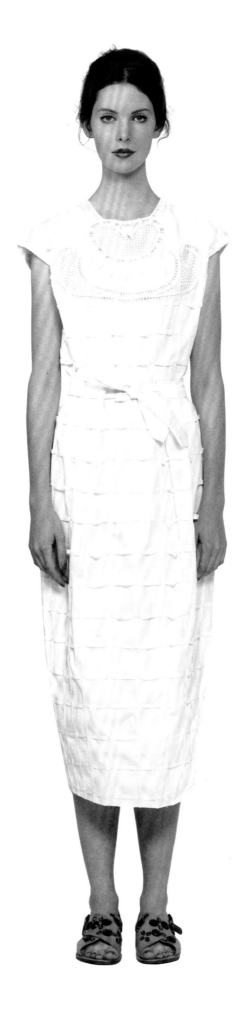

Easton Pearson, Spring/Summer 2013 Collection, Hideout Dress. Cotton, hand embroidered with glass and plastic beads. 123 × 15 cm (48 × 18 in.) © Easton Pearson 2013.

and feedback. While these models appear to be arranged in an ascending ethical order, there is an argument to be made that each has their place. Contexts will suit particular forms of partnership depending on factors such as degree of cultural difference, artisans' level of artistic interest and demands of the market. But underlying this is an ethical ideal of mutual respect, in which both partners are positioned as active agents with their own interests. We can see that an interest in craft provides for a more equal partnership than one based on purely economic interests. The dialogical relationship poses a particular challenge for ethics. While other models can be read relatively directly in terms of the separate interests of the artisans or designers, when they come together the values at play become subject to negotiation. Ethical principles must thus be constructed by mutual dialogue rather than specialist moral philosophy.

CRAFT-DESIGN PARTNERSHIPS

The history of Western fashion is replete with motifs and techniques borrowed from India. But rarely are sources acknowledged. While Australian fashion has sometimes sought to develop a distinct style in response to the natural environment, some designers have drawn inspiration from neighbouring cultures. A recent generation has taken it further through active collaborations with textile artisans.

EASTON PEARSON

The Australian fashion house with the longest history of working in India is Easton Pearson. The Brisbane studio was established by Lydia Pearson and Pam Easton, who have been working together since 1988. From 1990, they have been using the services of a friend's sister, Sudha Patel, in Mumbai to recruit textile artisans throughout India. In Kutch they work with the NGO Shrujan. Their current operation involves artisans working on their garments throughout India.

Easton Pearson's work with artisans is a signature aspect of their label. According to Queensland Art Gallery curator Miranda Wallace (2009), 'it is in the construction of the fabrics, the sourcing of the prints and the jewel-like complexity of the hand-finished detailing, that the true artistry of Easton Pearson's fashion lies.' India is described as their 'spiritual home'. (Wallace 2009: 18) In an interview with Sharia Bano (2012), they say of their Indian embroiderers, 'It's what really made us: it's what we are.'

Easton Pearson's work in India involves a distributed studio, where particular specialist techniques are sourced from different areas. For instance, one garment is made of silk brocade from Varanasi which is embroidered in Mumbai, adorned with buttons crafted by specialist Patwa, then cut and assembled in Brisbane. Occasionally there have been differences of opinion with the Indian artisans. Once there was an issue with the pale colours that they commissioned from artisans in Kutch, who disliked them in preference to bright hues. (McNeill 2011) In another instance their need to demonstrate the craftsmanship of their garments by showing marks of the handmade conflicted with the artisan's values. Ironically, their master embroiderer Mr Moti can sometimes be too perfect. As they said in a 2007 interview:

> [The craftsman] has the most beautiful, even hand and if you ask him to draw something it is symmetrical and it's even. That's not our way and we are constantly telling him, 'no Moti, not so precise. Look: like this … ' And if we leave him to his own devices, it always comes back perfect … he has [now] become used to it and doesn't mind doing it, but he still can't do it by himself: he has to have someone free him up, free his hand. (Bano 2012: 64)

Easton Pearson have achieved much success with their relatively timeless fashion. In 2009 their work was displayed in a solo retrospective exhibition at the Queensland Art Gallery. They have received many awards including the Fashion Award for the

Sara Thorn, *Mermaid* cushion, 2010. Ari hand
embroidery, felt. 40 × 40 cm (16 × 16 in.).
Photograph by James Widdowson.
© Sara Thorn.

2012 InStyle and Audi Women of Style Awards. Their work is a model of how artisan skill can add value to fashion design.

SARA THORN

The Melbourne-based fashion designer Sara Thorn brings a craft sensibility to her engagement with artisans. Largely self-taught, Thorn started her first business in 1983 in Melbourne as an independent fashion and textile designer with an interest in textile history. After several successful studios and labels in Melbourne, she took up the position of head designer at Stussy Sista, a sister brand to the iconic Stussy brand from California in 1995. She then moved to Europe where she designed textiles for Christian Lacroix in Paris, Michiko Koshino in London and Scottish tartans for Bella Freud in London in 1997–98. On her return to Australia in 2000 she became the creative director of the Sydney Fashion Week.

In 2001, a Churchill Fellowship enabled her to study jacquard silk weaving at the Lisio Foundation in Italy. She also attended a symposium on embroidery in Hyderabad and learnt about the diversity of traditional textiles in India and Asia from the artisans and historians. There she was introduced to a global network of those working with traditional textiles, such as Edric Ong from the World Crafts Council: 'Destiny called. It made me feel that this was a path I wanted to pursue.' (Thorn 2011)

She made some orders from that trip, but there were problems with quality and translation of ideas. Thorn felt the need to introduce her own designs, as products with an Indian look were perceived as cheap. But there were cultural issues with product development, such as rural women artisans who were uncomfortable embroidering an image of a topless mermaid. She also believes that designers need to be thoughtful of commissions that require set-up costs and loss of long-term local markets. In 2004, Thorn gave a series of workshops in Southern India to inform artisans about the realities of the foreign market: 'They had little familiarity with Western lifestyles and what the end use of their work was used for … They

were making table mats. One man put up his hand and asked, "Madam, what are these for?"' (Murray 2011)

In 2008 Thorn started the company Worldweave, with architect Piero Gesualdi, which produced homewares and accessories in India. Thorn decided to use established craft workshops such as a company specializing in traditional ari embroidery by machine. She felt this met the realities of manufacture while retaining the variation of individual expression: 'Out of ten cushions, each one has a different face.' The alternative for a designer like Thorn is to have her concepts realized by manufacture in China. But Thorn prefers to produce in India: 'I wanted to support Indian business and tradition because it's a democratic country and keeps traditions alive.'

While Thorn's work in India is sensitive to the realities of life as an artisan, she is also mindful of the limits of the Australian market. In the interests of effectiveness, she places business sustainability above museum-level authenticity.

CAROLE DOUGLAS

Over the past twenty years, Carole Douglas has developed long-term relationships with textile communities in Gujarat. During the 1970s she worked in rural Northern New Zealand running the art department of a district high school and later as the crafts co-ordinator of Northland Community College. She ran her own textile studio, played a leading role in the Crafts Council of New Zealand and worked closely with the (then) Department of Māori affairs on youth unemployment. In 1982 she won the first fibre arts award when the NZ Academy of Fine Arts accepted textiles as an arts genre, and several architectural-scale commissions followed.

On moving to Australia in 1986 she became increasingly involved in the environmental movement, with a particular focus on sustainability. Invited to attend a conference in Rajasthan, she stayed on to investigate natural dyes with the (late) Siddiquebai Mohamed Khatri of Kutch, a region near Pakistan and home to ethnically varied communities involved in the hand production

232

Tejsi Dhana Marwada, *My Community
Migration*, 2009. Raw sheep, goat and camel
yarns hand woven in Kukma, Gujarat, India.
162 × 224 cm (64 × 88 in.). Photograph
© Carole Douglas.

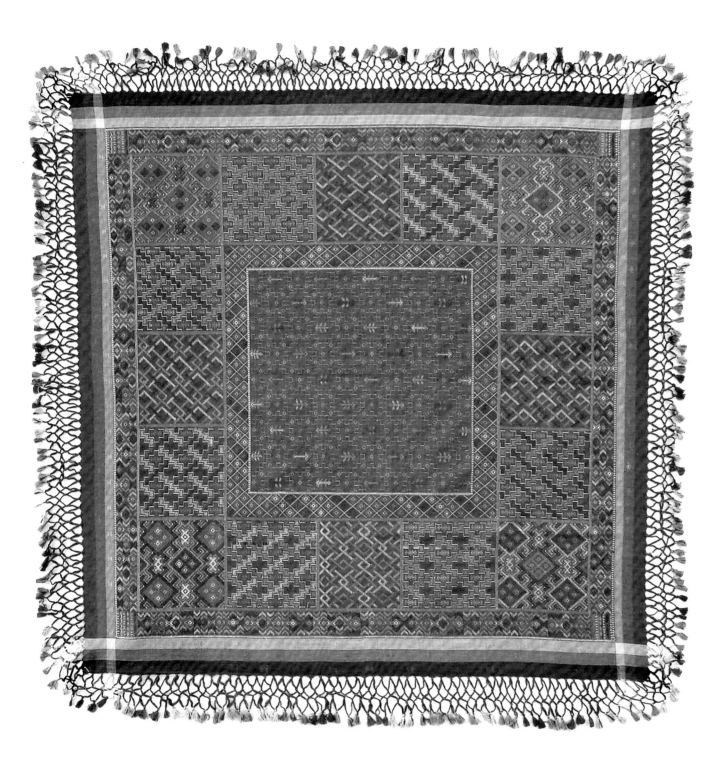

Vankar Chaman Premji, *Margada: Knowing Our Limits*, 2007. Local plant dyes on organic cotton and silk, handloom weaving in Bhujodi, Gujarat, India. 45 × 45 cm (18 × 18 in.). Photograph © Carole Douglas.

Abdulgafoor Daud, *From Heart to Head to Hand*,
2002. Rogan painting on silk made in Nirona,
Gujarat, India. 115 × 153 cm (45 × 60 in.).
Photograph © Carole Douglas.

of textiles. This early meeting led to a series of sustainability projects in Kutch.

In 2001 her work was disrupted by the devastating earthquake. In response to the disaster, Douglas organized an exhibition in Sydney. Over two years, she raised substantial funds, working closely with local NGOs and artisans to develop textile works that told stories of survival and aspirations. The participants had not previously produced narrative works. The show returned to India where it travelled to Ahmedabad and Mumbai where it is now housed at Chhatrapati Shivaji Maharaj Vastu Sangrahalaya or CSMVS (formerly the Prince of Wales Museum). During these years, she also developed textile tours as part of a longer-term livelihood initiative.

The narrative work continued in 2006 with a range of textile works created for an exhibition associated with the fourth UNESCO Education for Sustainability Conference. Working with the younger generation of Kutch artisans in liaison with the NGO Khamir and the Centre for Environmental Education, she conducted workshops which culminated in a series of works reflecting environmental themes.

Douglas' work is oriented around the needs of artisans. It is developmental work that seeks to improve livelihood with an emphasis on sustainability at all levels. Her own product ranges and exhibitions serve as her personal creative outlet and reflect her values. She is currently engaged in a cultural mapping project with pastoral communities in North Western India and is seeking parallels with similar issues in Australia.

LIZ WILLIAMSON

Following Douglas' path, a number of Indian-focused designers have emerged from the College of Fine Art, University of New South Wales. They have been led by Liz Williamson, Australia's most celebrated weaver. Williamson was inspired to take up textiles following her travels through Asia in the early 1970s. She since developed a very successful line of woollen scarves woven in her Sydney studio, as well as a series of works for exhibition reflecting on the techniques of repair such as washing, patching and darning. In 2008 she was awarded the distinction of Living Treasure of Australian Craft.

In 2001, Williamson was invited to participate in the Vital Traditions workshop organized by UNESCO in Vietnam and conducted a weaving workshop that included artisans from fourteen countries and focused on design processes. From this event Williamson developed a partnership with Irani Sen from Kolkata, who ran a weaving workshop in the West Bengal village of Fulia. 'This was a turning point. I could see how I could utilise my skills.' (Williamson 2012) The workshop looked to higher-end products that offered a bigger mark-up, as opposed to the quantities normally required for Fair Trade clients.

Williamson started to commission wraps and scarves woven by the cooperative in 2004. With each visit to Fulia, she spends time with the weavers introducing new designs. The first Woven in Asia range appeared in 2007 with the products consisting of designs woven with silk yarns based on the woollen design previously woven in Williamson's Sydney studio. Williamson undertakes all the finishing of these products, which are marketed through her studio and retail outlets in Australia.

Williamson was Head of the School of Design Studies at the College of Fine Art, University of New South Wales where she also coordinates the textiles program. Each summer, she teaches a Cultural Textiles course which involves travel to Gujarat in partnership with the National Institute of Design, Ahmedabad. The course introduces students to artisan textile production in Gujarat and offers a pathway for a new generation of Australian designers working in India.

DEBORAH EMMETT

In the 1980s, Deborah Emmett was printing textiles in Sydney for Phantom Textiles, which became the international Mambo brand. In 2000, while travelling through India, she began working with artisans in Jaipur, Rajasthan to develop her own designs in traditional wood block printing, bandhini and embroidery techniques.

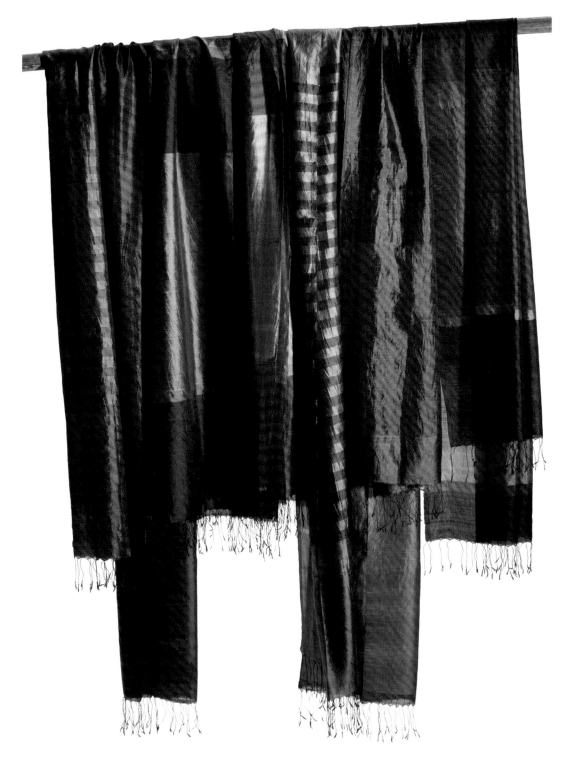

Liz Williamson,
Woven in Asia silk
scarves, 2011.
Photograph
by Ian Hobbs.
© Liz Williamson.

Deborah Emmett, coloured digital photograph of applique embroiderers near Barmer, Rajasthan, India, 2011. 30 × 20 cm (12 × 8 in.). Photograph by Deborah Emmett. © Deborah Emmett.

Bani Prasad, woodblock printer, prints Deborah Emmett's woodblock designs at Sanganer, Rajasthan, India, 2011. 30 × 20 cm (12 × 8 in.). Photograph by Deborah Emmett. © Deborah Emmett.

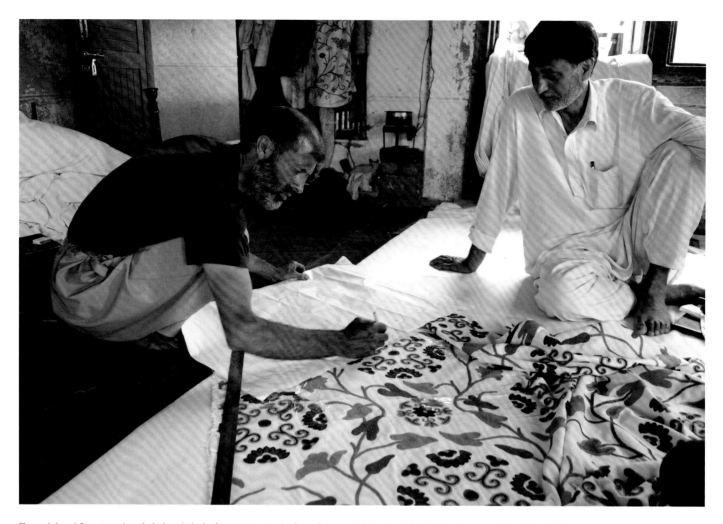

Fayaz Admad Jan, crewel and chain stitch draftsman or naqash, from Srinagar, Kashmir, India, 2012. Photograph by Deborah Emmett.
© Deborah Emmett.

These received a positive response back in Australia from retailers such as Von Trosker. Liz Williamson connected her with Irani Sen in Kolkata, who among others provided access to craftspeople that would enable her to further develop the range.

Emmett has since been working with textile artisans in Rajasthan and Kashmir. In Sanganer, she commissions carved woodblocks according to her specifications. She now lives between Sydney and Delhi, producing garments and soft furnishings for sale in Australia. Block printing survives despite being outmoded several times, previously by silkscreen and recently by digital production techniques. For designers such as Emmett, block printing still has a handmade feel that enhances the garment's authenticity and visual interest. Although

Emmett prefers high quality production, in some cases, Western designers seek to highlight the handmade look by asking for deliberate faults like misregistrations. This can sometimes be a problem for artisans who pride themselves on accuracy.

For Emmett, the contributions of artisans are a key part of her practice. Here she explains a scene of direct communication:

> When making new designs for crewel embroidery curtains the Kashmiri naqash or draughtsman studied my proposed designs and suggested subtle changes that would better suit the crewel embroidery stitch. After explaining that the embroidered fabric would be

Block printer, Bagru, Rajasthan, India, 2013. Photograph by Lauren Bennett. © Walter G.

made into three-metre length curtains he suggested the concentration of the design be reduced to make the product more affordable for the customer while still enabling the fabric to be hand embroidered. Time spent with the crewel embroiderers meant colour variations can be explained and adjustments made while an appreciation of their skills is ascertained. (Emmett 2012)

Emmett has an apartment in Delhi and regularly travels around India to work with artisans. Her blog Tradition Textiles contains images of the artisans that she deals with and descriptions of their work. (http://traditiontextilesandjewellery.com/blog/)

WALTER G

A number of Cultural Textiles alumni have gone on to develop textile projects in India. In 2010, Liz Williamson helped Lauren Bennett find an internship with Irani Sen's Craft Resource Centre (CRC). She then worked with vegetable dyers in Sanganer, Rajasthan. In 2011 she travelled with business partner Genevieve Fennel back to Sanganer for five months to locate and work with artisans. They met father and son traditional natural dyers Om Jo and Shankar, who they asked to develop a series of indigo prints using the traditional dabu technique of mud-resist block printing.

As they write, 'This technique, we knew, was just the medium to communicate the Indian

Walter G hand carved printing
blocks in Hanami design and
tray of pigment, Sanganer,
Rajasthan, India, 2013.
Photograph by Lauren Bennett.
© Walter G.

Walter G hand block printed
and indigo dyed fabrics.
Bagru, Rajasthan, India, 2013.
Photograph by Lauren Bennett.
© Walter G.

Printer sampling Walter
G designs with dabu
mud printing. Sanganer,
Rajasthan, India, 2013.
Photograph by Genevieve
Fennel. © Walter G.

Indigo dye vat. Sanganer,
Rajasthan, India, 2013.
Photograph by Lauren Bennett.
© Walter G.

heritage of pattern and textile in everyday life to the Australian market!' (Bennett & Fennel 2012) Attracted to the rawness of the fabric, they had problems initially coaxing Shankar to achieve the 'dirty indigo' effect they were looking for. The fabric was eventually used for a variety of products, including lampshades and umbrellas.

The Walter G website ('Walter G Hand printed textiles and furniture' 2013) celebrates the artisans they work with in a light-hearted way. Though the products don't list the makers involved, the website contains profiles of individual artisans and blog stories highlighting the pleasures of travelling around India in search of beautiful crafts.

ARTISANS OF FASHION

Alongside individual designers working in India is a significant campaign to raise awareness about the value and needs of artisans. In 2012, Caroline Poiner founded an initiative titled Artisans of Fashion with a mission to support vulnerable and landless communities in India whose lives depend on the traditional craft industry. Artisans of Fashion works alongside artisans to support business growth, positively impact the respective communities and provide access to global markets which would not otherwise be possible.

To launch the program, Artisans of Fashion set out to profile the presence of Indian artisan skills in Australian fashion. The core activity was a documentary journey through India with designer garments, Australian photographers and models. The photos showcased the garments in the rural context, back to the source of many of the traditional skills, with the aim of demonstrating how these ancient techniques can still capture the imagination of the contemporary design world. This presented quite a radical alternative to the metropolitan catwalk. Instead the clothes were contextualized by the exotic landscapes and scenes associated with their production by artisans.

Behind the scenes, new connections for Australian designers were being fostered in a micro partnership project run by Sydney designer, Julie Lantry. For instance, the fashion jeweller Michelle

Jank was paired with the fifth generation embroiderer Ashok Ladiwal from Vrindavan. The application of a traditional craft to contemporary fashion involved innovation. Rather than create detachable jewellery, Jank asked Ladiwal to embroider bird like forms on gauze, which became a dress. The collaboration was documented by photographer Robyn Beeche.

The final suite of photographs were exhibited in the Strand Arcade, the established centre of Sydney Fashion in conjunction with their 'Art of Authenticity' campaign. This was also featured in billboard posters around the city along with an editorial feature in *Marie Claire* magazine.

Artisans of Fashion is designed to appeal to the ethical consumer. Poiner quotes from the CIBJO (The World Jewellery Confederation) Responsible Luxury report: 'the awareness of the provenance and production process of a luxury item has become as important to the consumer as the actual product itself. Buying no longer just demonstrates financial or stylistic independence. Knowing its foundation signifies a social conscience, a duty of care and a deeper knowledge of craftsmanship, skill and quality.' (Kendall 2010)

The Artisans of Fashion (2013) website reveals the lie of the land in craft-design collaborations that bridge Global North and South. The Artisans tab takes the viewer to a map of India. Clicking on a map region leads to an outline of its particular crafts.

For example, the link for Madhya Pradesh includes an item on Chanderi cotton weavers with an image of man at his loom and a brief outline of the weaving technique. On the other hand, the Designers tab leads to a grid of nineteen fashion brands, such as Easton Pearson and Akira Isogawa. While the East is represented collectively by place, the West is designated by individual

OPPOSITE Artisans of Fashion. Clothes by Romance Was Born designers Luke Sales and Anna Plunkett with stylist Caterina Scardino, brocade woven near Varanasi, India, photographed on runway for Wills Lifestyle India Fashion Week 2013. Photograph by Graham Crouch / Australian High Commission.

Social sutra: a platform for ethical textiles in partnerships between Australia and India

Roopa Pemmaraju, Ngalyipi and Kurrkara fitted split dress, crêpe silk, based on painting by Judy Watson.
© Roopa Pemmaraju and Calantha Wardrobe Pty Ltd.

name. Unbalanced though this may seem, the map reflects the balance of tradition, tied to its place of origin, and modernity, which is fluid and abstract. While the blog and Facebook page feature images of finished garments on models, there are also images of artisans. Over a nine-month period in 2013, artisans featured in eleven out of a total of eighty-six images. Artisans of Fashion goes out of its way to promote producers, despite their less glamorous settings.

ROOPA PEMMARAJU

One of the ethical limits of Australian designers working with Indian artisans is the asymmetry of agency involved in the commissioning process. An exception to this is provided by one of the designers involved in Artisans of Fashion, Roopa Pemmaraju. Rather than a Western designer who focuses on the exotic East, she is an Indian fashion designer who draws from an indigenous culture in the West.

Pemmaraju studied in the Bangalore art institution Karnataka Chitrakala Parishath, which promotes local cultures. Before migrating to Australia, she worked in India for the fashion chain Tommy Hilfiger, helping it connect with the local Indian market. In developing her own designs, she drew from classical Indian culture, referencing temple sculptures. In Australia, she took a master's degree in Fashion at the Royal Melbourne Institute of Technology (RMIT).

While in Australia, she looked for its unique cultural sources, parallel to the place of tribal cultures in India. (Pemmaraju 2012) Her first engagement with Aboriginal culture entailed licensing designs from Jilamara Art & Crafts association in Tiwi Islands for digital printing onto garments. She has since gone on to work with the copyright agency Viscopy to license work by Aboriginal painters. Pemmaraju's Earth Collection draws on colours and textures that evoke the Australian landscape as reflected through Aboriginal art. This has proven to be a successful venture. Her work is stocked in the high-end retail chain David Jones.

The website link Meet the Artists takes the viewer to short profiles of Aboriginal painters and their particular dreamings. According to the website:

> Roopa Pemmaraju believes in Fair Trade and ethical dealings with artists and their communities. Royalties from the sale of each garment are returned to artists' communities. We are delighted to facilitate this exchange of artistic ideas and cultural heritage between two ancient ways of life. (Ethos 2013)

Working in the Bangalore studio are artisans from Kolkata, who specialize in skills such as zardosi embroidery and hand-dyeing. Mostly these artisans work on the fashion lines targeting the Indian market, though there are plans to introduce Aboriginal designs to handwoven saris. Though there is no information about production, the labels include the name and a portrait photo of the Aboriginal artist, along with the traditional story told by the painting.

In the article published by *The Australian* (Woolnough 2012), Pemmaraju identifies the core principle of her work: 'It's about bringing artisans and stories together. These clothes unite the stories found in Aboriginal art and in the production of the clothing in India.' The article focuses exclusively on ethical issues related to the use of Aboriginal designs. Pemmaraju's practice reflects the idea of indigenous-to-artisan that seeks cultural parity between India and Australia by linking their traditional cultures. The challenge is to find ways of telling the artisan story alongside that of the Aboriginal design.

BETTER WORLD ARTS

Pemmaraju's work does have precedents in the homewares produced by Australian company Better World Arts, established by Carolyn Wilson. Wilson's work in India arose out of her experience as a tourist in Northern India. Originally trained as a painter, Wilson decided to import Indian crafts back to Australia. However, at the time there was a great deal of competition in Adelaide, where she lived. She then found a Kashmiri family, the Sidiqs, who traded

ABOVE Better World Arts, *Family and Country*, 2009. Hand chain stitched wool on cotton. 40 cm × 40 cm (16 × 16 in.) © Damien and Yilpi Marks and the artist c/o Better World Arts.

RIGHT Better World Arts, *Family and Country*, 2009. Acrylic on cotton canvas. 122 cm × 91 cm (48 × 36 in.) © Damien and Yilpi Marks and the artist c/o Better World Arts.

in local crafts. Wilson was able to send over her own designs to be woven, which proved more successful than the traditional designs.

In 1996 she partnered with an Aboriginal community at Kaltjiti Arts, located at Fregon in the Anangu Pitjantjatjara/Yankunytjatjara Lands (APY Lands) about 200 kilometers south of Uluru. She saw potential in taking designs from Aboriginal paintings to be reproduced in Kashmiri handicrafts. There were some initial frustrations, as the colours did not match specifications, but this improved over time.

Such ventures have much to offer Aboriginal communities. In the typical community, the most common 'creative industry' is painting. But the market to collect these works of art is relatively finite. These communities do not have the tradition or capacity of manufacturing handcrafts to make products that can be used more commonly in everyday life, such as cushion covers and rugs. Instead, they license the designs, cultures and stories from their paintings, bringing income back into the community and disseminating their designs into other people's lives.

The arrangement has proved sustainable, with many sales through outlets such as museum shops. Better World Arts has been fêted with many awards. It has even been called 'the Body Shop of Aboriginal Art in Australia.' The model has been extended to include Peruvian jewellers and Tibetan artisans, leather workers in West Bengal using the revived Shantiniketan printing process and hemp rugs made in Central India. One of its stated aims is to preserve traditional village culture in Kashmir. As with Roopa Pemmaraju fashions, the labels on Better World Arts products highlight the Aboriginal painter who created the original designs, including a photo.

SUMMARY

The various projects by Australians all demonstrate a commitment to partnerships that have a long-term benefit for artisans. Artisans are commissioned primarily for their unique skills, rather than cheap labour. Yet the realities of the market reveal the limits of equal respect. Successful designers such as Easton

Pearson, Roopa Pemmaraju and Sara Thorn choose not to market their goods using the identities of the artisans who made them. The products of those designers who do profile individual artisans, such as Carole Douglas and Artisans of Fashion, take the form of awareness-raising campaigns.

There are many reasons for the relative invisibility of artisan labour. Fashion designers rarely show their production process. Displays of routine labour can detract from the glamour of the parade. Certain artisans can also be highly prized, and some designers are reluctant to expose themselves for fear of having their talent poached. In the case of India, there is also the risk that the consumer will lower their expectations of price given the perception of poverty. Some may fear poor quality, such as low colour-fastness and rough finishing. Despite the best intentions, at the moment many Australian designers seeking a sustainable business model do not foreground Indian artisans.

The exception is in blogs. Both Deborah Emmett and Walter G feature stories of their encounters with artisans on their websites. These kinds of back stories serve a consumer curious to know more about a product's origins, and therefore willing to explore the website, rather than those casually inspecting labels before a purchase. The rise of e-commerce platforms demonstrates the greater suitability of the internet as a medium of transparency than the bricks and mortar retail environment.

PLATFORMS FOR PARTNERSHIP

To help develop sustainable equal partnerships, a code of practice was developed including standards of best practice in partnerships between designers and artisans. This followed the precedent of the Protocols for Producing Indigenous Visual Arts and Crafts (Mellor & Janke 2001), which sought to encourage respect for traditional Aboriginal cultures. The development of a code of practice for Partnerships in Craft & Design has entailed a variety of discussion formats both in Australia and India. These include interviews, roundtables, workshops and public forums over three years (2011–13).

The code of practice (Code of Practice for Partnerships in Craft & Design 2013) was developed out of the reciprocal principles of honesty and respect. These were realized within an ethical matrix of rights and duties that involved the particular rights individuals and communities could claim. But according to the consensual model, these cannot be purely abstract rights such as might be embodied in an institution. For these rights to be realized, a reciprocal set of duties is necessary. For example, the 'right to be known' for artisans to have their names attached to products to which they have made a significant contribution is complemented by the duty of designers to acknowledge their sources. The openness of this code operates as a means of highlighting the distance between ethical ideals and reality. Roadblocks are identified that resist transparency. Rather than ignore these, integral to the process is the sharing of advice about how to work around these roadblocks.

A number of examples illustrate this process. While it might be assumed that all artisans would want to have their names on the labels of their products, the Indian potters in the 2011 Delhi roundtable argued that theirs was a collective process. The attribution should be for village or family, rather than an individual. In response, the protocol was introduced that there be consent for the information used in labelling. In the 2013 Sydney roundtable, a retailer objected to the duty of including information about who made the products in his story. He argued that customers may then take that information and go direct to the source, cutting him out of the equation. In response, various workarounds were developed, such as the introduction of a loyalty program for customers whereby those who return are entrusted with the background information. And in the case of designers, there was some reluctance to include information about their producer in case their hard-won loyalty was compromised by another designer competing for the producer's services. Here a solution was to bind designer and producer in a long-term partnership agreement whereby some of the payment would be given as royalties on future sales.

CONCLUSION

Since colonization, there has been an important turn in the politics of Indian textiles. To varying degrees, this begins with the replacement of hand skills by mechanized looms in Northern England, which reduced the Indian economy from that of secondary to primary producer. Independence from Britain in 1949 was associated with Gandhi's *swadeshi* movement to revive textile handicrafts. This was complemented by the world craft movement, which sought to preserve dying crafts.

Following this path, a number of textile and fashion designers from Australia are seeking to use the unique skills of Indian artisans through medium and long-term partnerships. These have the promise to realize more equal relationships, based on mutual respect between the risk of capital and the commitment of labour. But the effectiveness is limited by a system that is normally secretive about production and a market that gives low value to Indian-made products. Following the postcolonial process of formalizing standards for creative partnerships between indigenous and settler Australians, a draft code has been developed to identify best practice for partnerships that extend into India. At this stage, e-commerce is likely to be a platform where this kind of code can be effective.

Though these boutique design practices are limited in scale compared to the activity of textile corporations, they provide models for partnership that offer an alternative to the inequity that has led to tragedies such as the Rana Plaza collapse. And in a historical context, they reflect the shared postcolonial trajectories of countries such as Australia and India. There is still some way to go until true equity is reached, but the dialogue towards this has certainly started.

249

BIBLIOGRAPHY

Amin, S. (2010), *Global History: A View from the South*, Cape Town: Pambazuka Press.

Artisans of Fashion (2013), *Artisans of Fashion* <http://www.artisansoffashion.com> [Accessed 12 December 2013].

Australian National Maritime Museum (2013), 'East of India – Textiles, Tea and Horses' <http://www.anmm.gov.au/site/page.cfm?u=2119> [Accessed 1 December 2013].

Bano, S. (2012), 'Transnational Networks within the Australian Fashion Industry: Case Studies on Akira Isogawa, Easton Pearson and Vixen' <http://researchbank.rmit.edu.au/eserv/rmit:160352/Bano.pdf> [Accessed 1 December 2013].

Bennett, L. & Fennel, G. (2012), artist statement for Walter G in *Jugalbandi: Designed and Made in Australia and India*, Australia India Design Platform, Sydney, n. pag.

Berg, M. (2009), 'Quality, Cotton and the Global Luxury Trade', in G. Riello & T. Roy (eds), *How India Clothed the World: The World of South Asian Textiles, 1500–1850*, Leiden, Netherlands: Brill.

Booth, T. (2013), 'Here, There and Everywhere', *The Economist* <http://www.economist.com/news/special-report/21569572-after-decades-sending-work-across-world-companies-are-rethinking-their-offshoring> [Accessed 1 December 2013].

Brown, R. (2010), *Gandhi's Spinning Wheel and the Making of India*, London: Routledge.

Burke, J. (2013), 'Bangladesh Factory Collapse Leaves Trail of Shattered Lives', *Guardian* newspaper <http://www.theguardian.com/world/2013/jun/06/bangladesh-factory-building-collapse-community> [Accessed 1 December 2013].

Code of Practice for Partnerships in Craft & Design (2013), *Sangam Project* <http://sangamproject.net/code> [Accessed 12 December 2013].

Craft Economics and Impact Study: Volumes 1 & 2 (2011), Chennai: Crafts Council of India.

Craftisan (2013), <https://craftisan.in> [Accessed 1 December 2013].

Dhamija, J. (2007), *Kamaladevi Chattapadhyay*, National Book Trust, India.

Emmett, D. (2012), 'Fashion Design with a Conscience', *Sangam Project* <http://sangamproject.net/fashion-design-with-a-conscience> [Accessed 13 August 2013].

Escobar, A. (2010), *Encountering Development: The Making and Unmaking of the Third World*. Princeton, New Jersey: Princeton University Press.

Ethos (2013), *Roopa Pemmaraju* <http://roopapemmaraju.com/p/ethos> [Accessed 3 September 2013].

Etsy (2013), <http://www.etsy.com> [Accessed 1 December 2013].

GlobeIn – Discover Artisans and Buy Handmade Gifts from Around the World! (2013), <http://globein.com/authorized> [Accessed 1 December 2013].

Hegel, G.W. (1977), *Phenomenology of Spirit*, Oxford: Oxford University Press.

IOU Project (2013), <http://iouproject.com> [Accessed 1 December 2013].

Kendall, J. (2010), 'Responsible Luxury' <http://www.cibjo.org/download/responsible_luxury.pdf> [Accessed 1 December 2013].

Marx, K. (1853), 'The British Rule in India', *New-York Daily Tribune* <http://www.marxists.org/archive/marx/works/1853/06/25.htm> [Accessed 11 August 2013].

McGowan, A. (2009), *Crafting the Nation in Colonial India*, New York: Palgrave Macmillan.

McNeil, P. (2011), 'Old Empire and New Global Luxury', in G. Adamson, G. Riello & S. Teasley (eds), *Global Design History*, London: Routledge, 138–149.

Mellor, D. & Janke, T. (2001), *Valuing Art, Respecting Culture: Protocols for Working With the Australian Indigenous Visual Arts and Craft Sector*, National Association of the Visual Arts, Potts Point, NSW.

Murray, K. (2011), 'Sara Thorn in India – How to Follow Your Dream into the Real World', *Sangam Project* <http://sangamproject.net/sara-thorn-in-india-how-to-follow-your-dream-into-the-real-world> [Accessed 13 August 2013].

Murray, K. (2013), 'The Visible Hand: an Urban Accord for Outsourced Craft', in E. Grierson & K. Sharp (eds), *Re-imagining the City: Art, Globalization and Urban Spaces*, London: Routledge.

Parthasarathi, P. (2011), *Why Europe Grew Rich and Asia Did Not: Global Economic Divergence, 1600–1850*, Cambridge: Cambridge University Press.

Pemmaraju, R. (2012), interview with Kevin Murray.

Prasannan, P. (2009), 'Historical Issues of Deindustrialization in Nineteenth-century South India', in G. Riello & T. Roy (eds), *How India Clothed the World: The World of South Asian Textiles, 1500–1850*, Leiden, Netherlands: Brill.

Riello, G. (2009), 'The Indian Apprenticeship: The Trade of Indian Textiles and the Making of European Cottons', in G. Riello & T. Roy (eds), *How India Clothed the World: The World of South Asian Textiles, 1500–1850*, Leiden, Netherlands: Brill.

Riello, G. & Roy, T. (2009), *How India Clothed the World: The World of South Asian Textiles, 1500–1850*, Leiden, Netherlands: Brill.

Scrase, T.J. (2003), 'Precarious Production: Globalisation and Artisan Labour in the Third World', *Third World Quarterly*, vol. 24, no. 3: 449–461.

Sen, A. (2009), *The Idea of Justice*, London: Allen Lane.

Sennett, R. (2010), *The Craftsman*, London: Allen Lane.

Stiglitz, J.E. (2003), *Globalization and its Discontents*, New York: W.W. Norton.

Thorn, S. (2011), interview with Kevin Murray.

Wallace, M. (2009), *Easton Pearson*, Queensland Art Gallery, Brisbane.

Walter G. (2013), *Walter G Hand printed textiles and furniture* <http://walter-g.com.au> [Accessed 12 December 2013].

Williamson, L. (2012), interview with Kevin Murray.

Woolnough, D. (2012), 'Roopa Pemmaraju's Continental Drift', *The Australian* <http://www.theaustralian.com.au/executive living/fashion/roopa-pemmarajus-continental-drift/story-e6frg8k6-1226465908137> [Accessed 12 September 2013].

World of Good (2011), *World of Good on ebay* <http://worldofgood.ebay.com> [Accessed 21 May 2011].

INDEX